Big School, Small School

Big School, Small School

High School Size and Student Behavior

by Roger G. Barker and Paul V. Gump

in collaboration with
Louise Shedd Barker, W. J. Campbell, Wallace V. Friesen,
Eleanor R. Hall, William F. LeCompte,
and Edwin P. Willems

Stanford University Press
Stanford, California

Stanford University Press
Stanford, California
© 1964 by the Board of Trustees of the
Leland Stanford Junior University
Printed in the United States of America
ISBN 0-8047-0195-4
Original edition 1964
Reprinted 1972

Preface

BIG SCHOOL, SMALL SCHOOL is presented in four parts. Part I (Chapters 1 to 3) sets forth the general framework of theories and concepts within which the investigations were carried out and the findings interpreted. The relevant research literature is also reviewed in Part I. Part II (Chapters 4 to 8) reports the main empirical investigations; Part III (Chapters 9 to 11) presents supplementary studies that enrich the basic research; and Part IV is a summary and discussion of the findings with respect to the school size problem.

The reader who is not concerned with theoretical issues, or who wishes to return to them later, can begin the book with Part II, for all operations connected with the field work and analyses and all results are reported in the last three parts.

The research reported in this book was supported through the Cooperative Research Program of the Office of Education, U.S. Department of Health, Education, and Welfare (Project No. 594). This financial support and the cooperation of the University of Kansas are gratefully acknowledged.

In this series of interrelated studies the persons who undertook particular investigations, and who are the authors of the separate chapters, also worked on material presented elsewhere in the report. The whole research has been the work of the Midwest Psychological Field Station.

The office staff of the Midwest Field Station, Marjorie Reed, Isla Herbert, and Dorothy Streator, carried out crucial tasks in all phases of the work. In addition to these, Maxine Mize, LaVelle Anderson, Ruth Finley, Barbara Patrick, and Verna Mae Hundley assisted during times of pressing work.

A study that involves schools means inevitably some disruption of the schools' routines and is time-consuming for the school staff. The research workers met unfailing courtesy and genuine interest from the administrators, the teachers, and the students involved. They were all fellow researchers. As we list for each section the persons with whom we worked most closely, we wish to include in our thanks the many others in their schools and organizations who cooperated with us.

Chapter 3. Work on this chapter and Chapter 8 was supported in part by a Public Health Service Fellowship (MPM-15, 824) from the National Institute of Mental Health, Public Health Service, awarded to the author in September 1962.

Chapter 4. The following school officials were most helpful to us in connection with the behavior setting surveys: Phyllis A. Aley, Herbert A. Barkley, Ira N. H. Brammell, Lee R. Cashman, Basil Covey, Mrs. William Greer, Stanley Inwood, Frederic J. Ketchum, Walter C. Meyer, Charles Short, Henry Streator, L. L. Van Petten, Virgil Volland, E. B. Weaver, G. Murlin Welch, Lyle Welch, and Neal Wherry.

Chapter 5. William Harrison, an undergraduate research assistant, was responsible for the major part of the data collection for this chapter. He was appointed under the undergraduate research program of the University of Kansas supported by the Carnegie Foundation. Mrs. Fay Kampschroeder, Director of the Finance Section of the State Department of Public Instruction, helped us to get and understand the official school records of enrollment and attendance. C. H. Kopelk, Executive Secretary of the Kansas State High School Activities Association, allowed us access to the records of that organization. Myers Yearbooks, Inc., of Topeka kindly allowed us to use the yearbooks that they published for the eastern Kansas schools.

Chapters 6, 7, and 8. In addition to some of the school personnel mentioned above, Glenn E. Burnette, E. L. Farr, Kenneth H. Meyers, and William Robey were most helpful in the participation studies. Margaret Ashton, Guney Kozacioglu, and Oren Glick participated as graduate Research Assistants in phases of these studies.

Chapter 9. Kenneth Bontrager, Robert Clemons, J. Courtney, and Arthur Hedges are added to our roster of cooperative school personnel for the studies on school consolidation.

Chapters 10 and 11. The basic data of these chapters were collected and recorded by a staff of junior Research Assistants and junior clerical aides in the summer of 1959. The high school Juniors who were Research

Assistants were Lucy Barker, Roger Brammell, Ralph Frakes, Sonja Hampton, Nancy Hamon, Joye Hensleigh, LaVerna Kessinger, Marilyn Peck, and Larry Sheldon. The clerical aides were Carol Henninger, Jacquelyn Herbert, and Constance Matney. Robert L. Taylor collected the data for the employment study in University City.

Contents

PART I

THEORY

THE THEORETICAL concerns of the investigators had an important influence upon the decision to undertake the studies reported here and upon the design of the research. A full report, therefore, requires an account of the theoretical background of the studies. Part I of *Big School, Small School* provides this background.

The concepts and theories that prompted and guided these studies are empirically based; they are one of the fruits of a number of years of research into the everyday living conditions of children. The earlier investigations led us to consider the effects of group and institutional size upon the behavior of children, and the data we gathered presented us with some hard questions which we attempted to answer in terms of general theories. The studies reported here represent further tests of the theories in public high schools differing in number of students enrolled.

The research has more than a theoretical significance, however, for the problem of the effects of school size upon the behavior and experience of students is a very practical and urgent one. One of the prized experiences of a scientist occurs when his theories lead to predictions that can be tested with precision. When, in addition, these tests involve problems of practical importance, the experience is doubly prized, for the paths of pure and applied science do not often coincide. So we have seized the opportunity to investigate a general, theoretically important problem in connection with a particular practical issue. The results are reported in this volume.

Chapters 1 and 2 of Part I present the theoretical setting of the research, and Chapter 3 surveys the thinking and findings of others who have considered the problem of institutional size and individual behavior.

1

The Ecological Environment

ROGER G. BARKER

THE IDEA is expressed in many forms that the child, the school, and the community are parts of a complex, interdependent system, and hence that problems of education do not begin and end at the school door. And the view is widespread that, insofar as the school is concerned, it is the whole school that enters into the educational process, not only the individual pupil and his teachers. However, these undoubted truths have been without adequate conceptualization or empirical support, and so have had little effect upon the theory and practice of education. The intention of the studies reported here is to investigate these problems within a broad ecological context. We have approached them by way of two dimensions of schools and communities, namely, the number of persons making up the school or community (population), and the number of parts of the school or community (differentiation).

THE INSIDE-OUTSIDE PROBLEM

One of the obvious characteristics of human behavior is its variation. Every day of a person's life is marked by wide fluctuations in almost every discriminable attribute of his behavior: in the intelligence he exhibits, in the speed with which he moves, in the emotion he expresses, in the loudness with which he speaks, in the goals he pursues, in his friendliness, his humor, his energy, his anxiety. Even geniuses think ordinary thoughts much of the time; they, too, have to count their change and choose their neckties. Continuous records of the behavior of children show that the ever changing aspect of the child's stream of behavior is one of its most striking features: trouble and well-being, quietude and activity, success and failure, dominance and submission, correct answers and wrong answers, interest and boredom occur in bewildering complexity (Barker and Wright, 1955). Laymen know of this dimension of human variation from their own experi-

ences and observations; novelists, dramatists, and biographers have described it. But it is not prominent in scientific psychology.

Scientific psychology has been more concerned with another dimension
of behavior variability, namely, differences between individuals. It is one
of the great achievements of psychology that in spite of the variation of
every individual's behavior, methods have been devised for identifying
and measuring individual behavior constants. An important part of scientific psychology is concerned with the great number of behavior constants
that have been measured and with the relations between them.

It is unfortunate that these accomplishments have not been accompanied by equal progress in studying naturally occurring, individual behavior variation. But there is an incompatibility here: to achieve stable
behavior measurements, stable conditions must be imposed upon the person, and the same conditions must be reimposed each time the measurement is repeated. This method provides measures of individual constancies
(under the designated conditions), but it eliminates individual variations
(under different conditions) and it destroys the naturally occurring contexts of behavior.

The problem is not peculiar to psychology. The strength of a beam can
be measured only under specified conditions, and under the same conditions each time the measurement is made. But a beam has many strengths,
depending especially upon its structural context. The same is true, too,
of the meaning of words. Words have a range of meanings, the precise
meaning being determined by the context in which the word occurs. A
good dictionary gives a number of these meanings, the modal meanings;
but for greatest precision it uses the word in revealing contexts. A person
is like a beam or a word: he has many strengths, many intelligences, many
social maturities, many speeds, many degrees of liberality and conserva-
tiveness, and many moralities.

The general sources of intra-individual behavior variation are clear. A
person's behavior is connected in complicated ways with both his inside
parts (his neurons, his muscles, his hormones, for example) and his outside
context (the school class where he is a pupil, the game in which he is a
player, the street on which he is a pedestrian). The *psychological person*
who writes essays, scores points, and crosses streets stands as an identifiable
entity between unstable interior parts and exterior contexts, with both of

which he is linked, yet from both of which he is profoundly separated. The separation comes from the fact that the inside parts and the outside contexts of a person involve phenomena that function according to laws that are different from those that govern his behavior. Brain lesions, muscle contraction, and hormone concentration are not psychological phenomena. In the present state of our understanding, they involve laws that are utterly incommensurate with those of psychology. The same is true of the environment with which a person is coupled. The school class where he is a pupil, the game in which he plays, and the street where he walks all function according to laws that are alien to those that govern his own behavior. This is the inside-outside problem which Allport has discussed (Allport, 1955).

The outside context which constitutes the *ecological environment* is the focus of this research. The ecological environment consists of those naturally occurring phenomena (1) outside a person's skin, (2) with which his molar actions are coupled, but (3) which function according to laws that are incommensurate with the laws that govern his molar behavior (Barker, 1960). The ecological environment differs from the psychological environment (or life space) and from the stimulus, as the following discussion will make clear.

The fact that behavior varies under the influence of the alien, incommensurate outside contexts of the psychological person places psychology in a serious dilemma. How is a unified science to encompass such diverse phenomena? Neither physics, nor astronomy, nor botany has to cope with psychological inputs to the systems with which they deal. How can psychology hope to cope with nonpsychological inputs? This is our problem, and it is the reason why "the whole school" (an outside, nonpsychological phenomenon) is, as yet, little more than a slogan.

THE TAUTOLOGICAL PROBLEM

In order to study environment-behavior relations on any level, the environment and the behavior must be described and measured independently; otherwise one becomes entangled in a tautological circle from which there is no escape. Thus, for example, three children who were each observed an entire day were found to interact with 571, 671, and 749 different objects; the total numbers of interactions with these objects were 1,882, 2,282, and 2,490, and each of these interactions had a number of attributes (Schoggen, 1951; Barker and Wright, 1955). But these objects did not constitute the ecological environments of the children, for the behavior of the children provided the sole criterion for identifying and describing the objects. When one uses a person's behavior as the only evidence of what constitutes his environment, one deals with psychological variables, i.e., with life-space phenomena. The naturally occurring life space deserves investigation, but it is not the ecological environment, and the latter cannot be discovered by using the person's behavior as sole reference point. This is true, not because it is impossible to see all the behavior that occurs, but because the ecological environment comprises a different class of phenomenon, and can only be identified and understood independently of the behavior with which it is linked.

This confronts us with the essence of the ecological environment in its relation to people. One can easily conceive of the problems of students of light perception if they had no physical description of light, or only a physical description of light at the precise point of contact with the receptor. To understand this point of intersection, it is essential to know the structure of light, for the point of intersection takes part of its characteristics from the total wave, quanta, or matrix of which it is a part, and this cannot be known from the points of contact, i.e., the stimulus, alone.

This is a general problem in science. When we are concerned with the outside context of any entity, whether a behaving person, a supporting beam, or a word in a sentence, this context cannot be described in terms of the points of contact with the entity alone. The properties of the points depend upon the structure of which they are parts. Take the word "brought" in the succeedingly more inclusive contexts in which it occurs (from R. L. Stevenson, *The Pavilion on the Links*):

brought
were brought under
provisions were brought under cover
fresh provisions were brought under cover of darkness

The immediate points of contact between the word "brought" and its context are clearly insufficient to define this context; the properties of the contact points "were" and "under" depend upon the total sentence; in fact, "were" and "under" are not the context of the word "brought"; the whole

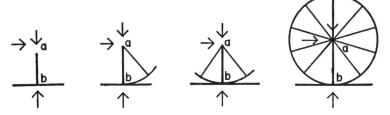

Fig. 1.1. The context of a supporting beam; an example.

sentence is the context. The contexts of all words in Stevenson's writings, and in all meaningful writings, occur in organized units that are larger than the preceding and succeeding connecting words.

Figure 1.1 illustrates another example. The supporting beam (a, b) and its momentary context are shown in the succeeding diagrams. The instantaneous behavior of the beam can be completely described in terms of the internal and external structural arrangements and forces existing for it at a particular instant without regard for what is outside of points a and b. However, if more than an infinitely small time interval is involved, more is required: it is essential to know the structural and dynamic contexts of the intersection points a and b. The properties of contact point b, in this case, can be defined in terms of its position on the rim of a wheel of a certain diameter and motion, and the properties of point a by its position as the center of the wheel. Knowing, for example, that b is on the rim of a wheel moving forward at 50 miles an hour tells us immediately that there will be a cyclical change in the forward movement of b between zero and 100 miles an hour, with corresponding changes in the strength and direction of the forces and in the behavior of the beam.

This is true of the ecological environment of persons, too. A person's momentary behavior is completely determined by his life space, but if we wish to understand more than the immediate cross-section of the ongoing behavior stream, knowledge of the ecological environment is essential. For example, giving and receiving love between mother and child is an important variable in some theories of psychological development. From the developmental viewpoint, such an exchange takes part of its significance from the total context of the mother's and the child's life. It is important to know the larger ecological situation within which this type of contact occurs, because this is often, technically, the only way to understand what actually happens at the momentary intersection between the person and the ecological environment. But, more important, knowledge of the ecological context is essential, because development is not a momentary phenomenon (in fact, most behavior in which we are interested is not momentary), and the *course* of the life space can only be known within the ecological environment in which it is embedded.

PROBLEM OF STRUCTURE

The most primitive and simple thing we know about the ecological environment is that it has structure; it has parts with stable relations between them. One task is to describe this structure.

It is clear that structure cannot be discovered by observing a single part, such as the point of intersection of the environment with a particular person, or by considering the parts separately, one by one. For example, a complete description of a player's behavior in a ball game, or the complete statistics of all the plays occurring in the game, do not reveal the game of baseball. It is the rules of the game, and the arrangement of things and people according to the rules, that constitute the essential, unitary ecological environment of the players; it is these that shape the life space of each player. By dealing with such contexts in terms of their discriminable parts, and processing them by probability statistics, we destroy what we are searching to discover. This approach has the value of a filing system, or of a concordance; but we cannot understand a book from its concordance. By these methods, the structure of the context is dismantled and rearranged; the structure is destroyed.

This does not mean, of course, that such investigations are without value. Important information about one level of a functioning system can be obtained when the system is dismantled. All sciences have structure-destroying methods and make valuable use of them. Essential components of the brain can be determined by excising and mascerating brain tissue and analyzing it by physical and chemical techniques, even though this ignores or destroys the brain's macro-structure.

But most sciences have, also, special nondestructive techniques for studying the structure of their phenomena. X-ray analysis, and electrical, magnetic, and resonance techniques are instances. A primary concern of geologists, oceanographers, cytologists, mineralogists, geneticists, and astronomers is precisely with the naturally occurring, unrearranged structure of things: from chromosomes to the solar system and beyond. So it is important for psychology to discover tender-minded nondestructive techniques for preserving intact naturally occurring behavior and its ecological environment. Here are some guides for this discovery from general ecological methodologies translated into terms of behavior phenomena.

1. The behavior with which one is concerned must be identified. There are many levels of behavior, each of which has a special environmental context. In the present case we are interested in molar behavior, in the behavior of persons as undivided entities; we are not interested in the behavior of eyelids or glands.

2. The problem of identifying and describing the ecological environment of behavior is an empirical one. It is necessary to observe and describe the environment in order to develop theories which later can guide further empirical investigation.

3. The identification of the ecological environment is aided by the fact that, unlike the life space, it has an objective reality "out there"; it has temporal and physical attributes.

4. Since the physical-temporal world is not homogeneous but exists in natural parts with definite boundaries, the ecological environment occurs in bounded units. Arbitrarily defined physical-temporal units will not, except by chance, comprise an environmental unit. Furthermore, the boundaries and characteristics of the ecological environment cannot be determined by observing the persons within it.

5. The individual persons within a bounded unit of the ecological environment differ in psychological attributes; their behavior in the same environment will, therefore, differ.

6. However, since people *en masse* can be expected to have common attributes, the inhabitants of identical ecological units will exhibit a characteristic overall extra-individual pattern of behavior; and the inhabitants of different ecological units will exhibit different overall extra-individual patterns of behavior.

7. In summary, the ecological environment of a person's molar behavior consists of bounded, physical-temporal locales and variegated but stable patterns in the behavior of people *en masse*.

These characteristics of the ecological environment and behavior are familiar to laymen. The dictionary defines common ecological words in terms of both their physical-temporal and their extra-individual behavior coordinates, thus,

ROAD: a track (physical attribute) for travel or for conveying goods (extra-individual pattern of behavior)

STORE: any place where goods (physical attribute) are kept for sale (extra-individual behavior pattern)

PARK: a piece of ground (physical attribute) kept for ornament or recreation (extra-individual pattern of behavior).

An analysis of all descriptions of behavior occurring in one newspaper revealed that about 50 per cent of the reports were in terms of ecological units, including their synomorphic behavior patterns (Barker and Wright, 1955); for example, "The Corner Drug Store will hold a sale on Friday and Saturday," "The Midwest High School Commencement was held last Tuesday." Such physical-behavioral units are common phenomenal entities, and they are natural units in no way imposed by an investigator. To laymen they are as objective as rivers and forests, and they can be defined by denotation; they involve, in the beginning, no theories or concepts; they are parts of the objective environment that are experienced directly, as rain and sandy beaches are experienced.

2

Ecological Units

ROGER G. BARKER

AN INITIAL practical problem of ecological research is to identify the natural units of the phenomenon studied. The essential nature of the units with which ecology deals is the same, whether they are physical, social, biological, or behavioral units: (*a*) they occur without feedback from the investigator; they are self-generated; (*b*) each unit has a time-space locus; (*c*) an unbroken boundary separates an internal pattern from a differing external pattern. By these criteria, an electron, a person, and a waterfall are ecological units. This is true also of most towns and cities; and within a city, it is true of a particular school, of the geometry lesson within the school, and of student Joe Doakes raising his hand to ask to recite. On the other hand, a square mile in the center of a city is not an ecological unit, since it is not self-generated; neither are the Republican voters of the city or the school system, since they have no continuously bounded time-space loci.

Many ecological units occur in circumjacent-interjacent series, or assemblies. A chick embryo, for example, is a nesting set of organs, cells, nuclei, molecules, atoms, and subatomic particles. In these assemblies, the number of included levels is sharply restricted (in the 14-day chick embryo, for example, there are nine or ten levels of units); at each level there are a limited number of discriminable varieties of units (at the level of organs in the chick embryo there are about 40 varieties of units); and within each variety there are differing numbers of individual units (within the organ variety *heart* there is a single unit). Within this arrangement, each circumjacent assembly is reciprocally linked with the interjacent units of which it is composed. This is clearly exemplified by the relation between words, punctuation marks, and sentences: words and punctuation marks form sentences from which, in turn, the words and punctuation marks derive their precise meanings.

This raises the theoretical problem, mentioned in Chapter 1, of accounting within a univocal explanatory theory for the reciprocal relations between different levels of phenomena. How, for example, can we account for the fact that a gas molecule behaves according to the laws of molecular motion and at the same time according to the entirely different laws of the jet of gas of which it is a part? How can the explanations of the movement of a train of wheat across the Kansas plains, given by an economist (a scientist of circumjacent assemblies) and by an engineer (a scientist of interjacent units), ever be incorporated into a single theory? Both the laws of economics and the laws of engineering are true; both operate in predictable ways upon the train, but they are as utterly incommensurate as the price of wheat in Chicago and the horsepower of the engine. How can we ever subsume the laws of motivation that are true for individual children and teachers and the principles of institutional operation within one system of concepts?

The difficulty in all of these cases resides in the fact that the "laws" that govern individual units are different from those applicable to the compound, circumjacent series, or assemblies, of units; yet units and unit assemblies are closely coupled.

Our work is in behavioral ecology, and we are concerned with molar behavior and the ecological contexts in which it occurs. The problem can be illustrated by an example (from Barker *et al.*, 1961):

Anne Matson was 10 years and 11 months of age and in the sixth grade of the Midwest public school. It was 2:09 P.M. and time for the daily music lesson with Miss Madison. The first five minutes of the record, made at the time (March 8, 1951), reported Anne's behavior as follows:

Mrs. Nelson said in a business-like manner, "All right, the class will pass."
Anne picked up her music book from her desk.
She stood.
She motioned urgently to her row, indicating that they should follow her around the front of the room.
The class filed out, carrying their music books.
Anne walked quickly to the music room; she was near the end of the single-file line.

2:10 The children seated themselves in a semicircle across the front of the music room.
Anne sat with Opal Bennet directly on her right and Rex Graw on her left.
Alvin Stone was one seat over from Rex.
Miss Madison, the music teacher, said briskly, "All right, let's open our books to page 27."
Anne watched Miss Madison solemnly.
Anne licked her finger.
She turned to the correct page.
Miss Madison asked the class, "How would you conduct this song?"
Immediately Anne raised her hand, eager to be called on.

2:11 Miss Madison called on Ellen Thomas to show how she would conduct this song.

Ellen waved her right arm in three-quarter rhythm.

Miss Madison watched Ellen critically.

With her hand still part way in the air, Anne watched earnestly.

Someone in the class objected that Ellen's beat wasn't quite right.

Persistently, Anne put her hand up higher, wishing to be called on.

Miss Madison called on Stella Townsend.

Anne put her hand down, disappointment showing in her facial expression.

Intently she watched Stella demonstrate the pattern for conducting the song.

Miss Madison called on Opal Bennet.

Anne didn't raise her hand.

(There was really no opportunity for hand-raising.)

She turned toward her right.

With interest she watched Opal demonstrate the way to lead the song.

Miss Madison demonstrated how three-quarter time should be led.

Anne watched with an interested expression.

2:12 She started to practice, moving her arms in the demonstrated pattern.

Some of the other children also started practicing.

Miss Madison said pedagogically, "All right, let's all do it together."

She stood sideways in a business-like way so that the children could see her hands.

She led the children as they all practiced conducting three-quarter time.

Anne let her fingers hang loosely in a consciously graceful manner.

With restraint and enjoyment she moved her arm up, down, and across in the correct pattern.

2:13 Miss Madison said, "Now we want one person to get up in front of the class and conduct."

Anne immediately raised her hand very eagerly straight up into the air.

On her face was a look of expectancy.

She held her hand in the air until Miss Madison called on Ellen Thomas.

Anne exchanged looks with Opal Bennet, apparently communicating about something of private significance.

She held her book up several inches off her lap expectantly.

She was sitting quite straight.

Miss Madison started the music on the piano.

Ellen started to conduct.

Anne sang the first few notes of the song.

Miss Madison stopped playing.

She showed Ellen how to begin the first beat.

As Miss Madison made the correction, Anne smiled sympathetically at Ellen.

Ellen smiled back.

Miss Madison resumed playing and Ellen conducted.

Anne sang.

2:14 Anne glanced alternately at her book and at Ellen, who was conducting.

She sang heartily and seemed to enjoy it a great deal.

This is an example of the dependent variable with which we are concerned, namely, a child's behavior. We might have obtained the data in another way; in fact, in the research to be reported, we secured information about the children's behavior and experiences by directly questioning them. For example, 16-year-old Joan Bell reported that she was "in the cast of the Junior Class Play" and that the best thing about it for her was "it gave me a chance to be someone else for a change."

We have raised the question: What are the ecological contexts of such behavior?

There are an infinite number of discriminable phenomena external to any individual's behavior. In the case of Anne Matson during the music class there were, for example, her neighbors Opal and Rex, the music book, the song on page 27, the piano, the fifth- and sixth-grade classroom across the hall, the cool overcast day, the town of Midwest, the country of U.S.A.; there were Anne's hand, the windows of the room, Andrea French sitting five seats away, Ellen's smile, and so on without limit. With which of these innumerable exterior phenomena was Anne's behavior linked? And were these phenomena related only via their links with Anne, or did they have a stable independent structure; were they an ecological assembly of units independent of Anne and her behavior?

How does one identify and describe the environment of behavior? Students of perception have been centrally concerned with this problem and they have had some success in dealing with it. When perception psychologists have turned from the nature of perception to the preperceptual nature of light and sound, they have discovered something very important about the ecological environment of vision and hearing: it is not random; it involves bounded manifolds of individual elements with varied and unusual patterns. The environment of vision and hearing has a structure that is independent of its connections with perceptual mechanisms. All science reveals that nature is not uniform; the environments of atoms and molecules, of cells and of organs, of trees and of forests are patterned and structured, and this greatly facilitates their identification.

It would appear that students of molar behavior might profitably emulate students of perception and look at the ecological environment of the behavior with which they are concerned, entirely aside from its connection with behavior. It is, in fact, one of the primary intentions of the present research to advance the science—for which we as yet have no name—that stands with respect to molar behavior as the physics of light and sound stands with respect to vision and hearing. For students of education this means that schools must be studied as carefully as the behavior of the individual children within them.

An analogy may help to make the problem clear.

If a novice, an Englishman for example, wished to understand the environment of a first baseman in a ball game, he might set about to observe the interactions of the player with his surroundings. To do this with utmost precision he might view the first baseman through field glasses, so focused that the player would be centered in the field of the glasses, with just enough of the environment included to encompass all his contacts with the environment, all inputs and outputs: all balls caught, balls thrown, players tagged, etc. Despite the commendable observational care, however, this method would never provide a novice with an understanding of "the game" which gives meaning to a first baseman's transactions with his surroundings, and which in fact, constitutes the environment of his baseball-playing behavior. By observing a player in this way, the novice would, in fact, fragment the game and destroy what he was seeking. So, he might by observations and interviews construct the player's life space during the game: his achievements, aspirations, successes, failures, and conflicts; his judgments of the speed of the ball, of the fairness of the umpire, of the errors of his teammates. But this would only substitute for the former fragmented picture of "the game" the psychological consequences of the fragment, and thus remove the novice even further from the ecological environment he sought. Finally, the novice might perform innumerable correlations between the first baseman's achievements (balls caught, players tagged, strikes and hits made, bases stolen, errors, etc.) and particular attributes of the ecological environment involved (speed of balls thrown to him, distance of throw, weight of bat, curve of balls, etc.). But he could never arrive at the phenomenon known as a baseball game by this means.

It would seem clear that a novice would learn more about the ecological environment of a first baseman by blotting out the player and observing the game around him. This is what the student of light and sound does with elaborate instrumentation, and it is the approach we have taken in the present studies.

It is not easy, at first, to leave the person out of observations of the environment of molar behavior. Our perceptual apparatus is adjusted by our long training with the idiocentric viewing glasses of individual observations, interviews, and questionnaires to see *persons* whenever we see behavior. But with some effort and experience the extra-individual assemblies of behavior episodes, behavior objects, and space that surround persons can be observed and described. Their nonrandom distribution and bounded character are a crucial aid. If the reader will recall a school class period, some of the characteristics of an environmental unit will be clearly apparent:

1. It is a natural phenomenon; it is not created by an experimenter for scientific purposes.

2. It has a space-time locus.

3. A boundary surrounds a school class.

4. The boundary is self-generated; it changes as the class changes in size and in the nature of its activity.

5. The class is objective in the sense that it exists independent of anyone's perception of it, *qua* class; it is a preperceptual ecological entity.

6. It has two sets of components: (*a*) behavior (reciting, discussing, sitting) and (*b*) nonpsychological objects with which behavior is transacted, e.g., chairs, walls, a blackboard, and paper.

7. The unit, the class meeting, is circumjacent to its components; the pupils and equipment are *in* the class.

8. The behavior and physical objects that constitute the unit school class are internally organized and arranged to form a pattern that is by no means random.

9. The pattern within the boundary of a class is easily discriminated from that outside the boundary.

10. There is a synomorphic relation between the pattern of the behavior occurring within the class and the pattern of its nonbehavioral components, the behavior objects. The seats face the teacher's desk, and the children face the teacher, for example.

11. The unity of the class is not due to the similarity of its parts at any moment; for example, speaking occurs in one part and listening in another. The unity is based, rather, upon the interdependence of the parts; events in different parts of a class period have a greater effect upon each other than equivalent events beyond its boundary.

12. The people who inhabit a class are to a considerable degree interchangeable and replaceable. Pupils come and go; even the teacher may

be replaced. But the same entity continues as serenely as an old car with new rings and the right front wheel now carried as the spare.

13. The behavior of this entity cannot, however, be greatly changed without destroying it: there must be teaching, there must be study, there must be recitation.

14. A pupil has two positions in a class; first, he is a component of the supra-individual unit, and second, he is an individual whose life space is partly formed within the constraints imposed by the very entity of which he is a part.

This entity stands out with great clarity, as we have pointed out in Chapter 1; it is a common phenomenon of everyday life. We have called it a K-21 *behavior setting* (see discussion on p. 27). We have made extensive studies of K-21 behavior settings and found much evidence that they are stable extra-individual units with great explanatory power with respect to the behavior occurring within them (Barker and Wright, 1955; Barker, 1961; Barker, 1963). It is the central hypothesis of our studies that K-21 behavior settings constitute the ecological environment of molar behavior, and the theory of them, based upon the earlier work, provides the guides for the investigations.

According to the theory of behavior settings, a person who inhabits and contributes behavior to one of them is a component part, a fixture of a behavior setting. As such, he is anonymous and replaceable, and his behavior is subject to the nonpsychological laws of the superordinate unit. At the same time, however, every inhabitant of a behavior setting is a unique person subject to the laws of individual psychology, where his own private motives, capacities, and perceptions are the causal variables. This is the classical inside-outside paradox, involving in this case persons who are governed by incommensurate laws on different levels of inclusiveness.

One of the sticking points of social and educational psychology is how to account for the consensus, the norms, and the uniformities associated with school classes, business offices, and church services, for example, and at the same time account for the individuality of the members. This problem cannot be solved by either individual or group psychology. It requires a different conceptual treatment, the unnamed science mentioned earlier. In the remainder of this chapter, we shall sketch the theory that has guided this research, and which appears to account for one small facet of this inside-outside paradox.

THEORY OF BEHAVIOR SETTINGS

In order to make the discussion more concrete, sample behavior settings from the high schools in which most of the research was done are listed. These are presented in groups of similar settings from different schools.

Biology and Health Classes, Mr. Campbell (Malden)
Chemistry, Biology, Physics Classes, Mr. Johnson (Midwest)
Physics, Biology, General Science Classes, Miss Smith (Vernon)
Physiology Class, Miss Williams (Walker)
Chemistry Classes, Mr. Jones (Capital City)

Vocal Music Classes, Miss Harris (Malden)
Vocal Music Groups, Miss North (Midwest)
Vocal Music Groups, Miss West (Vernon)
Vocal Music Group, Mr. Field (Walker)
Girls' Chorus Classes, Mr. McGregor (Capital City)

Basketball, Boys' A and B Teams and Girls' Team at Home (Malden)
Basketball, Boys' A and B Teams and Girls' Team at Home (Midwest)
Basketball, Boys' A and B Teams at Home (Vernon)
Basketball, Boys' A and B Teams and Girls' Team at Home (Walker)
Basketball, A Team at Home (Capital City)

After-Game Dance at Legion Hall (Malden)
Dance following Football Game (Midwest)
Sock Hop (Vernon)
Student Council Dance after Game (Walker)
Varsity Dance after Game (Capital City)

Junior Class Play (Malden)
Junior Class Play (Midwest)
Junior Class Play (Vernon)
Junior Class Play (Walker)
Junior-sponsored Play (Capital City)

High School Principal, Office (Malden)
Grade and High School Principal, Office (Midwest)
High School Principal and School Superintendent, Office (Vernon)
High School Principal, Office (Walker)
High School General Office (Capital City)

Pep Club Car Wash (Malden)
Junior Car Wash (Midwest)
Senior Car Wash (Vernon)
Junior Class Work Day (Walker)
Junior-Senior Prom Committee Car Wash (Capital City)

Home Economics Class to the City (Malden)
Drama Club to "My Fair Lady" (Midwest)
Constitution Class Tours State Capitol (Vernon)

Band Attends U.S. Navy Band Concert (Walker)
Science Students to Math, Science Day at University (Capital City)

Key Club Meetings (Malden)
Drama Club Meetings (Midwest)
Future Homemakers Meetings (Vernon)
Y Teens Meetings (Walker)
Thespians Meetings (Capital City)

Behavior settings such as these are organized assemblies of behavior episodes, physical objects, spaces, and durations. Few things can be clearer in terms of direct experience than their coercive power over individuals; no one dances in Mr. Johnson's chemistry class and no one carries out chemistry experiments at the Sock Hop. Despite this, behavior settings have largely escaped the attention of behavioral scientists. We have to look to novelists, dramatists, and pictorial artists for descriptions of them. It is interesting to note, however, that there is evidence of a concern by town planners, highway engineers, human factors scientists, industrial designers, and architects, for example, for a science of behavior settings.

Despite the primitive state of knowledge regarding behavior settings, earlier studies have provided a first step toward an understanding of them (Barker and Wright, 1955; Barker, 1960; Barker and Barker, 1961a). According to the theory developed, a setting is a homeostatic system with controls that maintain the setting intact and operating at a stable functional level under widely varying conditions. These forces have multiple, independent origins, and this is one reason for the stability of settings. Some of the controls reside within the setting itself; in a school class, there are the time schedule, the "rules," the arrangement of the room. Some controls involve input and feedback circuits which couple the setting with exterior conditions; the whole school has its independent schedule and regulations and ways of requiring conformity by the individual class. Other controls involve feedback loops linking the setting with its inhabitants and other of its interior components; the maturity of the pupils and the textbook are examples of interior controls.

A second part of the theory is this: a setting and the behavior episodes that comprise it stand in the relationship of *thing* to *medium,* respectively. The terms thing and medium are used here in the way Heider (1958) defines them. Things are entities that are *internally* constrained. They have internal forces that impose patterns upon their own internal components, and upon external entities that are coupled with them. A chair is a thing with respect to its own parts (its legs, its back, its arms) and it is a thing with respect to persons who sit upon it: its form is impressed upon them. A sentence is a thing with respect to the words that compose it and with respect to the meaning a reader gets from it. The components of a thing have little freedom; an increase in their freedom leads to the destruction of the thing. Things are not docile.

A medium, on the other hand, is *externally* constrained; its freedom is not limited by its own internal arrangements but by external forces that play upon it. The parts of a chair, when it is dismantled, and the words of a sentence, as they occur in a dictionary, have relatively high medium-quality. An appropriate external force may impose any of a wide range of forms upon them: the parts of the chair become a bed or a rose trellis; the words of the sentence express another idea. A medium is docile.

Thing-medium relationships of different sorts are common in nature. According to Heider's analysis, the possibility of perception at a distance depends upon it. Molecules of the air are media with respect to a vibrating tuning fork, which stands as a thing in relation to them. It is because of this relationship that the molecules can transmit the wave pattern imposed upon them by the fork. Small interjacent entities are frequently media vis-à-vis the circumjacent units they compose. A jet of gas issuing under pressure from a small opening of a container is an example: the molecules of the gas are the media of the jet. The jet is the superordinate thing; it constrains, according to the laws of gaseous jets, the behavior of the molecules, which still, however, behave according to molecular laws (of thermal agitation, for example).

In this and every case where a system is made up of an entity and its component media, the characteristics and laws of the interior elements, the media, are different from those of the entity, the things; yet the two are closely coupled. The laws of molecules are not the laws of gas jets. It is such facts as these that present all science with a fundamental problem: how to account for and incorporate phenomena as disparate as molecules and gas jets, words and sentences, behavior episodes and behavior settings within a single system of understanding.

According to Heider, a medium is always a composite entity, a manifold of elements; medium-quality is a property of the manifold, not of the elements separately. A single element of such a manifold has thing-properties to a high degree; a single molecule, a single word, a single music pupil, a single throw of a ball have limited medium-quality. Mutiple, independent elements are essential. Other things being equal, then, the number of parts of a manifold of entities is directly related to the medium potentialities of the manifold. A baby's single word provides it with a poor medium for expressing its much-more-than-single desires; 270 words at two years are a better verbal medium; with a 1,000-word vocabulary more can be said better. There are many ways in which the medium-quality of a medium is reduced; one of them is by a reduction in the independence, i.e., the flexibility of the parts; another is by a reduction in the number of elements in the medium manifold.

The third part of the theory of behavior settings can now be presented. There is for every homeostatic level of a setting an optimal number of elements in its internal, medium manifold. The Baseball Game calls for the behavior of 20 participants, 18 players, and two officials; in Midwest, the setting First Grade Academic Activities is believed to do best with the behavior of 23 inhabitants—22 pupils and one teacher. For the position of pitcher a variety of actions is required. However—and this is crucial—the homeostatic mechanisms of a setting operate to maintain the setting intact and its functional level essentially unchanged when the medium-quality of its component manifold is reduced by reason of a decrease in the number of its interior units below the optimal level. This can occur, of course, only within limits. But to the degree that it does occur, certain consequences follow for the persons who provide the behavior manifold of the setting. Two consequences may be stated as follows: (1) the *strength* of the forces acting upon the individual inhabitants, and upon particular behavior units, increases; and (2) the *range in the direction* of the forces acting upon the individual inhabitants, and upon particular behavior units, increases.

There is nothing mysterious about this; it is simple arithmetic: so long as the homeostatic controls maintain the functional level of the setting, the same pattern and strength of forces is distributed among fewer persons and behavior units. There are, in Allport's terms, fewer junction points, or encounters, but the same number of forces and events (1955). Each point is therefore the focus of more forces and the locus of more events. Accordingly, the fewer available persons are pressed more strongly to produce the same number and variety of behavior units, and fewer behavior units are pressed to produce the same number and variety of achievements.

We come now to the final link in the theory. A setting is a place where most of the inhabitants can satisfy a number of personal motives, where they can achieve multiple satisfactions; a setting contains opportunities. Furthermore, different people achieve a different cluster of satisfactions in the same setting. The unity of a behavior setting does not arise from similarity in the motives of the occupants. In the setting Baseball Game, for example, the pitcher will experience a complex system of social-physical satisfactions, depending upon what kind of person he is; his mother in the bleachers will at the same time have quite a different set of satisfactions; and the coach will have still others. But unless these and other inhabitants of the setting Baseball Game are at least minimally satisfied, they will leave the game, or will not return on another occasion, and the setting will cease. In other words, a setting exists only when it provides its occupants with the particular psychological conditions their own unique natures require. Heterogeneity in the personal motives of the individual inhabitants of a setting contributes to the stability of the setting.

Settings impose obligations upon their occupants too. These arise via the intrinsic structure of the setting and the inhabitants' perception thereof. If the inhabitants of a setting are to continue to attain the goals that bring them satisfactions, the setting must continue to function at a level that each occupant defines for himself. Every occupant of a setting, therefore, encounters two routes: One is the immediate, direct route to his goals; and the other route is directed toward maintaining the setting in such condition that the goals, and the routes to them, will remain intact. When an occupant of a setting sees that it threatens to change in such a way as to reduce the valence of the goals it provides him, or to increase the resistance of the paths to these goals, an increase occurs in the forces along the routes that maintain the setting. The amount and direction of the increase depend upon the degree of the perceived threat, upon the person's perception of its sources and the most promising ways of countering the threat, and upon the valence for the occupant of the goals within the setting.

The primary link between settings and behavior is via the inhabitants' cognitions of the relation between the goals and the routes the setting provides. The inhabitants of a setting need not comprehend the setting as a phenomenal unit of their own life spaces, but they must comprehend some, at least, of its structural and dynamic arrangements, and be aware of changes in them. Most settings include more than one member, so the perceptions mentioned do not involve a single person, but all members of the setting. One direction of most of the inhabitants' maintenance forces is toward getting others to act along maintenance channels too. These interlacings of obligations strengthen greatly the total coercive power of a setting and homogenize, so to speak, the source of its forces.

It is the resultant of such adjustment circuits that keeps a setting on a quasi-stationary level, or moving toward a more satisfying level for the inhabitants. Sometimes, of course, the forces along the maintenance routes are too weak, and the setting deteriorates.

SOME DYNAMICS OF INDIVIDUAL BEHAVIOR

Let us return to the consequences of a reduction of the number of interior elements of a behavior setting below that required by the homeostatic mechanism of the setting. We shall apply the theory to the case of two high schools similar in all respects except number of students and staff. Here is the argument:

1. People (students and staff) provide the component media of behavior settings of a school.

2. The behavior settings are homeostatic systems with optimal media requirements at each homeostatic level.

3. The homeostatic mechanisms maintain the functional level of the setting when the inhabitants fall below the optimum number, within a limited range.

4. The behavior settings of small and large high schools are equivalent in all respects, except that

5. the settings of small high schools are more frequently below the optimal level with respect to number of inhabitants than those of large high schools; therefore

6. the inhabitants of small high schools in comparison with those of large high schools are pressed (a) by stronger forces; (b) in more varied directions.

The phenotypic expression of these predictions takes many forms, which have been presented in detail elsewhere (Barker, 1960, pp. 30–33). We quote from that statement:

1. The behavior consequences of the stronger forces acting upon students of small high schools, in comparison with those of large high schools, will be:

  1.1 *Greater effort.* Greater individual effort can take the form of "harder" work or longer hours. The greater effort is directed both toward the primary goals of the setting and along the maintenance routes. When the assistant yearbook editor leaves, with no one available for replacement, the editor proofreads all the galleys instead of half of them.

  1.2 *More difficult and more important tasks.* There is in most settings a hierarchy of tasks with respect to difficulty and importance. The inexperienced sophomore has to take the lead role in the play when the experienced senior becomes ill.

The primary sources of these changes have been identified. They are greatly enhanced in social behavior settings by the individual's perception of increased rate of work by others, and by increased social pressure from others. One maintenance route for all members is to encourage and indeed to force others to work hard also. These ramifications of influence increase still further the strength of the claim; they also generalize the claim of a setting so it becomes a property of the whole setting.

2. Behavior consequences of greater range in the direction of the forces acting upon students of small high schools will be:

  2.1 *Wider variety of activities.* Each occupant is called upon to fill more positions and play more roles in the setting. The director of the small choir also plays the organ. This primary resultant has many ramifications and manifestations; it involves perception as well as overt behavior. The person sees himself as suitable for previously "inappropriate" tasks. It involves people as well as nonsocial situations. The person has to meet and interact with a greater proportion of the total variety of people present.

  2.2 *Less sensitivity to and less evaluation of differences between people.* This will usually be in the nature of ignoring differences previously noted, and exhibiting increased tolerance of those noted. It is a direct manifestation of the greater variety in the direction of forces; under their influence not only does the person see himself as suitable for new roles, but he sees others, too, as more widely suitable. Undoubtedly the increased strength of the behavior-setting forces aids this process, too. Recalcitrant media (the self and others) become more docile. Here we enter the field of values, at least on a functional level. When essential personnel are in short supply, it is necessary to "accept" those persons who are available and can do the job.

  2.3 *Lower level of maximal performance.* By reason particularly of the demands of great versatility, which introduce interfering skills, but also because of the greater effort and longer hours, with consequent fatigue, the maximal level of a person's achievement in any particular task is reduced. The soloist of the chorus who is also conductor, organist, and librarian is less able to excel in one of these tasks than if he were able to devote all of his time to it. This tendency may be enhanced in a social setting where an individual's performance requires others' support, as is often the case; it is easier to pitch a superlative ball game if the fielders can catch the ball.

3. Behavioral consequences of the joint influence of greater strength and greater range in the direction of forces acting upon students of small high schools will be:

   3.1 *Greater functional importance within the setting.* With increasing scarcity of population, the people who remain become ever more essential. A stage is sometimes reached where everyone is a key person; this happens when everyone in the setting is in one or more essential jobs, with no substitutes available.

   3.2 *More responsibility.* In striving to maintain the setting for his own personal reasons, the individual in a setting where population is scarce is also contributing something essential to the other inhabitants of the setting, who may have quite different interests and motives. A high school student wants to study second-year Latin, and by doing so assures Sue and Joe and Mary, who want the class, too, that it will be held. He, and all the others, achieve "Latin plus appreciation." Responsibility is experienced by a person when a behavior setting and what others gain from it depend upon him. This in most cases amounts to adding a new set of social goals to the setting, or of increasing the valence of an existing set.

   Both functional importance and individual responsibility are attributes experienced by a person himself, and by his associates. They do not occur to so large a degree in optimally populated settings, and not at all in overpopulated settings. A setting that is truly optimally populated does not burden itself with indispensable personnel; people are too unreliable. Substitutes, vice-presidents, committee members in excess of the quorum requirement, a second team: these are regular features of optimally manned settings.

   3.3 *Greater functional self-identity.* A decrease in the population of a behavior setting below the optimum for the setting *qua* setting is accompanied by a change from preoccupation with "What kind of a person am I?" and "What kind of a person is he?" to "What has to be done?" and "Who can do this job?" This is a major shift. It is closely related to the importance and variety of jobs to be done, but it is grounded also in well-established perceptual laws. A functionless person, as is necessarily true of many in an overpopulated setting, and to some degree in an optimally populated setting, has only personal attributes and *potential* functions (e.g., abilities, aptitudes). The only functional relations he can have are the interpersonal ones of being liked or not being liked, of being judged and evaluated by others and by himself. Thus, "What kind of a person am I? (is he?)" becomes of central importance; it creates a highly personal and egocentric situation. Here, too, the person is in the position of a figure against an undifferentiated background, where small differences are clearly seen. Individual differences become important, and the innumerable ways of sorting and classifying people become prominent.

But a person with a function, as is necessary in an underpopulated setting, is more than a person; he is a person in a complicated behavioral context, and he is judged within this context. Fine discriminations as to the kind of person he is are difficult to make. There is less possibility and need to classify functioning people with respect to the kind of people they are. The question becomes "Is the job coming off?" If it is an important job, and it is coming off, the person takes on the value of this achievement no matter what "kind of a person" he is. Personality analysis (by self and others), including subtle testing, sorting, and classifying people, is a feature of overabundantly populated settings.

3.4 *Lower standards and fewer tests for admission.* A baseball game of two members can scarcely maintain the semblance of the setting although it occurs in this emasculated form in Midwest, with a batter-catcher and a pitcher-fielder. The claim of such a setting upon potential participants is very strong indeed, so strong that it will accept, solicit, even impress a five-year-old player or a parent into the setting. We are all familiar with the change in personnel policies when the prime sources of manpower are withdrawn from settings, as during a war. Age, sex, and ability tests for admission to settings are changed and the formerly rejected members are welcomed: women operate lathes, 16-year-olds supervise work crews, and retired professors are reprieved. The lower selectivity of behavior settings relatively deficient in occupants is closely related to the greater range of direction of the forces operating upon them; see paragraph 2.2.

3.5 *Greater insecurity.* Under the pressure of engaging in more difficult and more varied actions, a person in an underpopulated setting is in greater jeopardy of failing to carry through his tasks. To his personal uncertainty is added that which arises from lack of reserves in the behavior setting as a whole. The latter amounts to increased dependence upon every other person carrying through his assignments.

3.6 *More frequent occurrences of success and failure.* The underpopulated setting, by providing a situation where high aspirations (in relation to ability) are encouraged in important actions, but encouraged without authoritative coercion, provides a place for the flowering of success experiences, and also of failure experiences. The underpopulated setting is one where self-esteem and social status can both flourish, and also wither. The degree of the success and of the failure a person achieves is related to his evaluation of the importance of the setting in which the experience occurs.

The last sentence raises an important issue: All of the consequences of underpopulated settings that have been mentioned have been made as relative statements: they describe the behavior to be expected in an underpopulated setting in comparison with that which occurs in the same setting with an optimal number of inhabitants to maintain its homeostatic level. It is assumed that the settings are equally valued in both cases. In circumstances where the "same" small setting was undervalued ("this doesn't amount to anything") or overvalued ("this is exclusive") relative to the "large" setting, some of the predictions would have to be modified.

This is the theory that has guided the research we have done; we have assembled data with respect to a number of the predictions derived from the theory.

IDENTIFICATION OF K-21 BEHAVIOR SETTINGS

The reader will find that the behavior settings which are identified and described in the schools and towns we have studied usually appear to be reasonable, common-sense parts (Appendix 4.1). It must be emphasized, however, that the identification and enumeration of K-21 behavior settings is a highly technical task. Many reasonable, common-sense parts of institutions and communities can be identified which do not possess the distinguishing characteristics of K-21 behavior settings. It is essential that the operations for identifying K-21 behavior settings, which are presented in detail in *Midwest and Its Children* (Barker and Wright, 1955, pp. 50–57, 489–95), be followed by investigators making use of them. The essential technical problem is to identify a single part as one or as more than one K-21 behavior setting; e.g., is the school office a single K-21 behavior setting or is it two K-21 behavior settings: the school principal's office and the secretary's office? This decision requires rating the K-value for the principal's office and secretary's office. The K-value is a rating of the degree of interdependence of the two parts in question. If the rating of K is below the cutting point we have chosen, i.e., 21, the two parts constitute a single setting; if the rating is above the cutting point, the two parts are separate K-21 behavior settings.

VARIETIES OF BEHAVIOR SETTINGS

The definition and description of behavior settings make it clear that all settings have the same fundamental structural and dynamical characteristics, but that beyond these definitive attributes behavior settings vary widely. Like cells, crystals, and fishes, they display many different properties. The varying properties of behavior settings make it possible to classify them narrowly or widely according to defined degrees of similarity upon one or several dimensions. Many classifications are possible and of value for particular problems. A number of different classifications are used in the studies that follow; the one most widely used is classification into *varieties* (Appendix 4.1).

The behavior settings listed on pp. 18–19 are grouped by varieties, and the behavior setting surveys given in Appendix 4.1 are organized by varieties. Behavior settings within one variety have a defined degree of similarity with respect to the following attributes: action patterns, behavior mechanisms, spatial arrangements, and behavior objects. The methods of rating these attributes of behavior settings, and the allowable intravariety variation in each, i.e., the required degree of similarity, are presented in detail in Barker and Wright (1955, pp. 57–58, 81–83). The permissible intravariety variation has been set at a level that produces varieties corresponding to classifications commonly made by laymen, e.g., Church Services and Classes, Lawyers' and Real Estate Offices, Food Stores. It should be clearly understood, however, that identification of varieties is made via precise predetermined criteria.

3

Review of Research

EDWIN P. WILLEMS

BEFORE WE describe the research on schools and communities differing in size, we shall summarize the results of the relevant empirical studies we have discovered in the literature. Few of these studies deal directly with schools or make explicit use of behavior settings as defined here, but all have implications for our work.

Thomas and Fink (1963) point out that two types of size effects are reported in the literature. The one type, which Allport (1955) has termed the "outside" view, considers the effects of size upon the group as a whole, e.g., group learning, group problem-solving, division of labor. The other type, Allport's "inside" view, deals with the effects of size upon individual members, their range and depth of participation in group activities, their feelings, their experienced pressures, and so on. The present review focuses on the second issue: the effects of size upon the behavior and experience of individuals.

LABORATORY STUDIES

On the basis of their review of laboratory studies of groups, Thibaut and Kelley (1959) conclude: "As the group becomes progressively smaller, its identity seems to become increasingly dependent on maintaining each one of its members" (p. 192). Elsewhere, Kelley and Thibaut (1954) conclude that with increasing size of groups, (a) the proportion of members who are "uncontributors" increases, (b) most active members become more and more differentiated from the rest of the group, and (c) most active members become more similar to each other at low levels of participation.

Bass and Norton (1951) trained outside observers to rate participants in group discussions in terms of the leadership ability demonstrated by their group participation. They found that the average leadership ratings on the group members decreased markedly with increases in group size. In other words, outside observers rated members of large groups as less active, less responsible, less effective, and less influential than members of small groups.

Summarizing communication patterns in small experimental groups, Bales (1952, p. 155) concludes:

> As groups increase in size, a larger and larger relative proportion of the activity tends to be addressed to the top man, and a smaller and smaller relative proportion to other members. In turn, as size increases, the top man tends to address more and more of his remarks to the group as a whole, and to exceed by larger amounts his proportionate share. The communication pattern tends to "centralize," in other words, around a leader through whom most of the communication flows.

Bales and Borgatta (1955) found that as group size increased, the numbers of persons who participated at low rates increased.

Taylor and Faust (1952) studied the effectiveness of individuals working alone, in groups of two, and in groups of four in solving the game Twenty Questions. Despite the small differences in group size, the following effects emerged: (a) The four-man groups required almost twice as many man-minutes to reach solutions as the two-man groups. (b) In the four-man groups, the individual who actually achieved the solution differed significantly from the rest of the group in his total amount of activity, e.g., asking questions, suggesting steps toward the solution. This difference did not arise in the two-man groups. This result agrees with Bales's (1952) finding of greater centralization of activity around a leader and with Kelley and Thibaut's (1954) observation of higher proportions of "uncontributors" in larger groups.

Comparing contrived discussion groups of different sizes in a Boy Scout camp, Hare (1952) found that there were more persons in larger groups who were dissatisfied with group discussions. In particular, he found in the larger groups, as compared with the smaller, that (a) there was less consensus about discussion issues; (b) group members changed less toward consensus; (c) group members felt less often that they had enough time for discussion; and (d) those who felt they did not have enough time for discussion were dissatisfied with the results of the discussions.

Holding constant the number of task roles available, Bales (1953) discovered that as size of group increased, the average number of persons playing such task roles did not increase correspondingly, i.e., smaller proportions of group members took part in group tasks.

Slater (1958) studied the evaluations of groups offered by members of laboratory groups differing in size. On postexperimental questionnaires, members of small groups were more nearly unanimous about positive evaluations of their groups (satisfactions) than were members of larger groups. Members of larger groups were more nearly unanimous in complaining about their groups than were members of small groups; the larger *groups* were seen as too hierarchical, centralized, and disorganized, and *members* of larger groups were seen as too aggressive, impulsive, competitive, and inconsiderate.

FIELD STUDIES

Baumgartel and Sobol (1959) conducted field research on the effects of the number of personnel at the airports of an airline and found size to be positively correlated with absenteeism. These researchers used the concept of "attractiveness" to account for their findings and hypothesized that in larger units individual employees operate under reduced attraction toward the work situation and make more choices to stay away.

In an attempt to relate size of organization to "satisfaction," Katz (1949) observed, in various industrial organizations, that (a) higher group cohesion arose in smaller organizations, (b) employees in small work groups were more "satisfied," and (c) individual workers in small groups assumed more importance.

Worthy (1950) concludes: (a) "Mere size is unquestionably one of the most important factors in determining the quality of employee relationships; the smaller the unit the higher the morale" (p. 173); (b) in the smaller units the employee's work becomes more meaningful to him; and (c) attraction to the organization and morale, or satisfaction, are negatively correlated to size.

Cleland (1955) predicted that personnel turnover, i.e., quitting and beginning, would be negatively correlated with size of industrial plants, but he found the reverse to be true; less turnover and absenteeism were found in smaller plants. Cleland explained this by the "intangible personal" approach, i.e., more intimate employer-employee and employee-employee relations, knowledge of personal circumstances, greater rapport, and an "open-door" policy, which was found more frequently in small plants.

Reviewing findings from British data on the effects of size, Revans (1958) noted that (a) the number of accidents per person increased with size in industry; (b) the probability of dying after an amputation increased with the size of the hospital; (c) the number of strikes in factories increased with size; (d) absence rates were positively correlated with size; (e) punctuality decreased with size; (f) buying of professional periodicals was negatively correlated with size of coal mines and commercial organizations; (g) output decreased with size; and (h) compensable accidents increased in rate with size. Revans explains these findings in terms of more "vertical" (supervisor-employee) and "horizontal" (employee-employee) separation, and lower supervisor ratios (more employees per supervisor) in large organizations.

According to Tallachi (1960), increasing size leads to (a) increased division of labor, job specialization, and status differentiation, which lead to (b) decreased satisfaction and morale, and thereby to (c) avoidance by absenteeism and turnover. In 93 industrial organizations, negative correlations were found between size and satisfaction, and again between satisfaction and absenteeism.

Indik (1961, p. 2) states:

> We are hypothesizing that the size of the organization as a social structural fact influences member participation *indirectly* through its effect on specific organizational processes such as those relating to communication, control, task specialization, and coordination. These processes, in turn, affect the degree of attraction among organizational members, the amount of intrinsic job satisfaction derived by the members, and the degree of bureaucratic inflexibility felt by members. It is these latter variables that directly affect member participation rates.

Indik found that size of 96 business organizations correlated positively with difficulty of maintaining communication among members and negatively with participation, suggesting that greater size led to difficulty in communication, less attraction, and less participation.

Campbell (1952), as reported in Hewitt and Parfit (1953), examined the effects of size of work groups on the incentive effect of group payment schemes. He found that as size increased (a) the per cent of workers who did not understand the scheme increased, and (b) those workers who did not understand the scheme became progressively less satisfied with it, indicating that larger groups contained higher percentages of workers who were dissatisfied with work payment schemes. These findings agree with Hare's contrived discussion groups (see p. 30).

Marriot (1949), as reported by Indik (1961), found in two automobile factories that there was a consistent negative relationship between the size of the work unit and individual "productivity," or output.

The Acton Society Trust studies (1953) set out to investigate morale as related to size, using various behavioral and attitudinal variables as indexes of morale. It was found that interest in affairs of the organization and knowledge of names of administrators were negatively correlated with size, and that acceptance of rumors was positively correlated with size. Voting on work unit issues, subscriptions to professional periodicals, output, and punctuality were negatively correlated to size. Absenteeism, accident rates, strikes, and waste were positively correlated with size. These findings were found to hold for various industrial and commercial organizations.

Hewitt and Parfit (1953) studied a factory of 1,000 employees and found a positive correlation between size of work "rooms," or units, and rates of nonsickness absence.

Eighty-three county welfare bureaus from the same state were studied by E. J. Thomas (1959). He discovered the following to be negatively correlated with size of the bureaus: (a) agreement among workers and supervisors on roles of social workers, (b) the number of activities seen as part of the social worker's role, (c) commitment to the ethics and ideals of social work, and (d) worker performance on the job, or output.

By having students from 25 different fields of study rate all the primary, reciprocal social groups of which they were members, Fisher (1953) found that as these groups increased in size, they met less frequently. Thus the respondents had less social contact with the larger groups.

Wright (1961) has used behavior settings in an extensive series of studies of the living habitats, behavior, and experience of children in large and small towns. He has found that children in large towns enter a wider range of settings, but that children in small towns (a) have more positions of importance in settings, (b) re-enter settings more often, (c) spend more time in community settings, (d) find more of the same persons using the settings they enter, and (e) are more familiar with objects and people in the settings of their towns. There is also more crossing of paths and more familiarity with the broader community in the small towns. In terms of interpersonal transactions, children in the small towns initiate more greetings to other persons, experience more greetings from others, and are involved in more total interpersonal transactions.

In two publications that develop the theory of behavior settings, Barker

(1960) and Barker and Barker (1961a) present data comparing an English town with an American town. The English town was found to have more inhabitants per behavior setting than the American town. Within the English town, in comparison with the American town, (a) residents spent fewer hours per person per week in behavior settings; (b) they filled fewer positions of responsibility in behavior settings; (c) a higher per cent of the town's behavior settings were segregated with respect to age and social class; and (d) fewer behavior settings involved and depended upon children and adolescents for their functioning. The Barkers (1961a) found that the children of the American town in comparison with the children of the English town (a) participated in a wider range of settings, (b) were excluded from fewer settings, and (c) filled essential positions in more settings; and that the old people of the American town (1961b) (a) participated in a wider range of settings, (b) participated to a greater depth of penetration, and (c) participated for longer periods of time. The Barkers conclude that since, in the American town, people, including the extreme age groups, were in shorter supply and greater demand than in the English town, the average person was functionally more important to the town and its behavior settings.

LeCompte and Barker (1960) found that (a) in Rotary clubs, size is negatively correlated with attendance; (b) in churches, size of membership is negatively correlated with Sunday School attendance; and (c) in high schools, size is negatively correlated with participation in music festivals.

Larson (1949) related size of high school to students' activities and relations to peers. A higher percentage of students in small schools as compared with medium and large schools reported that it was easy to make friends and that they liked all their school acquaintances. Higher percentages of students in large schools than in medium and small schools reported that they engaged in no activities or only one, and that they experienced difficulty in getting into activities.

Dawe (1934) studied the effects of kindergarten size and seating position upon the retention of material and the participation of individual children in discussion. Among 433 children in groups ranging in size from 15 to 46, she found that when the number of comments by individual children during a controlled discussion period was tabulated, increasing size led to (a) decreased total amount of discussion, (b) decreased per cent of children who participated, and (c) decreased average amount of participation per child. Dawe also observed a strong interaction between seating position (front, back, or center) and class size. Children in the front rows of small groups participated the most, while children in the back rows of large groups participated the least.

A questionnaire study by Anderson, Ladd, and Smith (1954), involving 2,500 high school graduates, found that the per cent of graduates who reported that their participation in extracurricular activities was "very valuable and useful" was negatively correlated with size of the school. Coleman (1961) found the following to be negatively related to size of high school: (a) per cent of boys who participated in football; (b) ability to name an outstanding fellow student in certain areas; and (c) consensus about persons in the student body who were outstanding in certain areas.

Isaacs (1953) reports that the per cent of retention (inverse of dropouts) is negatively related to size of high schools in Kansas.

A type of school study that is only distantly related to the research reported here will not be reviewed, namely, the effects of high school and class size on the academic achievement of students (Harmon, 1961; Feldt, 1960; Hoyt, 1959; Gaston and Anderson, 1954; Ross and McKenna, 1955).

RELEVANCE TO THE PRESENT RESEARCH

The theory developed in Chapter 2 predicts a number of overt and covert behavioral effects of behavior setting size. It is predicted that in relatively underpopulated settings there will be more effort expended in a wider range of activities than in more heavily populated settings. Individuals in underpopulated settings will have a higher frequency of difficult and important functions both in direct, consummatory actions and in behavior to maintain the settings. It is expected that the differences in expended effort and range of activity will have correlates in individual as well as social, or interactional, behavior relevant to the tasks of the setting or group and in both overt behavior and subjective experience. Findings cited above in the review of literature are discussed below in view of these expectations.

Frequency, depth, and range of participation. Persons in smaller groups and other social, organizational, and ecological units:

—are absent less often (Baumgartel and Sobol, 1959; Revans, 1958; Tallachi, 1960; Indik, 1961; Acton, 1953; Hewitt and Parfit, 1953; LeCompte and Barker, 1960);

—quit jobs and positions less often (Cleland, 1955; Tallachi, 1960; Isaacs, 1953);

—are more punctual (Revans, 1958; Acton, 1953);

—participate more frequently when participation is voluntary (Dawe, 1934; Larson, 1949; LeCompte and Barker, 1960; Wright, 1961; Coleman, 1961; Fisher, 1953);

—function in positions of responsibility and importance more frequently, and in a wider range of activities (Barker and Barker, 1961a, 1961b; Wright, 1961);

—are more productive (Revans, 1958; Thomas, 1959; Acton, 1953; Marriot, 1949);

—demonstrate more leadership behavior (Bass and Norton, 1951);

—are more important to the groups and settings (Barker and Barker, 1961a; Katz, 1949; Thibaut and Kelley, 1959);

—have broader role conceptions (Thomas, 1959);

—are more frequently involved in roles directly relevant to the group tasks (Dawe, 1934; Bales, 1953; Taylor and Faust, 1952);

—are more interested in the affairs of the group or organization (Revans, 1958; Acton, 1953).

Communication and social interaction. Small groups and other ecological and social units give rise to:

  —greater individual participation in communication and social interaction, and less centralization of the communication around one or few persons (Kelley and Thibaut, 1954; Bales, 1952; Bales and Borgatta, 1955; Taylor and Faust, 1952);

  —more greetings and social transactions per person (Wright, 1961);

  —facilitated communication, both through greater clarity and decreased difficulty (Campbell, 1952; Indik, 1961);

  —greater group cohesiveness and more frequent liking of all fellow group members (Katz, 1949; Larson, 1949);

  —greater ability to identify outstanding persons and higher agreement about such persons (Coleman, 1961).

The reported experiences of persons. Persons in smaller groups and other social and ecological units:

  —receive more "satisfaction" (Katz, 1949; Tallachi, 1960; Slater, 1958);

—speak more often of participation having been valuable and useful (Anderson, Ladd, and Smith, 1954);
—are more familiar with the settings (Wright, 1961);
—report being more satisfied with payment schemes and with the results of group discussions (Campbell, 1952; Hare, 1952);
—find their work more meaningful (Worthy, 1950).

Several of the authors postulate a negative relation between size and attraction toward participation and use the concept of attraction to explain their findings, e.g., in terms of attraction toward the work situation (Baumgartel and Sobol, 1959; Cleland, 1955), interpersonal attraction due to better communication (Indik, 1961), morale and attraction (Hewitt and Parfit, 1953; Worthy, 1950), and forces toward the direct, consumatory use of behavior settings (Barker, 1960; Barker and Barker, 1961a).

SUMMARY AND IMPLICATIONS

The studies that used contrived laboratory groups differ in as yet undefined ways from behavior settings, e.g., in "time perspective" (Kounin, 1961). However, the negative correlations between size of such groups and participation and involvement of individuals are in agreement with the theory of the present studies. The field studies that did not make use of rigorously defined ecological units provide further general support for the hypotheses, as do, also, the field studies using behavior settings.

In summary, all of the studies we have discovered are in general agreement with the theory. The investigations reported in this volume advance research upon the relationship between size of ecological unit and individual behavior by placing it within a more explicit theoretical framework, by deriving explicit, testable predictions from the theory, by defining ecological units more precisely, and by including a greater range of behavior attributes, both overt and subjective.

MAJOR FINDINGS

CHAPTERS 4 THROUGH 8 provide the major data for pursuit of the school size issue. Chapter 4 describes the schools and communities in which the major studies were carried out. Also reported here are findings regarding the relationship between school size and such environmental variables as number and variety of school parts (or settings), population per setting, and completeness of offerings in large and small schools.

The first study of individual student behavior in relation to high school size appears in Chapter 5. As an exploratory effort, these investigators took advantage of data already collected by schools or agencies connected with schools. Such material provided information regarding several hundred schools and many thousands of students. Results encouraged more controlled and more direct tests of size effects.

Chapter 6 presents data from a study of student participation in one large and four small high schools. Findings are relevant to the predictions that the versatility and importance of students' extracurricular activities are related to the size of their school settings. Once students' activities in their school settings had been described, it became feasible to investigate what these activities meant to their participants; accordingly, comparisons of the satisfactions of large and small school students are presented in Chapter 7.

Chapter 8 reports a theoretically derived test of the size theory as it relates to forces toward participation in school settings. Of special interest in Chapter 8 are the findings on ecological versus personal variables in relation to the student's felt obligation toward the enterprises of his school.

In a general fashion, the sequence of Chapters 4 to 8 is from the environmental bases for school behavior, to a description of overt student activities, to considerations of the subjective effects of school size. All studies relate to the theory of size effects explained in Chapter 2.

MAJOR FINDINGS

CHAPTERS 4 THROUGH 8 provide the major data for pursuit of the school size issue. Chapter 4 describes the schools and communities in which the major studies were carried out. Also reported here are findings regarding the relationship between school size and such environmental variables as number and variety of school parts (or settings), population per setting, and completeness of offerings in large and small schools.

The first study of individual student behavior in relation to high school size appears in Chapter 5. As an exploratory effort, these investigators took advantage of data already collected by schools or agencies connected with schools. Such material provided information regarding several hundred schools and many thousands of students. Results encouraged more controlled and more direct tests of size effects.

Chapter 6 presents data from a study of student participation in one large and four small high schools. Findings are relevant to the predictions that the versatility and importance of students' extracurricular activities are related to the size of their school settings. Once students' activities in their school settings had been described, it became feasible to investigate what these activities meant to their participants; accordingly, comparisons of the satisfactions of large and small school students are presented in Chapter 7.

Chapter 8 reports a theoretically derived test of the size theory as it relates to forces toward participation in school settings. Of special interest in Chapter 8 are the findings on ecological versus personal variables in relation to the student's felt obligation toward the enterprises of his school.

In a general fashion, the sequence of Chapters 4 to 8 is from the environmental bases for school behavior, to a description of overt student activities, to considerations of the subjective effects of school size. All studies relate to the theory of size effects explained in Chapter 2.

4

Structural Characteristics

ROGER G. BARKER • LOUISE SHEDD BARKER

THIS CHAPTER has two purposes: first, to identify the schools in which the
main studies were done; second, to define and explore in a preliminary way
some characteristics of schools which enter the other studies as major variables. In particular, this chapter will describe the relationship between
school size (enrollment) and the differentiation, population density, and
scope and specialization of school offerings.

THE SCHOOLS

Eastern Kansas is an area of mixed farming, cattle raising, and wheat
farming. The economy of the towns and cities is based mainly upon trade
with farmers, light manufacturing, government agencies, educational and
medical facilities, and military installations.

The region has a great variety of public high schools: central city high
schools, suburban high schools, county high schools, town high schools,
rural high schools. The high schools of eastern Kansas range in size from
18 to 2,287 students. We selected 13 of these high schools for intensive
studies, and 39 for special, limited investigations. Population data for the
13 schools and their communities are reported in Table 4.1. The school
enrollment is that reported by the State Department of Education as of
September 15, 1958; the community population is as of January 1, 1959.
During the three years these studies were under way, school and community populations fluctuated, but there were no marked changes. Population
data at the time of particular studies are given in the separate reports.
Brief descriptions of the 13 schools and communities follow.

Otan and *Dorset*, the smallest high schools, with enrollments of 35 and
45, respectively. These schools served towns with 199 and 169 residents,
together with the farm families in the surrounding rural areas. Otan appeared to be a declining town, partly because its existence was threatened

TABLE 4.1. POPULATION DATA FOR THE 13 SCHOOLS AND COMMUNITIES

School	School Enrollment Sept. 15, 1958	Population of Community Jan. 1, 1959
Otan	35	199
Dorset	45	169
Walker	83	450
Malden	92	507
Meadow*	113	—
Midwest	117	781
Vernon	151	1,150
Haven	221	2,907
Eakins†	339	551
Booth	438	3,004
University City	945	23,296
Shereton†	1,923	4,769
Capital City	2,287	101,155

* Meadow was two miles from the nearest town; it served four towns.

† High schools that served several communities in addition to the one in which the school was located.

by a proposed dam, and some students who would normally have attended Otan went to high schools in Vernon or Midwest, neighboring towns. Dorset showed no signs of decay.

Walker, Malden, Midwest, and *Vernon,* schools in the next larger size range, with enrollments of 83 to 151 students. These schools constituted the small school base for the main studies to be reported. They were all located in Midwest County, an exclusively rural county. Their communities were vigorous business, school, church, and social centers. The maximum distance between the towns was 19 miles. They were approximately 30, 25, 40, and 50 miles from cities of 100,000, 25,000, 30,000, and 800,000 population. The county and the town of Midwest (the county seat) have been described in some detail in Barker and Wright (1955) and Barker and Barker (1961a). Additional data are reported for these schools and towns in Table 4.2.

Walker, Malden, and Vernon had each passed bond issues and built new elementary school buildings within the previous three years; Midwest had built a new elementary and high school building. Walker, the smallest of the Midwest County communities, was the site of the County Hospital and

TABLE 4.2. POPULATION DATA FOR FOUR SMALL KANSAS
TOWNS AND HIGH SCHOOLS

School	Town Residents	Rural Area Residents	High School Enrollment	
			No.	Per Cent Rural
Walker	450	691	83	48
Malden	507	708	92	58
Midwest	781	807	117	59
Vernon	1,150	891	151	49

of two large nursing homes. Malden was the headquarters for the regional cooperative electrical distribution system, and the town was unusually well supplied with churches; there were four. Midwest, as the county seat, had a higher concentration of law offices, government offices, and county-wide meetings than the other towns. Vernon, the largest of the towns, had the greatest number of business establishments; it was the locus of the County 4-H Fair grounds, and was the only one of the four Midwest County towns on a railroad. The elementary education of Vernon was divided between the public school and a Catholic parochial school, the only nonpublic school in the four towns.

Meadow, a district (consolidated) school of 113 students. Meadow had been organized two years before our study to replace four town schools of about the size of Otan's school. The school building was situated in the country, two to eight miles from the four towns it served.

Haven, a high school of 221 students located in a city of 3,000 population. Students were drawn almost entirely from the town, which was a county seat and had some small industry. The Haven High School building housed the seventh and eighth grades as well as the high school, but the former constituted a separate administrative and functional unit.

Eakins, a district school of 339 pupils. Eakins served a large area of farms, and of small towns of 100 to 500 population. Most of its students were transported by bus, some a distance of 25 miles. Eakins was one of the oldest consolidated schools in Kansas.

Booth, a school of 438 students situated in a town of just over 3,000 population. Students were drawn from the town and the neighboring countryside.

University City, a school of 945 students housed in a new building. The city was the home of a state university, and it had some light manufacturing industry. It was a county seat. The population, not counting the university, was about 25,000.

Shereton, suburban high school of 1,923 students located on the border of a metropolitan area of 800,000 population. Shereton drew its students from a number of rapidly growing middle- and upper-class residential towns.

Capital City, a school of 2,287 students serving an entire city of 100,000. There were several junior high schools and one Catholic parochial high school in the city. The year following the study a second public high school was opened in Capital City. For purposes of this study, however, it was fortunate that the high school in Capital City was a community school, as were the high schools in most of the small towns. Capital City High School had an enviable reputation; it had won a number of national awards, which indicated that it was widely regarded as representing the best in American public secondary education. Capital City High School was the large school anchor for the principal studies.

Some further details about the schools are given in connection with the particular studies.

For our purposes, the essential features of the schools were (*a*) they all conformed to the standards of the same educational authority (the State of Kansas); (*b*) they all conformed to the mores of the same culture (eastern Kansas); (*c*) nine of the 13 schools served the total high school population of single communities; (*d*) they varied greatly in enrollment, namely, from 35 to 2,287 (see Table 4.1). These facts meant that we were able to investigate the relation between size of school and other institutional characteristics across a number of schools that were otherwise remarkably similar.

THE PARTS OF A SCHOOL

Considerable research has been done on the relation of size of institutions, including schools, to such structural features as the administrative hierarchy and channels of communication (Terrien and Mills, 1955; Tallachi, 1960; Indik, 1961; Cleland, 1955). Valuable as such studies may be, they do not investigate the aspects of school that have direct impact upon students. Students have immediate and continuous contact with parts of the school; they live in English classes, libraries, and football games, not in administrative hierarchies or communication channels. Our aim has been to study the parts of schools where children live their school lives.

So the first question we must answer is: What are the parts of a school? Perhaps the answer that most readily comes to mind is: School classes. But there are difficulties with classes as school units for the problems with which we are concerned. In the first place the classes are only one kind of school unit, or part. We are interested in every part of a school that children inhabit. Children do not live their school lives only in the classes they attend; they live, also, in the halls, in the assemblies, in the principal's office, in the vocal trio, in the shower room. But how are these to be dealt with in conjunction with classes? Are they equivalent to classes? Do Mr. X's algebra classes in room 7 = the graduation procession = the senior dance = the counselor's office = the semester examination period = the school lunch room = the student council meeting = the marching band practice? The problem of equivalence arises in connection with classes too. Are Typing I and Typing II one class or two? They are listed separately in the schedule, but they meet at the same time in the same room with the same teacher. What about Physics, which meets for book work and recitation in classroom 3 on Tuesday and Thursday and meets for laboratory work in room 9 on Monday, Wednesday, and Friday? Is this one class or two?

Other complications will occur to the reader. Institutional units that are equivalent in a fundamental sense within schools, between schools, and between schools and communities are essential if we are ever able to have a comparative science of schools, and of schools and communities. Classes are not adequate for this purpose.

What are the parts of a school? In addition to classes, answers have been given in terms of space, equipment, education of faculty, window area, curricula, and budgets. These approaches provide information about important problems, but they do not describe a school as it functions vis-à-vis its pupils; they are akin to describing a house in terms of the properties of the boards, bricks, pipes, and nails of which it is made. Schools and houses, as places where living and learning occur, are not revealed by procedures that dismantle them.

At this point the reader may wish to review the discussion of behavior settings (Chapter 2), for these are the school units in terms of which we shall analyze schools. Behavior settings have these values for our purposes:

(*a*) they occur within the same spatial-temporal manifold as the school itself; (*b*) they are parts of the school; they are within it; (*c*) they are natural (i.e., experimenter-free) parts of the school; (*d*) they occur on a level of inclusiveness immediately below the school; no other part of the same or greater degree of unity separates a behavior setting and the school; (*e*) they occur upon a level of inclusiveness immediately above the persons who inhabit the school; behavior settings intervene between pupils and teachers and the school itself; (*f*) all behavior settings have the same degree of internal interdependence, as measured by the K-21 rating; they have the same unity; (*g*) they have fundamental, common characteristics; they belong to the same class of phenomena wherever they occur (Barker and Wright, 1955; Barker, 1960); (*h*) behavior settings vary in the degree to which they possess various properties; it is via the variable properties of behavior settings that the school exerts its influence upon pupils and teachers; (*i*) it is also by way of their variable properties that classes of behavior settings with defined degrees of similarity can be identified.

Examples of behavior settings have already been given, and others will be presented later. The relationship between behavior settings and school classes will be considered here. The K-21 cutting point we have used for determining the limits of a behavior setting solves univocally the problems raised above in the following ways: Mr. X's algebra classes = the senior dance = the counselor's office = the school lunch room = the student council meeting. These settings are "equal" in the sense that each has that minimum degree of internal unity and external independence that meets the K-21 criteria.

However, Mr. X's algebra classes $\neq$ the graduation procession $\neq$ semester examination period. Application of the K-21 method reveals that the graduation procession is a part, a cytosetting, of the behavior setting Graduation Exercises. The semester examination period is not equal to Mr. X's algebra classes because it represents a number of parts of other settings; these parts are not independent of the classes for which they are terminal events. Analysis of the operations of Typing I and Typing II reveals interdependence to a degree that makes them parts of one setting. This is true, too, of the physics class and the physics laboratory.

Objections can be made to almost every "decision" of the K-21 behavior setting criteria on grounds that change from one instance to another. But one strength of the K-21 basis for identifying behavior settings is that the grounds for discrimination are held constant; the same criteria are always employed, and hence the same phenomena are identified in each case. Criteria for discrimination include interdependence variables in order to assure identification of parts with the same degree of unity. Decisions based on the K-21 analysis become univocal and, within the rating reliability, objective.

BEHAVIOR SETTING SURVEYS

The primary data of this study were complete catalogues of all the K-21 behavior settings occurring in each school for the school year 1959–60. Each catalogue, or behavior setting survey, was arranged by behavior setting variety (cf. pp. 27–28). Complete behavior setting surveys of two schools are given in Appendix 4.1.

Behavior setting surveys of the schools were made according to the directions given by Barker and Wright (1955, pp. 491–95). The general task in such a survey is that of identifying all of the supra-individual place-time-behavior units of a given degree of independence and internal unity. Field work problems are easier for a school than for a community inasmuch as the school building, the class schedule, the table of school organization, written information and directions for students, the school paper, and the school yearbook provide much of the essential information. Of great help to the field work in the present case was the complete, and thoroughly rechecked, behavior setting survey of one of the schools, Midwest, which was available to us at the beginning of the study. Since all the schools were basically similar, this survey served as a useful guide; it was like having an anatomical dissection chart of one specimen of a species to guide the dissection of other specimens. After the basic structure of a school was laid out on the basis of the source material mentioned above, a relatively small amount of field observation and interviewing of staff and students served to complete the survey.

THE RELATION BETWEEN SCHOOL POPULATION
AND SCHOOL DIFFERENTIATION

Data on the population and differentiation of the schools are reported in Table 4.3 and Figure 4.1. Differentiation (D) here refers to the number of parts or behavior settings that a school contains for one school year.

Population refers to number of students enrolled. The data show that across the high schools, when they are ordered by population, differentiation increased more slowly than population. The smallest school had 1.5 per cent of the population and 14 per cent of the differentiation of the largest school. The smallest schools had fewer students than parts and the

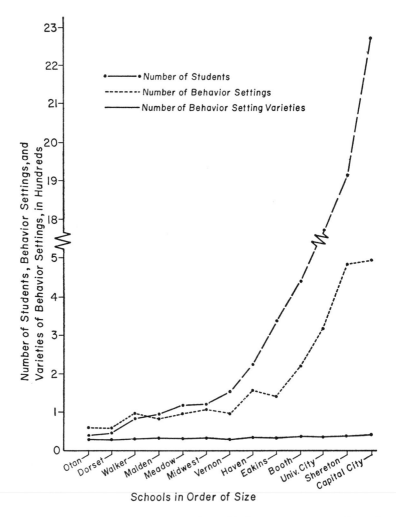

Fig. 4.1. Number of students, number of behavior settings, and number of behavior setting varieties for 13 schools.

TABLE 4.3. STUDENT POPULATION, NUMBER OF BEHAVIOR SETTINGS
OR DIFFERENTIATION, POPULATION/DIFFERENTIATION RATIOS,
AND VARIETIES OF SETTINGS IN 13 KANSAS SCHOOLS

School	Population (P)	Differentia- tion (D)	P/D Ratio	Varieties
Otan	35	60	0.58	29
Dorset	45	58	0.78	28
Walker	83	96	0.86	31
Malden	92	78	1.18	33
Meadow	113	94	1.20	32
Midwest	117	107	1.09	33
Vernon	151	98	1.54	29
Haven	221	154	1.44	36
Eakins	339	139	2.44	34
Booth	438	218	2.01	39
University City	945	312	3.03	36
Shereton	1,923	487	3.95	41
Capital City	2,287	499	4.58	43

largest had over four times as many students as parts. The actual ratios of
students to settings (P/D) are given in Table 4.3. P/D ratios are the average number of students per setting within individual schools; they are
equivalent to the average population density, as this is used by demogra-
phers. The P/D ratio ranged from 0.58 for the smallest school to 4.58 for
the largest school.

The P/D ratios tell nothing about the actual numbers of inhabitants in
the behavior settings of schools, since inhabitants are not fixed to settings;
every pupil inhabits a number of settings. To investigate the actual populations, we secured data for a sample of students in a sample of the settings
of seven schools. In Table 4.4 we report the mean and the median number
of Junior Class students inhabiting the extracurricular behavior settings
of these schools. These data refer only to those behavior settings inhabited
by one or more Junior Class students. In this sample of schools, the settings
of the small schools, with low P/D ratios, had fewer Junior student inhabitants than the settings of the large schools, with high P/D ratios.

Our first findings may be summarized as follows: (a) the large schools
had more parts than the small schools, but (b) the greater number of parts
of the large schools was not proportional to their greater number of stu-

TABLE 4.4. MEAN AND MEDIAN NUMBER OF JUNIOR STUDENT INHABITANTS
OF EXTRACURRICULAR BEHAVIOR SETTINGS FOR SCHOOLS
OF DIFFERENT SIZES AND P/D RATIOS

School	P/D Ratio	No. of Students	No. of Students in Behavior Settings	
			Mean	Median
Walker	0.86	16	10.6	11.8
Malden	1.18	18	11.5	13.7
Midwest	1.09	22	11.0	10.4
Vernon	1.54	36	17.0	13.0
Haven	1.44	50	23.1	20.9
Eakins	2.44	86	34.9	30.0
Capital City	4.58	714	105.5	37.0

dents, so that (c) large schools had greater average density of students per setting (P/D ratio) than small schools, and (d) they had a greater average number of student inhabitants per setting.

According to behavior setting theory, the population of a behavior setting and the P/D ratio of an institution are important aspects of the environments that settings and institutions provide their inhabitants (cf. Chap. 2). Our data establish the fact that, in the schools we have studied, these variables are positively related to school size. In the research presented in the other chapters of this report, some derivations from behavior setting theory are tested in schools of various sizes, using the P/D ratio as the independent variable. The present data demonstrate that within these schools, P/D is an index of the relative population of the behavior settings of schools.

RELATION BETWEEN SCHOOL SIZE AND
NUMBER OF BEHAVIOR SETTING VARIETIES

Schools have so far been described in terms of numbers of parts or settings; it is also possible to portray schools in terms of the range of differences represented in their array of settings. One index of this range is that of *variety* (see pp. 27–28). Mr. X's algebra classes and Mr. Y's trigonometry classes are two independent settings of one variety. Mr. X's algebra classes and the Homecoming Assembly are settings from two different varieties. The richness of the schools' offerings, as measured by the number and nature of the varieties present, is our next concern.

The data of Table 4.3 and Figure 4.1 show that there were more varieties of behavior settings in the larger than in the smaller schools, but that the increment was less for varieties than for settings, and much less for varieties than for school population. In other words, the schools differed more with respect to number of students than with respect to number of settings, and more with respect to number of settings than with respect to number of behavior setting varieties. When we compare the largest school with the smallest, we find that it contained 65 times as many students, 8 times as many settings, but only 1.5 times as many varieties of settings.

We turn next to a consideration of the nature of the behavior setting varieties in the small and large schools.

VARIETIES OF BEHAVIOR SETTINGS COMMON
TO SCHOOLS OF DIFFERENT SIZES

Forty-two different varieties of settings were present in the 13 schools, and of these, 19, or 44 per cent, occurred in all schools. Setting varieties found in every school might be thought of as the basic, or common denominator, settings. Within the society studied, such kinds of settings were probably essential if a school was to be a school. These common varieties are listed below. The numbers are the variety numbers; the letters in parentheses refer to variety groupings (see p. 54).

1. Athletic Contests, Indoors (A)
2. Athletic Contests, Outdoors (A)
20. Educational Groups, Academic (E)
22. Educational Groups, Home Economics (E)
24. Educational Groups, Physical Education (E)
25. Educational Groups, Shop and Agriculture (E)
29. Fire and Tornado Drills (O)
39. Government and School Offices (O)
41. Hallways and Coatrooms (O)
52. Libraries (E)
54. Meetings, Executive (Ex)
55. Meetings, Organization Business (Ex)
64. Open Spaces (Ex)
65. Outings (Ex)
70. Plays, Concerts, and Programs (Ex)
76. Recognition Programs (Ex)

80. Restaurants, School Lunch Room (O)
81. Restrooms (O)
83. School, Coaches' Rooms (O)

The common behavior setting varieties encompassed 65 per cent of the 2,300 behavior settings in the 13 schools; the number and per cent of settings within the common varieties are shown for each school in Table 4.5. It is clear that the per cent of behavior settings in common varieties decreased with school size. Conversely, the proportion of school settings beyond the common denominator group rose as school size increased. Nevertheless the degree of similarity of the schools with respect to varieties of behavior settings was much greater than their similarity with respect to population and differentiation. Within schools that differed in population by a factor of 65 and that differed in differentiation by a factor of 8, 44 per cent of the varieties were common to all schools and 47 per cent or more of the behavior settings of every school were in common varieties. If one compares individual large and small schools, the degree of commonality is even greater. Seventy-seven per cent of the behavior setting varieties present in Midwest High School (enrollment 117) and Capital City (enrollment 2,287) were common to both schools; all of Midwest High School's settings and 80 per cent of Capital City High School's were common varieties.

TABLE 4.5. BEHAVIOR SETTINGS WITHIN VARIETIES COMMON
TO ALL SCHOOLS

School	No. of BS	Per Cent of School's BS
Otan	48	80
Dorset	47	81
Walker	67	70
Malden	55	71
Meadow	67	70
Midwest	77	72
Vernon	82	84
Haven	125	81
Eakins	109	78
Booth	123	56
University City	206	66
Shereton	247	51
Capital City	233	47

Five varieties of behavior settings were absent from schools with fewer than 339 students, namely:

Educational Groups, Art (E)
Educational Groups, Swimming (E)
Doctors' Offices and Clinics (O)
Home Rooms (O)
Elections (Ex)

Driver Education did not occur in schools with fewer than 92 students, and Dances and Educational Groups, Music, did not occur in the smallest school, with 35 students.

Two of the behavior setting varieties were absent from the small schools for functional reasons. Elections did not occur in the small schools; nevertheless, student officers were elected in all schools. In the small schools the election of officers occurred within other, less specialized varieties of settings such as Meetings, Organization Business (e.g., Junior Class Meeting), and Plays, Concerts, and Programs (e.g., All-School Assembly). This is an example of the emergence in large schools of specialized varieties of settings from the less specialized settings of the small schools. The variety Home Rooms in the larger schools is another example of the same process of specialization. Lack of material resources was undoubtedly an important factor in the absence of Driver Education and Swimming from small schools, and insufficient manpower was involved in the absence of Art Classes and Doctors' Offices and Clinics from the small schools.

There were 14 other behavior setting varieties that were missing from some of the schools. The absence of these varieties was not clearly related to school size; they were absent from a single school only, or from schools of various sizes; the omissions appeared to be due to local, often temporary causes.

In summary, there were three varieties of behavior settings whose essential features were not available to the students of the small schools, namely, Swimming Classes, Medical Examinations and Service,* and Art Classes (i.e., painting, sculpture, and crafts; music and drama were present in all schools). No variety of setting was regularly absent from the large schools.

* Medical examinations for athletic participation occurred in the local doctors' offices.

NUMBER OF BEHAVIOR SETTINGS IN DIFFERENT CLASSIFICATIONS

It is of interest to know the extent to which schools of various sizes emphasized certain aspects of the environments they provided their students. One measure of emphasis is the proportion of a school's settings having designated characteristics. For example, do larger or smaller schools devote a greater proportion of their settings to extracurricular affairs? To investigate such questions we have grouped behavior setting varieties into four classes: (E) Educational behavior settings (all varieties of behavior settings that consisted of formal classes, with a teacher and pupils); (A) Athletic behavior settings (athletic games and contests); (O) Operating behavior settings (settings that maintained the school); (Ex) Extracurricular settings (all other settings). The grouping of the different varieties is indicated in the lists by the symbols E, A, O, Ex. The number of settings in each of these variety groupings is presented in Table 4.6.

A coefficient of concordance (Kendall, 1948) indicates that there was agreement among the schools in rank order of number of behavior settings in the four variety classes ($p < .001$). In general, the relative order of frequency within schools was Extracurricular, Educational, Athletic, Oper-

TABLE 4.6. NUMBER AND PER CENT OF BEHAVIOR SETTINGS WITHIN EACH SCHOOL WHICH FELL INTO FOUR VARIETY GROUPINGS

	Variety Grouping				
School	Educational	Athletic	Operating	Extracurricular	Total
Otan	12 (20)	10 (17)	11 (18)	27 (45)	60
Dorset	15 (26)	12 (21)	6 (10)	25 (43)	58
Walker	17 (18)	13 (14)	11 (12)	55 (57)	96
Malden	14 (18)	13 (17)	8 (10)	43 (55)	78
Meadow	20 (21)	15 (16)	11 (12)	48 (51)	94
Midwest	18 (17)	15 (14)	13 (12)	61 (57)	107
Vernon	18 (18)	17 (17)	8 (8)	55 (56)	98
Haven	27 (18)	20 (13)	14 (9)	93 (60)	154
Eakins	40 (29)	18 (13)	14 (10)	67 (48)	139
Booth	39 (18)	22 (10)	32 (15)	125 (57)	218
University City ..	56 (18)	53 (17)	57 (18)	146 (47)	312
Shereton	88 (18)	54 (11)	101 (21)	244 (50)	487
Capital City	108 (22)	50 (10)	114 (23)	227 (46)	499

Note: Figures in parentheses are percentages.

ating. However, inspection of the rank order matrix showed considerable deviation from this order within the larger schools. In the three largest schools the order was Extracurricular, Operating, Educational, and Athletic. A chi-square test of obtained vs. expected frequencies involving all the data of Table 4.6 indicates that the schools were heterogeneous with respect to actual frequency of settings within the variety groupings $(p < .005)$.

Analyses of each variety grouping separately across schools revealed that the frequency of settings varied more than would be expected in the case of Operating varieties $(p < .001)$ and Extracurricular varieties $(p < .02)$. Inspection of Table 4.6 shows that in the largest schools a greater proportion of all behavior settings fell in the Operating category. This finding is in accord with findings of industrial research, which indicate that specialized administrative and control personnel increase more rapidly than total personnel (Terrien and Mills, 1955; Haire, 1955). No pattern in the relation of school size to per cent of Extracurricular settings was apparent.

In summary, large and small schools were similar in their concentration of settings in the four areas. However, there was a significant trend for large schools to emphasize Operating settings more than small schools.

RELATION BETWEEN SCHOOL SIZE AND SCOPE OF
ATHLETIC BEHAVIOR SETTINGS

In the analyses above, behavior settings were grouped into broader categories than varieties. They can also be placed in narrower classes than varieties. Within any of the varieties we have identified there are subvarieties of behavior settings with greater intersetting similarity than within varieties. We have called these *equivalence groups,* or *kinds* of settings. The standing behavior patterns and the material supports of settings within the same equivalence groups can be exchanged between the settings with little disturbance; e.g., the setting Football Game, A Team, and the setting Football Game, Freshmen, are highly congruent and could be easily transposed.

A measure of the breadth or scope of behavior settings in a variety is the number of behavior setting equivalence groups it contains, i.e., the number of different kinds of behavior settings it encompasses. Thus, the behavior setting variety Athletic Contests, Indoors, in the town of Otan

TABLE 4.7. NUMBER OF BEHAVIOR SETTINGS AND NUMBER OF KINDS OF
BEHAVIOR SETTINGS (SCOPE) IN THE VARIETIES ATHLETIC CONTESTS,
INDOORS AND OUTDOORS, IN ORDER OF SCHOOL ENROLLMENT

School	No. of Settings	Scope	Per Cent of Maximum Scope
Otan	10	4	21
Dorset	12	4	21
Walker	13	3	16
Malden	13	4	21
Meadow	15	4	21
Midwest	15	5	27
Vernon	16	5	27
Haven	20	6	32
Eakins	18	4	21
Booth	22	7	37
University City	53	13	69
Shereton	48	12	64
Capital City	49	15	80

had two kinds of behavior settings: Basketball Games (four settings) and
Gym for Free Play (one setting). The scope of this variety in Otan was,
therefore, 2. Haven High School had the same two kinds of behavior
settings, and also a third, Wrestling, making a scope score of 3.

We have studied the scope of Athletic Contests, both Indoors and Outdoors, across the 13 schools. In the 13 schools, there were 19 different kinds
of behavior settings within the varieties Athletic Contest, Indoors and
Outdoors, as follows (each equivalence group included contests, games,
and practices, if the latter occurred):

Basketball   Aerial darts
Wrestling   Football
Handball   Touch football
Bowling   Tennis
Volleyball   Golf
Table tennis   Baseball
Badminton   Hockey
Trampoline   Free gym activities
Track   Swimming
Gymnastics

The total (summed) scope scores for the two varieties of Athletic Contests are reported for each town in Table 4.7. In this table, also, the num-

ber of athletic behavior settings is presented, and the scope score is given as a per cent of the possible maximum scope, i.e., 19.

These data show that the number of kinds of athletic behavior settings, i.e., the scope of athletic activities, increased by a factor of about 4, from 4 in the smallest school to 15 in the largest. At the same time, the total number of athletic behavior settings increased by a factor of about 5, from 10 to 49. The relation of scope scores to size presents a different picture of the relative richness of large and small school offerings from that of the relation of variety to size. It will be recalled that variety from smallest to largest school increased by a factor of only 1.5. These data on scope within athletic varieties would indicate that the richness advantage of a large

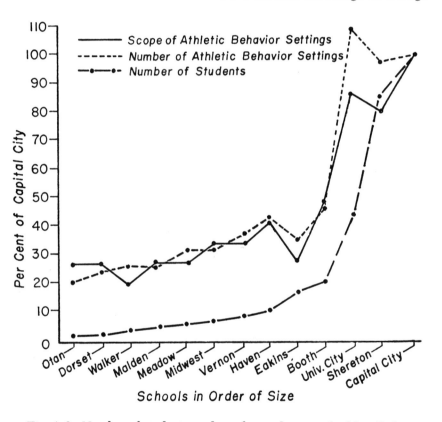

Fig. 4.2. Number of students, and number and scope of athletic behavior settings expressed as per cent of data for largest school.

school is one of heterogeneity within varieties rather than the more diverse richness of many varieties. Thirteen of the 19 kinds of athletic behavior settings did not occur in schools with 151 or fewer students, namely:

Wrestling	Gymnastics
Handball	Aerial darts
Bowling	Tennis
Volleyball	Golf
Table tennis	Swimming
Badminton	Hockey
Trampoline	

The data concerning school size, and number and scope of athletic behavior settings are presented graphically in Figure 4.2. Here all data for each school are presented as proportions (per cents) of the data for the largest school. These data make it dramatically clear that the schools did not differ so much in terms of number and kinds of athletic behavior settings as in terms of number of pupils: the largest school contained 65 times as many students, five times as many athletic behavior settings, and four times as many kinds of athletic settings as the smallest school.

RELATION BETWEEN SCHOOL SIZE AND SCOPE
OF ACADEMIC BEHAVIOR SETTINGS

Athletic behavior settings do not usually contain subparts, or cyto-settings, with sufficient completeness to allow them, under any circumstances, to be differentiated as separate, independent settings. The audience of a basketball game without the game is not a viable unit. This is not true of some other cytosettings. The pharmacy and the fountain of a drugstore have enough completeness in themselves to survive as independent settings under the proper circumstances. This is true, too, of some parts of a church worship service: the choir might sing alone, for its own satisfaction. There are many such cytosettings within the K-21 behavior settings of the variety Educational Groups, Academic.

For example, Mrs. S's shorthand and bookkeeping classes meet at the same time and place under the same leadership; thus, they are parts of one behavior setting. Either class could exist alone, however, and each represents a different kind of curricular activity. A measure that counts these classes as separate and different would reflect a school's scope of academic offerings.

In order to study the scope of academic activities we identified all the cytosettings of the 13 schools that had the potentiality of independent existence; this was done on the basis of our general experience: any cytosetting we had known to exist in some school as a separate setting was so identified. After identifying these cytosettings within the 13 schools we placed them in equivalence groups, or kinds of academic activities, exactly as we did with the athletic behavior settings. There were, in the 13 schools, 34 kinds of academic activities within the variety Educational Groups, Academic, as follows:

English	American History
Journalism	American Government
Public Speaking	World History
	Economics
General Mathematics	Sociology
Algebra	Psychology
Geometry	Occupations
Trigonometry	
Probability and	Latin
Statistics	Spanish
	French
General Science	German
Chemistry	
Physics	General Business
Geography	Typing
	Shorthand
General Biology	Bookkeeping
Physiology	Business Law
Botany	Office Machines
Health	Retail Selling

The number of academic behavior settings and their scope are reported in Table 4.8; scope is presented, too, as a per cent of the maximum possible scope, i.e., 34.

As with athletic contests, the scope of activities within the academic behavior settings changed with the size of the school, from 13 in the smallest school to 30 in the largest, i.e., by a factor of 2.3. At the same time the number of academic behavior settings changed from 8 to 64, i.e., by a factor of 8. These data are presented graphically in Figure 4.3, where all data for each school are presented as proportions (per cents) of the data for the largest school. The curves show that the small schools were not so small in terms of number and kinds of academic activities as they were in size, and that the scope of academic activities varied less with school size

TABLE 4.8. NUMBER OF BEHAVIOR SETTINGS AND NUMBER OF KINDS OF CYTOSETTINGS (SCOPE) FOR THE VARIETY EDUCATIONAL GROUPS, ACADEMIC, IN ORDER OF SCHOOL ENROLLMENT

School	No. of Settings	Scope	Per Cent of Maximum Scope
Otan	8	13	38
Dorset	5	12	35
Walker	8	14	41
Malden	5	12	35
Meadow	10	15	44
Midwest	8	13	38
Vernon	7	14	41
Haven	13	19	56
Eakins	23	20	68
Booth	21	23	68
University City	30	23	68
Shereton	60	27	79
Capital City	64	30	88

than did number of academic settings. The largest school had 65 times as many students, 8 times as many academic behavior settings, and 2.3 times as many kinds of academic activities as the smallest school.

Nine of the 34 cytosetting equivalence groups were not represented in any school with fewer than 151 students, namely:

Probability and   Geography
  Statistics   Spanish
Economics   French
Sociology   German
Psychology   Retail Selling

Six of the equivalence groups occurred within the larger schools as differentiated cytosettings, but they were present in less specialized forms in the smaller schools. These were:

Journalism   Business Law
Public Speaking   Office Machines
Physiology   Occupations

The remaining 19 equivalence groups of cytosettings were represented in schools of all sizes and were common to schools of 220 and over.

The smaller schools were deficient, in comparison with the larger schools, with respect to specialized mathematics, specialized social and behavioral sciences, foreign languages, and specialized business classes.

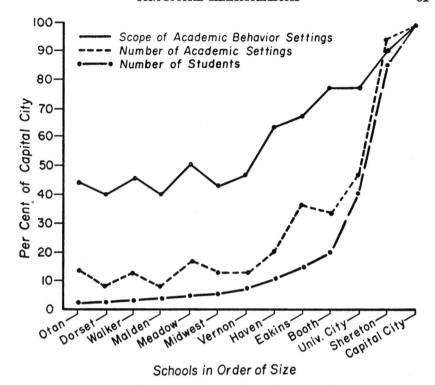

Fig. 4.3. Number of students, and number and scope of academic cytosettings expressed as per cent of data for largest school.

RELATION OF SCHOOL SIZE TO OTHER SCHOOL
CHARACTERISTICS—A SUMMARY

The data assembled indicate that as the schools increased in size, they increased in differentiation, but at a much slower rate. Accompanying the increase in number of settings was a corresponding increase in population density: the theoretical number of persons per setting, as represented by the P/D ratio, increased with size; the actual number of persons inhabiting settings also increased.

There is also evidence that increase in school size was accompanied by a change in the proportion of settings with certain functions. Specifically, the large schools invested a larger proportion of their settings in operating processes. This finding indicates that the larger schools had a different shape as well as a greater mass.

The extent to which school size was related to the richness of offerings depended upon the measure of richness employed. The variety index, which reflects only major degrees of diversity among settings, showed relatively little richness difference between large and small schools. When heterogeneity within varieties was investigated, it was found that large schools provided about four times as many kinds of athletic settings and twice as many kinds of academic cytosettings as the smallest schools.

In general, the smaller schools managed to sustain a large proportion of the types of offerings provided by the larger schools.

THE SCHOOL SIZE ILLUSION

To an outside observer, a school with many students is impressive: its imposing physical dimensions, its seemingly endless halls and numberless rooms, its hundreds of microscopes, its vast auditorium and great audiences, its sweeping tides of students, all carry the message of power, movement, vitality, purpose, achievement, certainty. In contrast, a small school with its commonplace building, its few microscopes, its dual-purpose gym-auditorium half-filled with students who assemble and depart, not in tides but in a tangle of separate channels, is not impressive. The members of the field-work team never ceased to marvel that the directly experienced differences between large and small schools were, in these respects, so compelling, like the differences between a towering mountain and an ordinary hill, between a mighty river and a meandering brook.

But to an inside participant the view is different. When the field workers were able to participate in the functioning behavior settings of schools, they saw the small schools as in some respects more coercive and dominating than the large schools, and the studies presented later in this report amply confirm this impression. There is, indeed, an inside-outside perceptual paradox, a school size illusion.

The data on school structure that have been presented in this chapter lay the groundwork for the explanation of this illusion. We have discovered that small high schools are, in fact, not so small on the inside as they are on the outside. In terms of number of behavior settings, number of varieties of behavior settings, and number of inhabitants per setting—interior characteristics not easily seen from the outside—small schools differ less from large schools than in terms of number of students and amount of space, which are perceptually salient external attributes of schools. Here is one basis of the school size illusion. But, more important, these findings raise the question of which are the stronger variables so far as students are concerned, the inside ones or the outside ones, and how they operate upon students. These are the problems of the chapters that follow.

5

Participation in Interschool Events and Extracurricular Activities

ROGER G. BARKER • ELEANOR R. HALL

THIS CHAPTER reports the results of our first reconnaissance of the problem of school size and student behavior. It makes use of data from the reports of government agencies, school organizations, and schools. The available data were fragmentary, but their meaning was clear within the narrow limits to which they applied, and they were decisive in convincing us that our theoretical analysis of the effects of school size upon the lives of high school students was promising. The more systematic investigations reported in the chapters that follow constitute replications and extensions of these first efforts, using more adequate data and methods.

SCHOOL SIZE AND PARTICIPATION IN INTERSCHOOL EVENTS

The Kansas State High School Activities Association organizes and supervises a great number of interschool contests, exhibitions, and festivals. In addition to sports events, regional and state competitions are held in the fields of drama, group and individual musical performance, and debating. The Activities Association also arranges conferences for school journalists and student government officers. It has, in addition, a program of interschool social and recreational activities.

The Association keeps careful records of the participation of each school in its programs, and in the case of the events concerned with drama, music, journalism, and student government the records include the number of individual participants from each school. We have used these records as measures of the extent of participation in the corresponding behavior settings of the member high schools.

Data were available from the Activities Association for 218 three- and four-year schools in eastern Kansas ranging in enrollment on September 15, 1958, from 18 to 2,287, and totaling 38,172 students. In using these data we

TABLE 5.1. NUMBER OF STUDENTS AND SCHOOLS IN STATED
SCHOOL SIZE-CLASSES

School Size-Class	School Size (No. of Students)		No. of Students	No. of Schools
	Range	Mean		
1	18–60	42	3,139	75
2	61–97	76	4,420	58
3	101–50	115	4,370	38
4	159–285	217	4,334	20
5	334–539	423	4,226	10
6	547–743	611	4,277	7
7	773–974	889	4,443	5
8	1,346–1,923	1,541	4,622	3
9	2,054–2,287	2,171	4,341	2
			38,172	218

have made no distinction between three- and four-year high schools. The 218 schools were divided into nine school size-classes, with a comparable number of students in each class. For each school size-class, the size range, the mean number of students per school, the total number of students, and the number of schools in the class are presented in Table 5.1.

The number of students from each of the 218 schools who participated in 1959 in district competitions and conferences concerned with dramatics, group musical performance, individual musical performance, school journalism, and student government affairs are reported in Table 5.2.

TABLE 5.2. NUMBER OF STUDENT PARTICIPANTS IN INTERSCHOOL
EVENTS FOR DIFFERENT SCHOOL SIZE-CLASSES

School Size-Class*	Dramatics	Journalism	Student Government	Music	
				Individual	Group
1	46	26	9	121	647
2	126	8	48	182	1,616
3	117	113	113	136	1,345
4	100	36	51	145	1,346
5	48	40	42	64	563
6	55	46	23	62	299
7	45	63	52	47	228
8	54	40	27	70	619
9	20	31	8	38	69

* See Table 5.1.

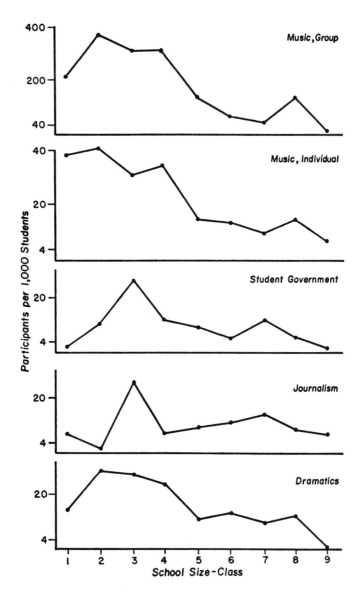

Fig. 5.1. Participation by high school students in district meetings. Number of participants per thousand students enrolled in the schools of different sizes. (See Table 5.1.)

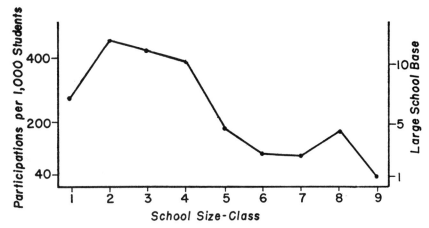

Fig. 5.2. Participation of high school students in district meetings; combined data. (See Table 5.1.)

The number of participating students per thousand enrolled in the schools of each size-class have been calculated from the data of Tables 5.1 and 5.2. The resulting participation rates are plotted in Figure 5.1. The five participation curves have two features in common: (*a*) the number of participants per thousand students is smallest in the largest schools, and (*b*) the number of participants per thousand is greatest in either the second or the third size-class (mean size 76 or 115); all the curves reach a peak in the smaller, but not in the smallest schools.

The general similarity of the separate curves justifies combining them; this has been done by summing the number of participants across events (Table 5.2), and converting to number per thousand enrolled in the schools of each size-class (Table 5.1). It should be clearly understood that the combined participation curves (Figure 5.2) do not report the number of different individuals who participated in district events, inasmuch as the same person could take part in more than one event; rather, the curves represent the number of district "participations" per thousand students. Two scales are provided for Figure 5.2: (*a*) participations per thousand students enrolled, and (*b*) participations per thousand expressed in terms of the rate for the largest class of schools, i.e.,

$$\frac{\text{rate for schools of class } X}{\text{rate for schools with largest enrollment (class 9)}}.$$

Statistical tests have not been applied to the data of Table 5.2. We look upon the data for the different events as independent tests of participation, and the five curves, therefore, as replicative. Their essential similarity leads us to conclude that in the schools involved, participation in district music, dramatic, journalistic, and student government events was more frequent in high schools within the 61-285 size range than in the smaller or the larger schools. If we take the data of Figure 5.2 as the most adequate, we find that participations in the five district events amounted to about 40 per cent (400 per 1,000) of the enrollments within school size-classes 2, 3, and 4 (61-285 students), that there was a sharp drop from these levels to school size-class 5 (334-539 students), and that the schools in classes 2, 3, and 4 had over ten times the rate of participation as the largest schools.

Although these findings are in line with the theories of school structure and behavior setting dynamics reported in Chapters 1 and 2 of this report, they can only be considered as suggestive and worthy of further exploration; there are inadequacies in the data and uncontrolled variables in the research design.

One of the latter is the possible different significance of district inter-school events for schools of different sizes. Perhaps large school administrators and students do not value district meetings so highly as small school administrators and students; perhaps large schools aspire, rather, to state and national competitions. One bit of evidence on this issue is the number of schools that entered the district events. One might expect schools that devalued the district meetings to enter, as schools, with less frequency than schools that valued them. The data of Table 5.1 show that there were 116 schools in the size-classes 2, 3, and 4; there were therefore $5 \times 116 = 580$ possible school entrances in the five events. In fact, there were 222 such entrances, i.e., 40 per cent of the possibilities. For the four largest school size-classes, there were 85 possible school entrances, and 57 actual entrances, i.e., 67 per cent of the possibilities. The large schools entered, as schools, in the district events even more widely than the small schools; this does not look like devaluation.

But rather than speculate about possible unknown factors we shall turn to another kind of public data.

It is the custom in the high schools of eastern Kansas to publish in a school yearbook the pictures of the graduating Senior students and a list of the extracurricular activities of each Senior during his high school career. The activity data are supplied to the yearbook by each student. We were able to obtain yearbooks for 36 high schools; the data that follow were secured from these yearbooks.

We have defined extracurricular activities as these were defined and recorded by the students themselves, according to standards that were common over the region of the 36 schools. Extracurricular activities fell into seven groupings, or kinds: members of school clubs, officers of school clubs and classes, members of athletic teams, cheerleaders, members of casts of school plays, members of staffs of school papers and yearbooks, members of music groups. The enumeration of a student's activities included each activity reported by him for each school year. Examples of the activity reports of two students follow. The numbers following an activity refer to the high school year in which the activity was undertaken.

Vernon High School Senior Boy
    Football—1,2,3,4
    Basketball—1,2,3,4
    Baseball—3,4
    Track—1,2,4
    Class President—1
    V-Club Treasurer—3
    V-Club President—4
    V-Club—2,3,4
    Boys' Glee Club—2,3,4
    Mixed Chorus—2
    Junior Play—3

Capital City High School Senior Boy
    Football—1,2
    Boys' Pep—2,3
    Track—1
    Band—1,2,3
    President Trojan Amateur
      Radio Club—3
    Orchestra—3
    Operetta Orchestra—3

Each year in an activity was scored one; these scores were 24 and 11.

Most of the yearbooks we secured were for four-year schools. We adjusted the data for the few three-year high schools by increasing the three-year activity score by 18.7 per cent, which was the proportion that Freshman activities bore to Sophomore, Junior, and Senior activities in four-year schools.

TABLE 5.3. NUMBER OF GRADUATING SENIORS AND EXTRACURRICULAR
ACTIVITIES FOR STATED SCHOOL SIZE-CLASSES

School Size-Class*	No. of Schools	Senior Class Size		Mean No. of Activities per School, for 4 Years	
		Range	Mean	Range of School Means	Mean of School Means
1	4	5–11	8	17–28	21.5
2	5	14–20	17	13–19	15.0
3	11	14–37	24	9–30	18.5
4	4	48–56	51	13–20	16.5
5	7	68–112	84	9–16	12.3
6	1	—	160	—	11.8
7	2	143–221	182	8.7–10.2	9.4
8	1	—	458	—	9.1
9	1	—	591	—	9.6

* See Table 5.1.

The data on school size and average number of extracurricular activities are presented in Table 5.3, where the schools are grouped into the same size-classes as in Table 5.1.

The mean number of activities are presented graphically in Figure 5.3; both the mean for each school and the mean for the schools of each size-class are presented. The product-moment correlation between school size and the average number of activities reported by Senior students is $-.51$ ($p < .01$).

The per cents of Senior students reporting no extracurricular activities, three or fewer activities, and 21 or more activities are presented for schools of four size ranges in Table 5.4. Chi-square tests were made of the actual

TABLE 5.4. PER CENT OF SENIOR STUDENTS REPORTING VARIOUS NUMBERS
OF EXTRACURRICULAR ACTIVITIES DURING FOUR-YEAR SCHOOL CAREER
FOR SCHOOLS WITHIN STATED SIZE RANGES

Size Range of Schools	Total No. of Senior Students	Per Cent Reporting No Activities	Per Cent Reporting 0, 1, 2, or 3 Activities	Per Cent Reporting 21 or More Activities
34–100	163	1.2	5.5	44.2
104–150	219	0.5	7.8	34.2
211–474	793	5.5	20.6	23.5
618–2,287	1,573	10.9	26.7	14.2

number of students reporting (*a*) no activities vs. one or more activities, (*b*) three or fewer activities vs. four or more activities, and (*c*) 20 or fewer vs. 21 or more activities. In all cases chi square exceeded chance expectation ($p < .001$). Inspection of the data of Table 5.4 shows that the small schools had relatively few students reporting no activities and three or fewer activities, and that they had relatively many students reporting 21 or more activities. The relationship between school size, as the schools were grouped in Table 5.3 and Figure 5.3, and per cent of students in each school size group reporting three or fewer activities and 21 or more activities is represented in Figure 5.4.

We conclude that the Seniors of the small schools reported more extracurricular activities than the Seniors of the large schools by a factor of over two to one. This confirms the data on interschool events, though the magnitude of the school size difference is less and there is no evidence that the smallest schools were deficient with respect to total extracurricular activities, as they were with respect to interschool events.

Extracurricular activities of the schools were classified into seven different kinds (cf. p. 69). The number of different kinds of activities in which a student engaged during his school career constitutes an index of his extracurricular versatility. The maximum versatility score was 7 and the minimum was 0; in the illustrative cases, above, the versatility score is 5 for the Vernon High School boy and 4 for the Capital City High School boy. In Table 5.5 the mean versatility scores of the graduating Seniors

TABLE 5.5. MEAN VERSATILITY SCORES OF SENIORS, AND PER CENT OF SENIORS REPORTING FIVE OR MORE KINDS OF EXTRACURRICULAR ACTIVITIES FOR STATED SCHOOL SIZE-CLASSES

School Size-Class*	Mean Versatility Score	Per Cent of Seniors Reporting 5 or More Kinds of Activities
1	4.78	53
2	4.29	41
3	4.24	48
4	3.15	21
5	2.81	11
6	2.99	12
7	2.73	10
8	2.39	3
9	2.17	4

* See Table 5.1.

and the per cent of the Seniors with versatility scores of 5 or greater are presented for the nine school size-classes. These data are corrected for the three-year schools. The data of Table 5.5 are presented graphically in Figure 5.5.

There is a rank-order correlation (T; Kendall, 1948) of .93 between average size of school and average versatility scores of Senior students ($p < .005$).

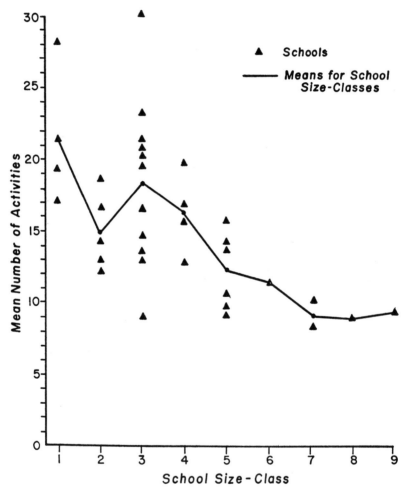

Fig. 5.3. Mean number of extracurricular activities reported by graduating Seniors in schools of different sizes. (See Table 5.1.)

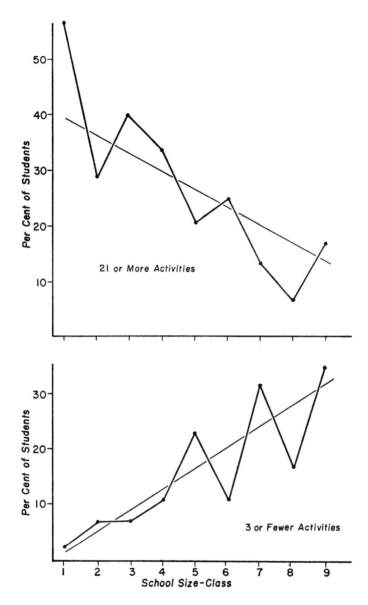

Fig. 5.4. Per cent of graduating Seniors in schools of different sizes reporting three or fewer activities and 21 or more activities during four-year school career. (See Table 5.1.)

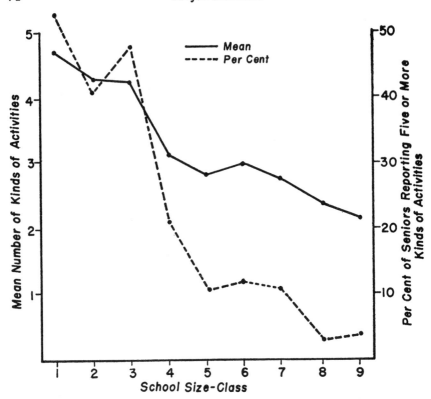

Fig. 5.5. Extracurricular versatility of graduating Seniors in schools of different sizes. (See Table 5.1.)

We were impressed to find this clear evidence of greater participation in school activities by small school students than by large school students in all the public records available to us. The differences were so great as to suggest not only that they were statistically significant differences but that they pointed to a different way of student life in small and large schools.

6

Participation in Nonclass Settings

PAUL V. GUMP • WALLACE V. FRIESEN

IT SEEMS obvious that a school that brings together a large number of students can offer its pupils a richer array of activities than can a smaller school. Methods and findings described in Chapter 4 indicate that larger schools did offer a more extensive group of class and nonclass settings. The extra richness was perhaps less than might have been expected; certainly it did not keep pace with increase in size. For example, when the smallest and largest schools were compared (see Table 4.3), population increased by a factor of 65, number of different settings by a factor of 8, and number of different varieties of settings by a factor of only 1.5.

On the other hand, we knew nothing about the relation between number of students, number and variety of behavior settings, and degree of participation of individual students in the array of activities the schools provided. The present chapter reports an investigation of this problem, using as subjects high school Junior* students within the nonclass behavior settings of five schools. Nonclass settings were investigated because the most adequate field methods made use of the free decisions of students with respect to entering or not entering, and of participating or not participating, in behavior settings. It was essential, therefore, to avoid settings where the students' participation was determined by school officials. In some of the settings included in the investigation, such as required assemblies, attendance was required, but more active participation, such as being on the program, was voluntary. In this chapter, therefore, the term behavior setting refers to the nonclass settings of the schools.

The particular purposes of the study are: (a) to describe similarities and differences in the richness of nonclass offerings in large and small schools; (b) to determine the extent to which such offerings were actually used by large vs. small school students; and (c) to compare the quality of participation in the settings of large and small schools.

* Juniors: Students in the 11th grade; modal age of 16 years.

Behavior setting theory predicts that the participation of large and small school students should differ in extent of penetration into behavior settings. The derivation of this prediction follows.

When enrollments of schools increase, the numbers of their settings do *not* increase proportionately. This failure of numbers of settings to keep pace with numbers of persons results in more persons being available per setting (see Chapter 4 for data). Behavior setting theory also proposes that a minimum number of important functionaries is required to operate settings of a given type. As more persons become available above this minimum, there is a reduction in forces on any one person to engage in the central and important setting functions. In a large school, students are exposed to long sequences of settings with relatively large numbers of inhabitants. It is therefore predicted that such students, on the average, will engage in comparatively few behaviors that are important to these settings. In the small school, students continually participate in settings that have few inhabitants, that are undermanned; as a result there are strong pressures on and invitations to these small school students to penetrate these settings, to take over significant tasks.

The basic units for the analyses of the behavioral predictions are behavior settings. The behavior setting surveys employed by the present study will be discussed in the first section of this report.

SURVEYS OF BEHAVIOR SETTINGS

One large and four small schools were investigated; the large school, Capital City,* had an enrollment of 2,287; the smaller schools, Malden, Walker, Midwest, and Vernon, had enrollments of from 83 to 151. For many comparisons, the four smaller schools were pooled together and labeled Midwest County Schools.

Behavior setting surveys of these schools supplied the basis for assessing the availability of activities. For the present study, the surveys included only settings that occurred in the three-month period from the opening of school until the middle of December and that were freely

---

* Since only one school provided data for the high end of the size continuum, it was important that this school adequately represent other large schools. As stated in Chapter 4, Capital City High was a community school, thereby providing a balanced subject population; it was a school with an "enviable reputation"; data on the number and variety of its behavior settings indicated that it compared favorably with the other large schools studied.

TABLE 6.1. NUMBER OF JUNIORS, NUMBER OF NONCLASS BEHAVIOR
SETTINGS AVAILABLE TO JUNIORS, AND RATIOS OF JUNIORS TO
THE SETTINGS FOR EACH SCHOOL

School	No. of Juniors	No. of BS	Juniors/BS (P/D Ratio)
Walker	16	45	.36
Malden	18	41	.44
Midwest	21	54	.39
Vernon	36	54	.67
Midwest County average	22.7	48.5	.47
Midwest County total	91	194	
Capital City	794	189	4.20

accessible to Junior students. Behavior settings that were routinely used by all students, such as hallways and restrooms, were omitted from the behavior setting lists.

For each school, settings that operated during the time period studied comprised approximately 80 per cent of a full year's settings, indicating that the samples of settings were proportional from school to school and that each list was comprehensive enough to represent the school year. Sample lists of complete school behavior settings are given in Appendix 4.1; sample lists of the nonclass settings are found in the record forms presented in Appendix 6.1. In Table 6.1, the number of Juniors, the number of nonclass behavior settings, and the ratios of the Junior students to settings are presented.

This table demonstrates that in the large school there was a greater number of Juniors who might be expected to attend each nonclass setting than in the small schools. This difference is in accord with the theory, and it provides the basis for expecting a greater proportion of the Juniors of the small schools than of the large school to perform tasks of importance in the school's settings. Data concerning the number of Junior students actually present in the nonclass settings of the schools are given in Table 6.4 (p. 83).

Variety of Nonclass Activities

One issue of the investigation was that of the richness of activity offerings in the large and small schools. There were 189 nonclass behavior settings usable by Juniors in the large school and an average of 48.5 in the small schools. If richness means numbers, then it is clear that the large school provided the greater richness of opportunity. However, two settings can be different in terms of independence and yet very similar in terms of kind. A principal's office and a head counselor's office are independent but highly similar. A principal's office and a pep club lounge are independent but dissimilar. Clearly, if richness means diversity, a more discriminating measure than independence is required. This is provided by the concept of behavior setting *variety*, described in Chapter 2. It will be recalled that *variety* measures are directed to differences in kind. With such an index the question can be asked: What varieties (types) of nonclass settings were available to Juniors in the Capital City and Midwest County schools?

Table 6.2 lists the 33 varieties of nonclass settings that were present in the five schools. It can be seen that there were more gaps in the variety offerings of the small schools than of Capital City High. The extent of this difference in variety offerings is indicated in Table 6.2 by the number of varieties in each school; this number is also expressed as per cent of the total number of varieties in the five schools and as per cent of the varieties in Capital City High.

Capital City High School provided its Juniors with 88 per cent, and the small schools with 66 per cent (mean) of the behavior setting varieties that occurred in all the schools. The small schools provided approximately 75 per cent (mean) of the number of varieties offered by Capital City High.

What were the specific advantages offered by the large school's greater variety? Variety identification numbers (see Table 6.2) and examples of settings in the varieties that were unique to Capital City High are as follows:

Variety Number	Examples of Behavior Settings
18	School Nurse's Office
20	All City Debate Clinic
23	All City Orchestra Clinic
24A	Swimming Meet
57	Chess Club Meeting
69	Photographic Rooms

A number of these unique settings appear to be somewhat peripheral to life in school in that they were established for quite special groups.

In order to deal more economically with the varieties, the schools'

TABLE 6.2. VARIETIES OF NONCLASS BEHAVIOR SETTINGS AVAILABLE TO JUNIORS AT CAPITAL CITY AND MIDWEST COUNTY HIGH SCHOOLS, SEPTEMBER–DECEMBER, 1960

Variety No.	Variety Name	Presence in				
		Capital City	Walker	Mal-den	Mid-west	Ver-non
1	Athletic Contests, Indoors	x	x	x	x	x
2	Athletic Contests, Outdoors	x	x	x	x	x
8	Book Exhange, Rentals	x			x	
15	Dances	x	x	x	x	x
17	Dinners, Banquets	x	x		x	x
18	Doctors' Offices, Clinics	x				
20	*Educational Groups, Academic	x				
22	*Educational Grps., Home Econ.	x				x
23	*Educational Groups, Music	x				
24	*Educational Grps., Phys. Ed.	x	x	x	x	x
24A	Swimming	x				
25	*Educational Grps., Shop, Agric.	x				x
26	Elections	x			x	
28	Fairs, Circuses, and Carnivals	x	x	x	x	x
35	Food Sales	x	x	x	x	x
36	Fund and Membership Drives	x	x	x	x	x
39	Government, School Offices	x	x	x	x	x
48	Initiations		x			x
52	Libraries	x	x	x	x	x
54	Meetings, Executive	x	x	x	x	x
55	Meetings, Organizat'n Business	x	x	x	x	x
56	Meetings, Social-Cultural	x	x	x	x	x
57	Meetings, Social-Recreational	x				
65	Outings	x	x	x	x	x
68	Parties	x	x	x		x
69	Photographic Rooms	x				
70	Plays, Concerts, Programs	x	x	x	x	x
80	Restaurants	x	x	x	x	x
81	Lounges, Student		x		x	
83	School, Coaches' Room	x	x	x	x	x
84	School, Custodians' Room		x	x	x	x
85	School, Special Days		x			
95	Volunteer Work, Fund Raising	x	x	x	x	x
33		29	24	19	22	22
	Per cent of total	88%	73%	58%	67%	67%
	Per cent of Capital City	100%	83%	66%	76%	76%

* In a complete list of school settings, these variety titles would include school classes; their presence here indicates that the school had a nonclass setting of the indicated variety, e.g., both Capital City and Vernon had the setting Future Homemakers of America, Regular Meeting, which was judged to belong to the variety Educational Groups, Home Economics. For other examples, see Appendix 4.1.

TABLE 6.3. NUMBER OF NONCLASS SETTINGS IN EACH SUPERVARIETY
FOR CAPITAL CITY AND MIDWEST COUNTY HIGH SCHOOLS

Supervarieties of settings	Capital City	Schools within Midwest County			
		Walker	Mal-den	Mid-west	Ver-non
Required Assemblies (all assemblies at which attendance was required).......	4	4	4	4	2
Operational Settings (school offices, lunchrooms, clinics, etc.)..	30	6	5	8	5
Athletics (football, basketball, wrestling, etc.)	31	8	8	9	8
Parties and Dances..............	17	5	6	4	10
Government (student council, executive committees)	18	3	2	3	3
Journalism Settings (newspaper staff, annual staff).............	4	0	1	2	1
Voluntary Work Settings (magazine sale, food sale, car wash, etc.)...	14	4	4	7	10
Outings (trips to places for music, art, drama).............	8	2	3	5	4
Club Meetings (Pep Club meetings, special interest clubs, etc.)......	29	4	2	5	5
Voluntary Programs (plays, music programs which were not required)	33	9	6	7	6
Smoking Room	1	0	0	0	0
Total 189		45	41	54	54

behavior settings were coded into larger categories or *supervarieties*. The supervarieties clustered the settings according to a common-sense idea of the reason for the existence of the settings. The supervarieties are identified and the number of settings falling into each are presented in Table 6.3 for each school. This table shows that all five schools offered activities in nearly all of these common-sense classes of settings.

These data make it very clear that although the large school had many more settings, the small schools dispersed their smaller number of activities into nearly as many varieties and supervarieties of settings as the large school.

USE OF BEHAVIOR SETTINGS

Method

Subjects. The small school sample consisted of all 91 Juniors enrolled in four high schools of Midwest County. The large school sample contained 604 Juniors from Capital City High School. Of the 794 Juniors enrolled at Capital City High, there were 122 Juniors who were not at school or had schedule conflicts when we collected the data at Capital City; 64 were excluded because they were non-Caucasian (all Juniors in Midwest County were of the Caucasian race), and four subjects were rejected because of evidence on their questionnaires that cast serious doubt on the truth of their answers.

Procedure. The Juniors from each of the five schools were given a complete list of the nonclass behavior settings in their school during the previous three months, since the beginning of school. Most of these Behavior Setting Reports were administered in study halls; special times and places were provided for those students without a regular study hall period. With the list of their school's settings provided, the students were simply asked to indicate which settings they had entered during this time; the question was "Were you there?" After completing this procedure the students were instructed to explain what they did in each setting they had entered. The complete instructions and sample questionnaires from Capital City and Midwest High School may be found in Appendix 6.1.

Unlike many other studies of behavior within institutions, the reports of activity did not involve unaided memory, or reflections contaminated with likes and dislikes. Rather, each student in a particular school was given a map of the settings which constituted his potential activities for three months. Moreover, the settings represented units whose equivalence and independence could be determined by use of the K-21 Behavior Setting Index (see Chapter 2 for a more complete discussion). Thus each student had an identical opportunity to recall every one of his activities over the period covered by the setting list.

Coding the quality of participation. Each student's report of his actions in each setting was coded for the degree of importance and centrality of his position in that setting. The four levels of participation were based on the levels of penetration into settings as defined by Barker and Wright (1955). Briefly, the students' activity in settings was rated as follows:

1. A customer, ordinary member, or part of an audience in a setting.

2. An active, responsible member in a setting which, by its nature, required that each member accept responsibility for contributing action. Examples: Basketball Practice, Junior Play Practice.

3. A performer at a low level; subject held an important or responsible position in a part of the setting that was not directly involved in the central activity. Examples: working at concession stands at Basketball Games, ushering at the Junior Class Play.

4. Performer in the central activity; subject was directly involved in the maintenance or control of the setting. Examples: players in Football Games, president of a Y-Teens Meeting.

In this chapter, responses to a setting coded 1 and 2 will be combined and defined as *entries*. Responses coded 3 and 4 will be combined and defined as *performances*, or *setting performances*. When only Level 4 performances are discussed, they will be called *high-level performances*. When entries or performances are combined (codes 1 through 4), they will be referred to as *participations*.

Results

Setting size. The median number of Juniors in each setting at Capital City High was over three times as great as the median number in small school settings (see Table 6.4, line 1). Thus the prediction that the large school settings would be relatively highly populated is verified.

Participation in settings. Line 2, Table 6.4 indicates that on the average, the large school Juniors entered and participated, on some level, in six more settings than did the small school Juniors. The significance of this difference was $p < .001$. Because of the heterogeneity of the large and small school variances, a chi-square median test was employed for the comparisons in Tables 6.4 and 6.5.

Participation in School Offices, attendance at Required Assemblies, and the Smoking Room did not represent what is ordinarily thought of as extracurricular activity. Accordingly an *extracurricular* index was developed; this index reflects participation in all the remaining supervarieties

TABLE 6.4. SIZE OF BEHAVIOR SETTINGS AND MEAN
PARTICIPATION OF JUNIORS

	Walker	Malden	Midwest	Vernon	Midwest County (Mean)	Capital City
1. Median number of Juniors per behavior setting	11	13	8	11	11	36
2. Mean number of *nonclass* settings in which Juniors participated (includes Offices, Required Assemblies, Smoking Room)	30.2	26.4	26.7	24.7	26.4	32.9
3. Mean number of *extracurricular* settings in which Juniors participated (omits School Offices, Required Assemblies, Smoking Room) ...	22.4	18.3	18.1	19.5	19.4	18.4
4. Extracurricular participation scope: mean number of different super-varieties attended ..					6.5	5.4

of behavior settings: Athletics, Parties and Dances, School Government
Settings, Journalism Settings, Voluntary Work Settings, Outings, Club
Meetings, and Programs. In line 3 of Table 6.4 it can be seen that the
small school students participated in the extracurricular settings just as
frequently as did large school students. The equality in this respect is
somewhat misleading. The distributions of the per cent of Juniors who
participated in different numbers of extracurricular settings are presented
in Figure 6.1. It is very clear from this graph that the population of the
large school was widely dispersed from the mean; a relatively large proportion of students engaged in ten or fewer settings, while a small proportion participated in over 37 settings, more than any small school stu-

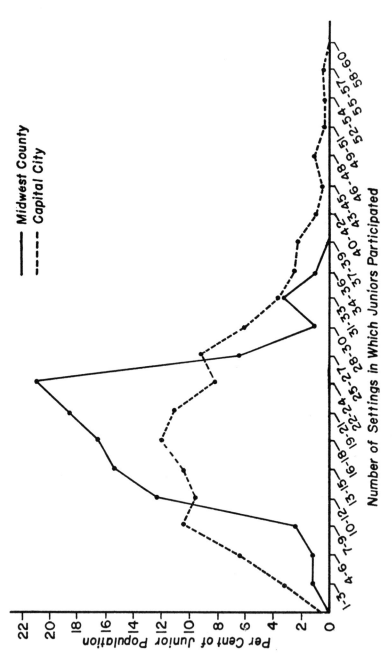

Fig. 6.1. Per cent of Midwest County and Capital City school Juniors who participated in stated numbers of extracurricular behavior settings.

dent. This small portion of the large school sample elevated the group mean. In contrast, nearly all small school students participated in ten or more settings, and only a small proportion of the sample participated in an excessively large or small number of settings.

The small school students participated in a slightly greater number of supervarieties of behavior settings than the large school students (Table 6.4, line 4) ($p < .001$). Thus, although the means would indicate a similar *number* of extracurricular setting participations, the small school Juniors participated in more *kinds* of these activities.

The data presented thus far have demonstrated that the students' participation in settings of the large school did not coincide with the larger number and wider variety of settings offered. Rather, Juniors in the large school participated in about the same number of extracurricular behavior settings as did the small school Juniors. Only in the case of Required Assemblies and in the school's Operational Settings (Offices) did the large school students participate more frequently. The students in the small schools actually participated in a wider variety of extracurricular activities in spite of the greater variety provided by the large school.

The small school students participated in a higher proportion and a wider variety of the settings available to them. The hypothesis of greater numbers of forces toward entry into the small schools' settings is tested directly in Chapter 8; however, this finding lends support to that hypothesis.

Penetration into settings. Up to this point only the number and range of participations have been presented. Nothing has been said about the quality of these participations. The most central hypothesis of this investigation was that the quality of participations would differ between large and small school students. It was predicted that small school students, in relation to those of the large school, would penetrate their settings more deeply and would occupy more positions of importance and responsibility. Data for the test of this hypothesis are displayed in Table 6.5 and in Figure 6.2. The table yields information on central tendency; the figure shows data on variance.

Table 6.5, line 1, indicates that the large school Juniors entered settings as audience persons or as members only with much greater frequency than small school Juniors ($p < .001$). In contrast, line 2 demonstrates that the Juniors in the small schools held responsible positions with more than twice the frequency of the large school Juniors ($p < .001$). Furthermore, line 3

TABLE 6.5. PENETRATION QUALITY OF PARTICIPATIONS IN SETTINGS BY
THE JUNIORS AT MIDWEST COUNTY AND CAPITAL CITY HIGH SCHOOLS

| | Mean Number of Settings in Which Juniors Participate at Designated Levels | |
Level of Participation	Midwest County	Capital City
1. Entry only: Levels 1 and 2..............	17.7*	29.4
2. Performance: Levels 3 and 4.............	8.7	3.5
3. High performance: Level 4 only..........	3.6	.6
4. Number of different supervarieties in which performances occurred...........	3.7	1.6

* The separate small schools are not presented in this table, since examination of
the separate means revealed almost no differences between the four small schools.

indicates that small school Juniors held high-level performances six times
as frequently as did large school Juniors ($p < .001$).

Figure 6.2 presents the distributions of the number of settings in which
each subject of the two populations performed. Almost 30 per cent of the
large school Juniors performed in no settings at all, while 2 per cent of
the Juniors from the Midwest County schools failed to perform in any
settings. Put another way, the majority (58 per cent) of students in the
large school performed in three or fewer settings, while most (80 per cent)
small school students performed in four or more settings. It is clear, then,
that the large school Juniors had relatively superficial and inactive contact
with their settings, while the small school Juniors were more actively contributing to the functioning of their settings.

Returning to Table 6.5, line 4, it can be seen that the variety of activities in which the Juniors from the large school performed was less than half
the variety in which small school Juniors held responsible positions when
this is measured by supervarieties ($p < .001$). Not only did more small
school Juniors perform in a greater number of settings than did large school
Juniors, but they also held these responsible positions in twice as many
kinds of activity.

Performance in supervarieties. The superiority of performances for
small school students is clear; the question arises as to whether this relatively high level of performance was generally distributed throughout all
parts of the schools' nonclass settings or whether it resulted from particu-

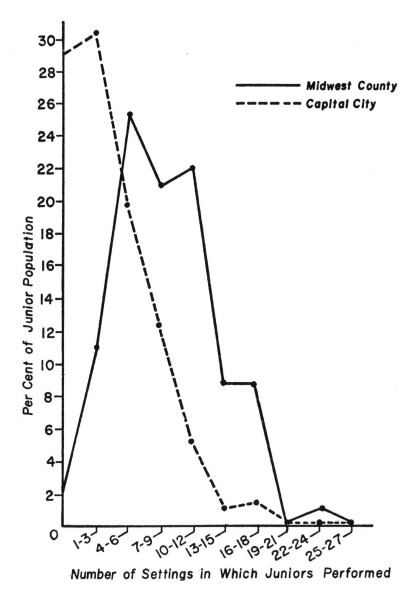

Fig. 6.2. Per cent of Midwest County and Capital City school Juniors who performed in stated numbers of behavior settings.

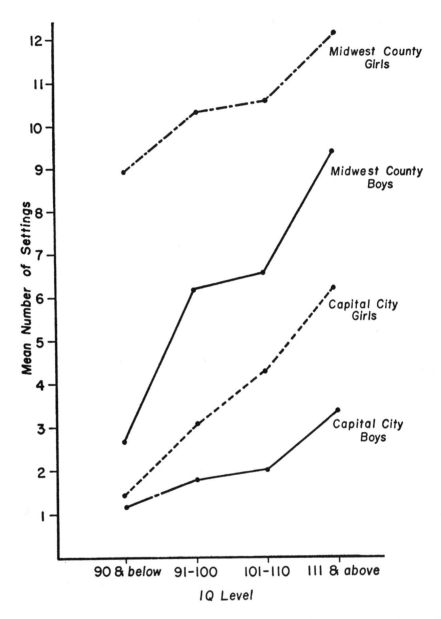

Fig. 6.3. Mean number of behavior settings in which stated sex, IQ, and school groups were performers.

larly high performance opportunities in specific areas. It is well realized, for example, that in small schools a greater proportion of students is invited, sometimes pressed, into performance roles in athletics. To test the spread of performances over areas of school life, comparisons were made between the large and small schools on the proportions of total performances in each of the ten supervarieties. For example, the proportion of total performances devoted to Athletics in the small schools was compared with this proportion in the large school. Results showed that the proportions were quite similar in six areas: Required Assemblies, Athletics, Government Settings, Journalism Settings, Meetings, and Voluntary Programs. The large school had proportionately (not necessarily absolutely) more performances in Operational Settings and in Parties and Dances; the small schools had proportionately more performances in Voluntary Work Settings and in Outings. When these latter settings are removed from the comparison, the small schools still average more than twice as many performances as the large school. The evidence supports the conclusion that the performance superiority of the small schools was reasonably consistent throughout the nonclass areas of school life.

Sex and IQ. In order to study the effects of school size on subgroups of the sample populations, the boys and girls of both schools were divided into four IQ groups for comparison. The mean number of settings in which performances occurred for boys and girls of each intelligence group is presented in Figure 6.3 for the large school and the small schools. Several general results are clear from these data:

1. When school size and IQ classifications were held constant, girls performed significantly more often than boys. (There was one exception: in the large school, dull girls did not perform significantly more frequently than dull boys.)

2. Brighter students performed more frequently than duller ones. Computation of tests between bottom and top halves of the IQ distributions in relation to performance yielded statistical significance for boys in both schools and for girls in Capital City; the test comparing bright and dull girls in Midwest County failed to reach statistical significance.

POPULATION, SETTINGS, AND PERFORMANCES: A RECAPITULATION

At this point it may be helpful to relate findings on performances to the ecological factors from which they spring. According to the theory

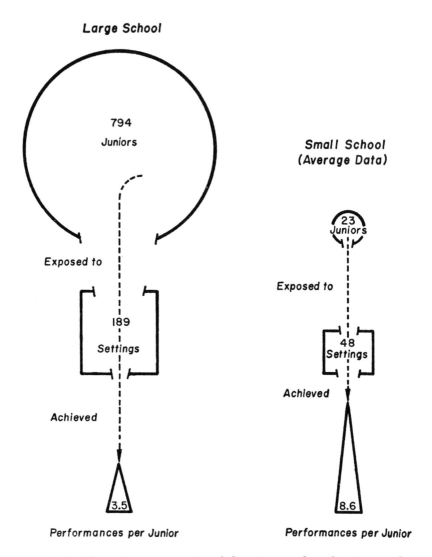

Fig. 6.4. Schematic representation of class size, number of settings, and performances per student.

utilized here, performance rates are higher in small schools than in large schools because of the different relationship between number of persons and number of settings in the two institutions. When many persons are exposed to a limited number of settings, the performance opportunities and obligations for any one person are reduced; when few persons are exposed to relatively numerous settings, such opportunities and obligations are increased. A graphic presentation of this relationship and of its outcome in actual performances per student appears in Figure 6.4.

PERFORMANCE AS A FUNCTION OF SIZE: ADDITIONAL DATA

During the course of another study, data equivalent to the performance data of the present investigation were obtained from Juniors in four additional schools. Compared with the small schools of the present study, two of these additional schools (Dorset and Hearn) had smaller enrollments, and two (Haven and Eakins) had larger enrollments. Since the large and small schools in the main study differed radically in enrollments, the additional data made it possible to test the effects of school size at additional points on the school size continuum.

To control for differences in time periods for the participation reports in the various schools, ratios of extracurricular performances to total extracurricular participations were calculated. This proportion of performances to participations by Juniors is plotted as a function of school size in Figure 6.5. Data in the figure indicate that as school size increased, there was a decrease in the proportion of encounters of students with settings which involved behaving in the central and important tasks of the behavior settings. Almost one-half of the extracurricular participations of students in the very small schools (Dorset and Hearn) were performances. This proportion falls to around the 40 per cent mark for the schools in the 83 to 221 range, and it then falls to about 30 per cent for the medium-sized school (Eakins); it falls again to about 15 per cent for students in the very large school (Capital City). Since data in Table 6.4 demonstrate no significant differences in rates of extracurricular participation between large and small schools, the decreasing proportions of performances in Figure 6.5 suggest that as school size increased, the frequency of performance decreased. Inspection indicates that a rapid deceleration in performance rates begins in the school size interval following 339.

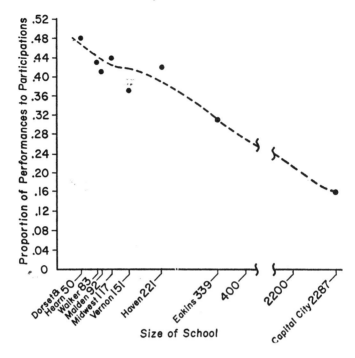

Fig. 6.5. Proportions of performances to participations in extracurricular settings by Juniors as a function of school size. The figure of 50 for Dorset and Hearn is the mean enrollment for the two schools.

ESSENTIAL FINDINGS

This study has demonstrated that a large school provides a somewhat larger number and wider variety of nonclass activities than a small school. But in spite of specific large school advantages in the variety of settings, the small school makes the same general kinds of activities available to its students. Moreover, the small school provides a higher proportion of settings to the number of students; this has the following consequences for the students' participation in activities:

(a) Small school students participate in the same *number* of settings commonly regarded as extracurricular as do large school students.

(b) Small school students participate in a wider *variety* of extracurricular activities than do the students in a large school.

(*c*) A much larger portion of small school students hold positions of importance and responsibility.

(*d*) Finally, small school students hold responsible and central positions in a wider variety of activities than do students in a large school.

Investigation in the present chapter has been directed to the number and kind of student participation in the nonclass settings of the schools studied. The question naturally arises as to the meaning of this participation to the students. What did they get out of their activity? It is to this issue that the next chapter is addressed.

7

Satisfactions Derived from Nonclass Settings

PAUL V. GUMP • WALLACE V. FRIESEN

EVIDENCE presented in Chapter 6 indicated the following:

1. Small school nonclass behavior settings contained a median of 11 Juniors per setting; large school settings a median of 36. In terms of the theory, the small school settings were relatively undermanned.

2. Small school Juniors occupied positions of centrality and responsibility in an average of 8.6 settings, large school Juniors in an average of 3.5 settings. In terms of the theory, small school Juniors occupied over twice as many performance positions as did large school Juniors.

These findings present the description of the ecological conditions and the overt behavior of the student population; they provide objective anchors for a more phenomenal inquiry. The central question of this chapter is what participation in settings meant to large and small school Juniors.

Effects of undermanned behavior settings were predicted in Chapter 2 of this report. Many of these hypotheses are predictions of overt behavior; however, they can also be related to experiences of setting occupants. Thus, when the theory predicts that occupants of undermanned behavior settings will engage in "more difficult and more important tasks" (Derivation 1.2, p. 24), it is to be expected that Juniors in small schools will report setting experiences that reflect feelings of challenge or importance. The present investigation tests the prediction that small school Juniors will report different patterns of satisfactions derived from nonclass behavior settings than large school Juniors.

SCHOOL SIZE AND REPORTED SATISFACTIONS

Data-Gathering Procedure

In the spring of 1961, there were 88 Juniors in the Midwest County high schools. A group of 88 Capital City Juniors was carefully selected to match this Midwest County sample on variables of sex, IQ, and race.

The senior investigator assembled the subjects in small groups of 15 to 25 and thanked them for their earlier, valuable help in connection with the Behavior Setting Report (Chapter 6). Their cooperation was requested for a final step in the investigation: reporting what their participation in behavior settings had meant to them.

Each student's Setting Report was returned to him and he was asked to refer to this as he responded to the following:* (1) which of the settings he had entered were especially good, satisfying, worth while—"plus"; (2) what he did, or what went on, that made these settings good—"plus"; what he enjoyed or got out of the setting.

In order to encourage conscientious and detailed replies to the second item, the investigator offered the following suggestions:

When trying to explain what's good about an activity, there are two ways of thinking that can help. You know that we all have desires, needs, wants. We can think of which of our desires or needs gets satisfied in the activity and explain it that way. The other way to look at an activity or setting is to think about the setting itself; it has a number of parts or aspects. Try to recall which part in particular was good, satisfying, worth while, and write about that. Using these two helps, you should be able to explain in a way so we can understand what the activity or setting meant to you.

The satisfaction-report protocols yielded a selection of one to eight "good settings," with an average of 2.5 settings per respondent. Almost all students made some attempt to explain why their selected settings were remembered as satisfying. Content analysis of the explanation "why it was good" provides the basic data for this report.

Content Analysis

The code for analyses of the student responses was empirically derived. An *a priori* framework for coding was avoided because it seemed desirable to obtain a code that remained quite close to students' ideas and feelings. This method left opportunity for results that might not have been predicted by the theory.

A large number of subject protocols were studied. From this "listening to" the students' responses, it seemed that several satisfactions frequently appeared in a single answer. When this occurred, each satisfaction was

---

* A copy of the report form is given in Appendix 7.1.

marked off as a separate unit. Thirty-nine different categories of satisfaction units were eventually identified. The number of different satisfactions yielded by this approach was somewhat burdensome, but this disadvantage was accepted in order to achieve a coding scheme whose categories required a minimum of interpretation by the coder.

The actual coding scheme is described below, with definitions of the coding categories and examples of units.

Categories	Definitions and Examples
1. Physical Competence	Increase in or maintenance of physical fitness or skill. *Tadpole Club.* ". . . improves your swimming ability." *Home Football Game.* ". . . keeps your reflexes alive."
2. Emotional Competence	Improved self-confidence or reduction of emotional blocks. *Junior Class Play.* "It gave me more confidence."
3. Social Competence	Increase in getting along well with others, in handling oneself in different situations. *Swimming Team Practice.* ". . . and I learned to get along with other people." *Basketball Games at another school.* "It also helps you adjust to different surroundings than you are used to."
4. Other Competence	Becoming able to do new tasks, or to do old tasks better. *'Blithe Spirit'—Play.* "I learned the ways and functions of a good light director." *Christmas Program Rehearsal.* "I learned what I was doing wrong and how to improve my voice and project sound."

In the competences above, the subject reports maintenance or increase in capacity. In the next five categories the subject indicates that he was exposed to, or learned *about*, various factors. There is no direct evidence of a capacity increase. Since students are exposed to many things in their settings, it is very easy to say one "learned about" these things.

5. Learn About— Social	Opportunity to learn about formal and informal social relationships, to know more of human nature. *Junior Class Meeting.* "It gives a chance to learn parliamentary procedure." *Girls Intramural Basketball.* "I can learn what other girls are like."
6. Learn About— Skill	Learning about various skills but with no direct statement of capacity increase. *Junior Class Play.* "Here we learned many things about acting." *Swimming Meet.* "I like to see good divers and swimmers; after seeing the way they do it, I try to improve myself."

Categories	Definitions and Examples

7. Learn About—
Cognitive
Areas

Learning about knowledge areas, as opposed to social and skill areas.
Debate Tournament. "I learned more about the U.N."
Science Office as a Proctor. "I learned more about biology and physiology than in any regular class."

8. Learn About—
Vague

"Learning about" inferred from general statements that the setting was "educational," "interesting," etc., but with no particulars given.
Trip to Leavenworth. "I learned a lot of interesting things that I didn't know before."
Science Club Meeting. "This presented very educational and worth-while information."

9. Learn About—
Future

Learning things that may help with educational or occupational planning.
Career Day. "It provided information on careers that students very possibly would later engage in."
Guidance Office. "I like having a place to go where people can help me decide where to apply to college."

10. Challenge

Satisfaction in hard work, self-test, attempts to progress.
Junior Class Magazine Sale. "This gave me a chance to see whether or not I am a good salesman. I now believe that I am."

11. Competition

Zest in the same struggle or test situations as in challenge, but the opposing forces are from people.
Basketball Intramurals. "I like tough hard competition and I usually get it."
Junior Class Magazine Sale. "I liked having the competition of fellow classmates."
Football Games. "I liked it because of the joy of a good hard tackle or because you have stopped a play."

12. Success

Positive outcome of individual or group endeavors: a good job, a successful job.
Swimming Meet. ". . . results were obvious" (referring to very successful interschool contest).
Football Games. "I knew we had a good show to put on."

13. Contribution
to Others

Important help to social cause or group. Does not include peripheral assistance like cheering for or being a customer; these latter units are called Support Indicators (24).
Principal's Office. "I enjoy helping out down at the office—I really enjoy helping teachers and the principal."
Wrestling Match. "It also enables me to help the school and coach."

Categories	Definitions and Examples

14. Big Participation

Doing a lot, or doing something important.

Science Club Meeting. "I got the speakers for all of these meetings, for one thing."

Pep Club Rally. "I was one out of four cheerleaders that got before the student body and led cheers at pep assemblies and also cheered at all the games, at all home and away games."

15. New Experience

Enjoyment of novel events, places, activities.

Homecoming Parade. "This was something new for me."

Junior Class Play. "It gave me a chance to be someone else for a change."

16. New People

Meeting, or knowing for first time, people one has not known before.

General Office Proctor. "I like this little job because I get to know all kinds of people."

Band Day–K.U. "I met many other young people . . . with whom I became good friends."

17. Escape

Escape from usual routines. Much like New Experience except that the *new* is not the focus; the escape from the *old* is the pleasure.

Regular Assembly. "I enjoyed them because you are dismissed from class to go."

Basketball Game at another school. ". . . but the main reason, I think, was to get out and go some place, because in a blue-nosed town like this it's hard to have any fun."

18. Something to Do

Enjoyment in "doing something." The qualities of this something are not stated; the main idea is that doing something is better than doing nothing.

General Office Proctor. "It gives me something to do with my spare time."

Art Exhibit. "It passes the time when I arrive at school early."

19. Competition— Vicarious

Observing struggle and competition.

Football Game. "I enjoy watching the team pit its skill against opposing schools."

20. Excitement

Pleasure in being stirred up, usually through watching others; enjoyment of suspense—as a pattern—whether or not excitement is mentioned.

All School Election. ". . . the fall elections have excitement to them."

Basketball Game. "The suspense of who is going to win or lose."

21. Vicarious Valence

Liking for the "show" put on by others; more specific satisfaction not stated.

Freshman Initiation. "It's fun to see some of those poor freshmen all messed up, going through what we had to go through."

Football Game. "I did enjoy watching it."

Categories	Definitions and Examples
22. Action Valence	Liking for the activity engaged in; more specific kind of satisfaction not indicated. *Swimming Practice.* "I also enjoy swimming very much, so I do a lot of swimming." *Junior Class Play.* "I enjoyed being in the Junior Class Play very much. We had a lot of fun putting it on."
23. Unspecified Valence	Satisfaction with setting seems clear but not specific; the vicarious-action distinction is uncertain. *Football Game.* "I like football because you can have a lot of fun going to football games."
24. Support Indicated to Others	Giving minor or token help or support. *Basketball Game.* ". . . to cheer our team on." *All School Elections.* ". . . to support (by vote) friends."
25. Support from School Adults	Support from key adults in school. *Coach's Room.* "I like the way he left his door wide open. He was always ready to discuss problems you might have."
26. Support from Others	Support from peers and from nonschool groups. *Basketball Game.* "It was a lot of fun playing when you knew the fans were behind you."
27. Be Valued	Being in the focus of attention, a status person, receiving an honor or prize. *Homecoming Parade.* "It also gave me recognition among the people and students of the school." *Football Game.* "A boy can gain respect and attention by playing football."
28. Informal Affiliation	Companionship, fun with others, conversation. *Varsity Dances.* "I deeply appreciated the friendly and informal attitude of those present." *Basketball Practice.* "You get to see your friends after school."
29. Affiliation— Group	Being part of an organized action group; satisfaction in functioning together. (Reserved for face-to-face type of group membership—not for large masses or for affiliation to institutions.) *Student Council Meeting.* "The experience of being active in student government with other students." *Junior Play Practice.* "The class worked together as a group, which I enjoyed very much."
30. Affiliation— Crowd	Attachment to, or the immersion in, large groups; a "herd" feeling—no evidence of personal or face-to-face relationships. *Basketball Game.* "I like the 'companionship' of mingling with the rest of the crowd."

Categories	Definitions and Examples
31. Affiliation— School	Feeling of a bond with the school awakened; enjoyment of the pride and vigor of "school spirit." *Representative Council Meeting.* "This gave me more of a feeling of belonging—Capital City High was more 'my' school." *Basketball Games at another school.* "I also enjoy going to away games because the school spirit is carried by everybody whether we are winning or losing."
32. Little Participation	Opportunity to participate, but report doesn't imply a very important participation. *Varsity Dances.* "Let you participate in class functions." *Junior Class Meeting.* "It gives you a chance to take part in different activities in school."
33. Have-a-Say	Chance to say what one wants or thinks; "having a vote" included here. *All School Election.* "It made each student feel he had something to say about how he would be governed." *Cheerleader Tryouts.* "I enjoyed the tryouts . . . because we, the student body, had a chance to pick the girls."
34. Supply-Work	Appreciation of a place for supplies; or a place in which to work efficiently or pleasantly. *Library.* "Besides, it is a lovely place to study before and after school." *Coaches' Room.* "My like for dextrose and salt tablets is pretty strong. This is the only place . . . that I can obtain them."
35. Uplift	Assistance toward higher moral or cultural values. Settings were sometimes said to provide appreciation of books or art, or to offer spiritual rewards. *Y-Teens Noon Meeting.* ". . . gave me spiritual strength for the day." *Wrestling Match.* "I feel it makes a better man of me."
36. Points	Extrinsic satisfaction through credits for attendance or service; a rare category but very clear. *Pep Club Meeting.* "You get to build up points for honor pep or honor C."
37. Milieu Knowledge	Learning "who's who" or "what's what" within the school. *Swimming Meet.* "I enjoyed this because I found out who was on the team." *Regular Assembly.* "They let everyone know what is going on about them."
38. Psychological Release	Inner tensions relieved or put aside. *Wrestling Practice.* ". . . a wonderful way to relieve tension without bad results." *Pep Club Meeting.* ". . . offers an opportunity to relax and enjoy things."

Categories	Definitions and Examples
39. Others Get Value	Any one of a variety of values mentioned, but phraseology implies that the person writing the answer is not the person obtaining the value. (The units in this category were not used in most comparisons.) *Basketball Games—by Capital City Girl.* "They are good exercise for the boys and it gives them encouragement when people are yelling for them to win."
X No Unit	A plus setting identified but satisfactions not described. (Not used in any comparison.) *Homecoming Parade.* ". . . followed in car, full distance."

Results

On various reliability checks, two coders assigned satisfaction units to the same category, with 80 to 85 per cent agreement. The basic results of the coding analyses are given in Table 7.1. The frequencies in this table are the number of subjects who reported at least one satisfaction in the stated category.

In Table 7.1, Categories 1 through 31 are grouped into seven clusters for ease of understanding and interpretation. Categories 32 through 39 represent miscellaneous kinds of units which appeared infrequently. The common thread in each cluster may be defined as follows:

Competence cluster (categories 1–4). The student reported some kind of capacity maintenance or improvement achieved through his experience in the setting. The Competence cluster was reported most frequently by Juniors in the small Midwest County schools.

Learn-About cluster (categories 5–9). This cluster deals with learnings that are more in the nature of new awareness than of capacity improvement. Juniors from the large and small schools reported the Learn-About cluster with about equal frequency.

Big Action and Test cluster (categories 10–14). This includes identified satisfactions derived from having participated in the challenging aspects of a setting or group, from having met the test. In many protocols, references to meeting the test and to the importance or largeness of one's contribution appeared together. That is, a Junior would report that helping to put on an affair was a challenge and that it also gave him a feeling of making a significant contribution to his school or class. Small school Juniors reported satisfactions in the Big Action and Test cluster more frequently than did large school Juniors.

TABLE 7.1. NUMBER OF JUNIORS REPORTING ONE OR MORE UNITS
OF SATISFACTION-DESIGNATED CATEGORIES

No.	Label	Midwest County Juniors	Capital City Juniors	P Value (Chi Square, Yates)	Group Using Category Most Frequently
1.	Physical Competence	11	2	.05	M
2.	Emotional Competence	10	0	.01	M
3.	Social Competence	11	2	.05	M
4.	Skill Competence	5	0	*	M
5.	Learn About—Social	10	10		
6.	Learn About—Skill	7	3		
7.	Learn About—Cognitive	13	13		
8.	Learn About—Vague	8	7		
9.	Learn About—Future	10	9		
10.	Challenge	24	4	.001	M
11.	Competition	17	3	.01	M
12.	Success	15	2	.01	M
13.	Contribution	23	14		
14.	Big Participation	13	7		
15.	New Experience	13	13		
16.	New People	20	13		
17.	Escape	13	10		
18.	Something to Do	5	6		
19.	Competition—Vicarious	10	20	.10	CC
20.	Excitement	9	20	.05	CC
21.	Vicarious Valence	25	47	.01	CC
22.	Action Valence	47	26	.01	M
23.	Unspecified Valence	31	29		
24.	Support to Others	11	15		
25.	Support from Adults	3	3		
26.	Support from Others	5	0	*	M
27.	Be Valued	14	3	.02	M
28.	Informal Affiliation	22	28		
29.	Action Group Affiliation	23	3	.001	M
30.	Crowd Affiliation	3	8		
31.	School Affiliation	3	18	.01	CC
32.	Little Participation	2	4		
33.	Have-a-Say	2	11	.05	CC
34.	Work and Supply Places	5	6		
35.	Uplift	10	2	.05	M
36.	Points	0	5	*	CC
37.	Milieu Knowledge	1	10	.02	CC
38.	Psychological Release	4	11		
39.	Others Get Satisfaction	7	5		
X	Selected Good Settings without a Unit	2	10		

Note: M—Midwest County; CC—Capital City.
* Low-frequency categories used exclusively by one population.

Novelty cluster (categories 15–18). This refers to aspects of novelty or escape from the usual. This cluster was employed with similar frequency by large and small school Juniors.

Vicarious Enjoyment cluster (categories 19–21). The basic idea here is "observer satisfaction," often derived from witnessing events. Large school Juniors most often reported satisfactions in this cluster.

Valence cluster (categories 22–23). These two categories are similar in that they deal with a rather general liking for a setting. Liking for the action in a setting (Action Valence) was a small school satisfaction, while unspecified liking was equally divided between the student populations.

Social Rewards cluster (categories 24–31). These have been grouped together because they refer to pleasures of sociality. However, inspection of the data suggests that different types of social satisfactions were enjoyed by the large and small school groups. While Support from Adults (category 25) and Informal Affiliation (28) appeared with similar frequency, small school Juniors reported more Support from Others (26), Being Valued (27), and Action Group Affiliation (29). Large school Juniors, on the other hand, reported enjoyments of belonging to the mass (30) or institutional (31) entities of crowd and school (Crowd and School Affiliation).

The miscellaneous, infrequently used caategories, 32–39, yielded some suggestive comparisons. The Uplift satisfaction (35) came predominantly from small school students; typical of large school Juniors were the chance to Have-a-Say in school affairs (33), to get information about what goes on in the school (37), and to accumulate Points (36).

Following is a summary of the major differences between small and large schools in the use of clusters and categories:

Satisfactions more frequent in the small schools were Competence, Big Action and Test, Action Valence, Group Action, Be Valued, and Uplift;

Satisfactions more frequent in the large school were Vicarious Enjoyment, Large Entity Affiliation (Crowd and School), Milieu Knowledge, and Points;

Frequently reported satisfactions that seemed of similar importance in large and small schools were Learn-About, Novelty, Informal Affiliation, and Unspecified Valence.

These findings indicate that there were marked differences in the kinds of satisfactions reported by matched groups of large and small school Juniors. The relevance of these differences to the theory of undermanned behavior settings is the next concern.

Discussion in Terms of Theory

It has been predicted that when conditions produce undermanned behavior settings, forces result that invite and press participants to engage in more difficult, more responsible, more central tasks. It has already been established that small school students, in comparison with large school students, participated in relatively undermanned settings within the school and occupied performance positions more frequently. The question at issue is whether the experiencs of small school Juniors were those that might be predicted from the theory.

The specific prediction from the theory of undermanned behavior settings stated in Chapter 2 are numerous and interrelated; at this point it is pertinent to restate a few that seem relevant to the data at hand and to juxtapose the findings reported above. Three of the predictions are stated in behavioral terms, to gether with their phenomenal counterparts, as reported in the satisfaction of the subjects.

Undermanned, i.e., small school, behavior settings in comparison with large school settings resulted in the following:

1.2 Inhabitants engaging in more difficult and more important tasks.
   Small school Juniors reported the satisfaction cluster Big Action and Test more frequently than large school Juniors; this suggests that small school students had more demanded of them in settings. Specifically, the data on Challenge and Competition seem to reflect the fact that small school students experienced more feelings of satisfaction going with hard work and with demanding tests of ability.
3.1 Inhabitants enjoying greater functional importance, and
3.2 . . . more responsibility.
   In an overall way, the greater use of Big Action and Test by small school Juniors suggests satisfactions arising out of functional importance and responsibility. Specifically, there were strong trends for small school Juniors to employ the categories of Contribution and Big Participation. On the other hand, large school Juniors emphasized satisfaction commensurate with low functional importance and low responsibility; this group emphasized the onlooker satisfactions of the Vicarious Enjoyment cluster.
   Results in the Social categories suggest that the small school students experienced satisfactions congruent with their functional importance, while

the large school students experienced more rewards of "herd association." Small school Juniors were impressed with the pleasures of being part of an organized action group (invariably a face-to-face group), while large school students reported the satisfactions of being part of a crowd or school.

Superficially, the large school students' emphasis on the category Have-a-Say seems to indicate that they experienced some importance in their settings. However, the Have-a-Say category usually arose from being one of hundreds of students to vote in an election. A reasonable inference is that the Have-a-Say emphasis meant that large school Juniors felt they lacked importance and control in most settings and that they appreciated those settings that offered the minuscule control of a vote.

3.6 Inhabitants experiencing more occurrences of success and failure.

The categories Success and Be Valued both related to frequency of success experiences. (The category Be Valued refers to honors and awards that result from success.) Small school Juniors reported such satisfactions much more often than did large school Juniors.

Three category comparisons have not yet been discussed: Uplift, Points, and Milieu Knowledge. The fact that small school Juniors emphasized Uplift suggests no compelling hypotheses to the investigators.

The superiorities of the large school on the Points and the Milieu Knowledge categories do seem capable of interpretation. The point system exists in both the large and small schools. It is a device to encourage students to participate in activities that might not be attractive enough without such an extrinsic reward. It is speculated that small school students were satisfied enough by intrinsic rewards to ignore the Points issue. Support for this notion is offered in Chapter 8, where it is demonstrated that students in the small schools reported greater numbers of attractions (own forces) toward participation in behavior settings than did students in the large school. A few of the large school students, however, failing to achieve significant intrinsic rewards, may have reported the Points as one thing they did get out of the setting.

The interest of large school students in Milieu Knowledge seems to point to the complexity of the larger organization and to the partial lack of awareness of its inhabitants about important persons and affairs. Because of the relative incomprehensibility of the larger milieu, its students appear to have appreciated those settings (often assemblies) where they learned such things as who were class officer candidates, who were the athletes in various sports, and what were the clubs available. It seems reasonable to suppose that Milieu Knowledge relates to the size issue via

Category No.	Category Name	Difference
*22	Action Valence	24
*29	Action Group Affiliation	23
*10	Challenge	23
*11	Competition	16
12	Success	15
27	Be Valued	13
2	Emotional Competence	11
1	Physical Competence	10
3	Social Competence	10
*13	Contribution	10
35	Uplift	9
*16	New People	8
14	Big Participation	7
4	Skill Competence	6
26	Support from Others	5
6	Learn-About Skill	4
17	Escape	3
*23	Unspecified Valence	2
8	Learn About—Vague	1
9	Learn About—Future	1
5	Learn About—Social	0
7	Learn About—Cognitive	0
15	New Experience	0
25	Support from Adults	0
18	Something-to-Do	−1
34	Work and Supply Plans	−1
32	Little Participation	−2
24	Indicate Support	−4
30	Crowd Affiliation	−6
36	Points	−6
*28	Informal Affiliation	−7
38	Psychological Release	−8
37	Milieu Knowledge	−10
33	Have-a-Say	−10
*19	Competition Vicarious	−11
*20	Excitement	−13
*31	School Affiliation	−17
*21	Vicarious Valence	−25

Note: The amount of the difference is expressed as per cent of 88 (the number of subjects in each group). M—Midwest County; CC—Capital City.

* Category reported by 20 per cent or more of the subjects of the group that most frequently reported the category.

the complexity of the total milieu, rather than the size of the particular setting for which the satisfaction was reported.

The preceding emphasis on differences between schools should not obscure the fact that comparisons of setting satisfactions also revealed some similarities. Both groups frequently used their nonclass settings for Novelty and Escape, and for Informal Affiliation. However, these seem to be rewards that are available to occupants of any position in a setting. Contrasts occurred most frequently for those categories where peripheral or central positions might be expected to make a difference. The small school students most frequently occupied performance (central) positions; they emphasized satisfactions related to competence, activity, self-testing, and face-to-face action groups. Large school students more frequently occupied nonperformance (peripheral) positions; they emphasized satisfactions related to passive observance and to belonging to large or mass entities.

A Descriptive View of Large School–Small School Comparisons

For those interested in a comparison of the two groups without clustering of categories and theoretical ordering, the data in Table 7.2 are descriptive. In this table, satisfaction categories are placed in order, from those more "favored" by the small school Juniors to those more "favored" by the large school Juniors.

Two comparisons can complete this description of differences in satisfactions. Compared with the large school Juniors, small school Juniors tended to report more units ($p < .10$); and, what is more significant, the small school students used more different categories to describe their satisfactions ($p < .01$). The latter finding can be expressed another way: compared with students of the large school, the Juniors of the small school experienced a greater range of satifactions from their participation in the nonclass school settings.

SETTING SATISFACTIONS AND SETTING POSITION

Discussion thus far has demonstrated that small school Juniors reported a satisfaction pattern quite different from that reported by large school Juniors. It has also been established that small school Juniors more frequently engaged in active, important, responsible positions in their settings (Chapter 6). The remainder of this report will test the hypothesis that these differences in position within settings determined the school differences in satisfaction patterns.

The approach to the test of the hypotheses was twofold. The first question was whether individuals reported different satisfactions from peripheral than from central behavior setting position. The second question was whether control of setting position would diminish or eliminate the difference in satisfaction patterns between large and small schools. Thus, analysis of the causal reationship of setting position to satisfaction pattern involved two steps: first, effects of degree of penetration were tested, with school size held constant; second, effects of school size were tested, with degree of penetration held constant.

Satisfactions and Behavior Setting Position, with School Size Constant

The matched samples of 88 students from the large and small schools served as subjects. As might be expected from the data on performances, a relatively small number of large school students described satisfactions from settings in which they had occupied central positions. Thirty-seven students who had relatively high performance rates were added to the Capital City sample in order to make it possible to compare satisfactions from all performance levels in that school.* Although the addition of these subjects resulted in a Capital City group with an atypically high performance rate, this did not bias the results, since comparisons were made between levels of performance within schools and between schools at the same level of performance.

It will be recalled that Chapter 6 (p. 82) discussed setting positions in detail. Level 1 included audience persons and relatively inactive group members (play attender, stamp club member); Level 2 referred to the participators in active group endeavors (member of intramural team); Level 3 included low-level performers (pep club member); and Level 4 was reserved for those who had penetrated the setting most deeply (proctors, cheerleaders, varsity team members, etc.). In the following comparisons of setting positions, Level 1 is the Peripheral Position, Levels 2 and 3 combined form the Middle Position, Level 4 is the Central Position.

The satisfaction categories compared were those that had yielded significant differences between the large and small school students and that

---

* These subjects filled out satisfaction report forms at the time of the initial survey and under the same conditions as the 88 matched subjects.

were used with reasonable frequency by at least one of the school groups. The first comparison determined, for each school group and for each of the three positions, the percentage of total units that fell in a given satisfaction category. All subjects were used in this comparison; results are given in Table 7.3.

If position centrality within behavior settings determined kinds of satisfactions in accordance with the hypothesis (p. 104), categories 1 through 5 in Table 7.3 should show increasing proportions from peripheral to central positions; categories 6 and 7 should show decreasing proportions. With the minor exception of category 4 (Group Action) in Capital City, the expected patterns were quite general for both school groups.

While the picture that satisfactions followed setting position is quite clear from Table 7.3, the data suggest that the school size groups emphasized particular satisfactions to different degrees at the same setting posi-

TABLE 7.3. SATISFACTIONS REPORTED BY MIDWEST COUNTY AND
CAPITAL CITY JUNIORS IN RELATION TO CENTRALITY OF POSITION.
PROPORTION OF ALL SATISFACTIONS AT A GIVEN POSITION
WHICH FELL INTO VARIOUS CATEGORIES

Satisfaction Cluster or Category	Peripheral Positions	Middle Positions	Central Positions
1. Competence			
Capital City	.01	.03	.05
Midwest County	.02	.08	.13
2. Big Action and Test			
Capital City	.03	.09	.26
Midwest County	.03	.23	.30
3. Action Valence			
Capital City	.04	.10	.13
Midwest County	.07	.16	.16
4. Group Action			
Capital City	.01	.01	.01
Midwest County	.02	.04	.08
5. Be Valued			
Capital City	.00	.03	.02
Midwest County	.01	.04	.04
6. Vicarious Enjoyment			
Capital City	.27	.16	.04
Midwest County	.17	.10	.04
7. Big Affiliation			
Capital City	.08	.04	.01
Midwest County	.03	.01	.00

TABLE 7.4. FREQUENCY OF THE DESIGNATED CATEGORIES OF SATISFACTION
REPORTED BY JUNIORS WHO OCCUPIED BOTH PERIPHERAL AND
CENTRAL BEHAVIOR SETTING POSITIONS

Satisfaction Cluster or Category	No. Giving Most Units in More Peripheral Positions	No. Giving Most Units in More Central Positions	p (Sign Test)
1. Competence			
Capital City	3	4	
Midwest County	1	20	.001
2. Big Action and Test			
Capital City	4	24	.001
Midwest County	3	41	.001
3. Action Valence			
Capital City	9	19	.05
Midwest County	9	25	.01
4. Group Action			
Capital City	1	1	
Midwest County	2	17	.001
5. Be Valued			
Capital City	0	3	
Midwest County	1	9	.02
6. Vicarious Enjoyment			
Capital City	28	7	.001
Midwest County	22	6	.02
7. Big Affiliation			
Capital City	8	4	
Midwest County	3	0	

tion. For example, Competence was emphasized more at the central position by small school Juniors than by large school Juniors, while Big Affiliation was more heavily employed at the peripheral position by large school Juniors than by small school Juniors.

The significance of the differences appearing in Table 7.3 were not testable, since satisfactions rather than persons were the basic units. In order to make statistical tests of the differences, a method in which each subject served as his own control was used. Subjects were selected from both school groups who reported satisfactions from at least two different behavior setting positions. For each subject, the analysis determined whether a larger proportion of units of a given satisfaction category were reported for peripheral or central setting positions. For example, a student might report two Vicarious Enjoyment units from two peripheral positions, no Vicarious Enjoyment units from one middle position, and one Vicarious Enjoyment unit from two central positions. For this subject, Vicarious Enjoyment was most heavily emphasized for the most peripheral position. (A very few cases reported an equal proportion of units in all three positions, or the greatest proportion in the middle position; these cases were considered ties, or "no case.") Probability tests were based on the Sign test of the significance of frequency of direction. Table 7.4 reports the results of this analysis.

Data in Table 7.4 suggest that when units were employed with enough frequency to test, setting position affected reported satisfactions. Inspection of the data indicates that those clusters of satisfactions related to involvement, action, challenge, and test were associated with the more central setting positions, while satisfactions related to onlooking, watching, and "herd association" were associated with the more peripheral setting positions.

Satisfactions and School Size, with Setting Position Constant

The previous comparisons indicated that behavior setting positions were associated with similar satisfaction patterns in both large and small schools. The next step in testing the contribution of setting position to the differences in the pattern of satisfactions in the large and small schools was to compare satisfactions between large and small schools when the small schools' superiority with respect to positions centrality was controlled. A simple device was used: comparison of satisfactions between the school size groups for peripheral, middle, and central behavior setting positions. To accomplish this, separate analyses for school size were calculated within each of the behavior setting positions.

Data in Table 7.5 indicate that Capital City students reported their

TABLE 7.5. NUMBER OF BEHAVIOR SETTINGS REPORTED BY LARGE AND SMALL SCHOOL JUNIORS IN WHICH THEY PARTICIPATED AT PERIPHERAL, MIDDLE, AND CENTRAL POSITIONS

School Group	Peripheral Positions	Middle Positions	Central Positions
Capital City	278	70	41
Midwest County	114	54	109

satisfactions in connection with many more settings in which they held peripheral positions, and that Midwest County reported for relatively more settings in which they held central positions. Since the number of positions reported influences the number of satisfactions reported, it was necessary to use the following controls in the analyses of peripheral and central positions: (a) one analysis compared large and small school students who reported *very few* settings in which their participation was peripheral or central; and (b) a second analysis compared large and small school students who reported *several* settings in which they participated at a peripheral or central position (no such control was necessary in the middle position, where position frequency was similar).

If no significant differences emerged between schools for any setting position, this would indicate that the differences between schools rested exclusively upon the differences in setting position occupied by students. If significant differences emerged, this would not be evidence that centrality of position was not a factor in satisfaction; the importance of setting position has already been demonstrated. Such a result would rather indicate that other factors, beyond behavior setting position, contributed to the satisfaction differences that emerged when large and small schools were compared.

Table 7.6 displays results of the 26 comparisons for which there were sufficient data for statistical tests. It will be noted that only one of these 26 reached statistical significance of .05 or better. In general, it is quite clear that the obtained differences in satisfaction patterns between school groups did *not* appear when the variable of setting position was held constant and when results were controlled for frequency of report. Most of the school size differences in satisfactions can be explained by reference to the degree to which large and small school students occupied different behavior setting positions.

The major exception to this general conclusion occurred on Group Action; there was evidence that the small school students reported more of this "teamwork pleasure." It may be that the smaller settings in Midwest County encouraged more comradeship in work and competition. It is possible that the larger settings in Capital City made it more difficult for even performers to feel togetherness in action.

A trend for Big Affiliation to be a large school satisfaction can be attributed to the greater difficulty a student experiences in feeling that he is a part of his school. Because the school presents so many different persons

TABLE 7.6. SIGNIFICANCE OF DIFFERENCES IN SATISFACTIONS DERIVED
BY CAPITAL CITY VS. MIDWEST COUNTY JUNIORS WHEN
SETTING POSITIONS WERE SIMILAR

Kind of Satisfaction	Peripheral Positions	Middle Positions	Central Positions
1. Competence		NS	NS/NS
2. Big Action and Test	NS/NS	M > CC, $p = .10$	NS/NS
3. Action Valence	NS/NS	NS	NS/NS
4. Group Action	NS/	M > CC, $p = .10$	M > CC $p = .02$ / NS
5. Be Valued		NS	/NS
6. Vicarious Enjoyment	NS/NS	NS	NS/
7. Big Affiliation	CC > M $p = .10$ / NS		

Note: Each entry under peripheral and central positions includes two results: the one
on the left is for subjects who reported few participations at the stated position; the
one on the right is for subjects who reported several. Where no results are reported,
frequencies were not high enough to be tested. NS means not significant. M—Midwest
County; CC—Capital City.

at many dispersed places, it may be difficult to encompass the school psy-
chologically. If this speculation is correct, large school students would
be particularly appreciative of those settings in which school unity and
spirit were deliberately emphasized. It was true that such satisfactions
were always mentioned in connection with all-school assemblies, rallies,
and athletic events. Such settings have the potential for encouraging the
feeling of belonging to the massive and "powerful" institution.

SUMMARY

It was hypothesized that small and large school Juniors would report
different kinds of satisfactions from their experiences in the nonclass
behavior settings. This hypothesis was confirmed. Specifically, Juniors
from the small schools reported more satisfactions relating to competence
development, to challenge and big action, to group action and to "uplift"
values; large school Juniors reported more satisfactions dealing with vicari-

ous enjoyment, with large entity affiliation, with learning about their school's persons and affairs, and with gaining "points" via participation. It was further hypothesized that the school differences in satisfactions were causally related to differences in the extent to which Juniors occupied central positions in school settings. It was possible to show that when Juniors in both large and small schools occupied the more central positions, they emphasized satisfactions of big action and test and of action valence, and they de-emphasized vicarious pleasures. The expected emphasis upon competent development when in a more central position was confirmed for the small school Juniors but appeared only as a slight trend in the larger milieu. Thus, there was considerable evidence for the prediction that satisfactions obtained in school settings were significantly influenced by the positions occupied within the settings.

The final question was whether the obtained differences in satisfactions between large and small school Juniors would emerge if the variable of setting position was not permitted to function. It was found that most of the tested differences in large and small school satisfactions did *not* occur when differences in setting position and in the number of settings reported were held constant.

The burden of the evidence reported, then, supports the conclusions that large and small school Juniors derived different satisfactions from their nonclass behavior settings and that these differences were causally related to differences in the number of students who occupied more central, important positions and the number of such positions held by each student.

The present investigation was directed toward *differences* in satisfactions. It was also true that Juniors from the large, as well as from the small, schools enjoyed many satisfactions of learning, of social interaction, and of novelty. The nonclass settings of both kinds of schools evidently provided many significant rewards.

The question might be raised: Which school size provides the "better" nonclass experiences for its Junior inhabitants? To the extent that one believes that the satisfactions related to competence, challenge, activity, and group affiliation are better than those related to vicarious enjoyment and to large entity affiliation—to this extent, small school Juniors reported better experiences than did large school Juniors.

8

Forces toward Participation in Behavior Settings

EDWIN P. WILLEMS

THE RESEARCH presented in this chapter* followed the theory and predictions of the first two chapters in two directions: first, it investigated "the real reasons for, or pulls toward" participating in voluntary school behavior settings as reported by students in large and small schools; second, it compared the reports of students who were relatively adequate academically (regular students) with the reports of students who were relatively unsuited for academic life (marginal students). The reports were coded as forces toward participation in designated behavior settings.

In Lewinian theory, the concept of *force* is defined as tendency to change, and has the conceptual properties of direction, strength, and point of application (Lewin, 1938, 1951). A number of empirical *symptoms* of tendency to change may be coordinated to the concept (Lewin, 1938). One of these symptoms is exemplified, with reference to the behavior setting Junior Class Play, by a student's statement, "My home-room teacher urged me strongly to go to the play." This statement reports that, at a particular point of application ("me"), there was a tendency to change ("go"), in a certain direction ("to the play"), with a designated strength ("strongly"). In this study, experiential symptoms of forces were secured by asking students, "What, if any, were for you real reasons for or pulls toward taking part in this activity?" (a precisely designated behavior setting). Each different reason reported was recorded as a separate force, and the total number of reasons were taken as a measure of the combined strength of all forces toward participation in the behavior setting.

Lewin (1951, p. 260) differentiated among three kinds of forces: (*a*) *own* forces, corresponding to the wishes, wills, and needs of the person himself (attractions), (*b*) induced forces, arising from the wishes and wills of some other person or persons, and (*c*) impersonal forces, arising

---

* The research is presented in more detail in a thesis on which this chapter is based (Willems, 1963).

from the impersonal environment. Here, induced and impersonal forces were combined into one class of *foreign* forces (pressures).

The *marginal students* of the study were those who had characteristics typical of students who drop out of high school without finishing the course of study, and the *regular students* were those who had characteristics typical of students who complete high school.

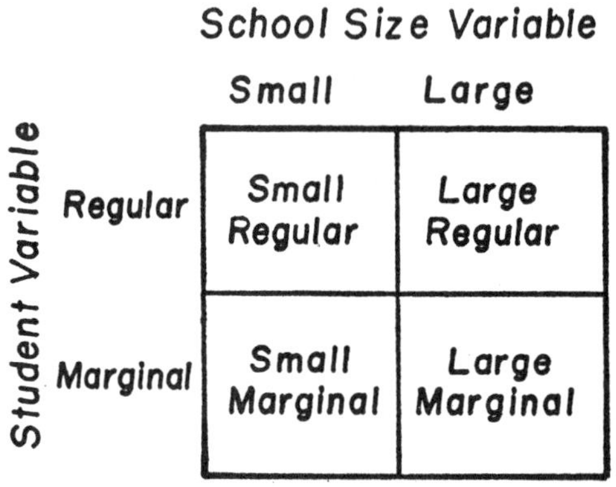

School Size Variable

Fig. 8.1.
Design of the study.

Figure 8.1 illustrates the basic design of the study. School size (large vs. small) and kind of student (regular vs. marginal) were studied for their association with forces toward participation in behavior settings. It has been shown (Chapter 6) that students in small schools, where settings were relatively underpopulated, engaged in central, important, responsible, or leadership functions (performances) more frequently than their large school counterparts. These relationships are in accord with the theory that has been presented, and they tend to validate its derivations. The present study was an attempt to penetrate these broad correlations and to investigate some of the effects of school size upon the kinds of forces students experience toward participation in behavior settings. The data of the study were relevant, also, to two related problems: the influence of school size upon the responsibilities felt by students, and the relation between number of reported forces toward participation and actual participation in behavior settings.

METHOD

The basic data were the number of "reasons or pulls" reported by each student toward taking part in designated behavior settings. Data were secured from 40 subjects (10 per cell in Figure 8.1) for the following classes of behavior settings in their respective schools: (a) five actual settings, i.e., behavior settings that had already occurred and that were equivalent across the schools; (b) those settings of the five actual settings that the subject had entered during a three-and-a-half-month period; (c) one hypothetical setting, a setting that had not occurred in any school; and (d) the most meaningful setting, i.e., the school setting listed first by each subject among those that were especially attractive and worth while to him.

Choice of Schools

The schools of this study were the same ones used in the studies reported in Chapters 6 and 7. There were the four small schools, with an average P/D ratio of 1.17 (Walker, Malden, Midwest, and Vernon), and the one large school with a P/D ratio of 4.58 (Capital City). The large school had roughly four times as many students available per setting as the small schools. Table 4.3 in Chapter 4 provides the detailed population and differentiation data.

Choice of Students

Junior students from the schools were subjects for the study. These students had taken part in the research reported in Chapters 6 and 7 three months previously.

The procedure for selecting marginal and regular students was entirely empirical. From a review of the literature on factors that characterize students who do not complete high school, and drawing especially on a study by Thomas (1954), the following cluster of five variables was chosen as predictive of this tendency to drop out of high school: (1) low IQ, (2) poor academic performance as indicated by grades, (3) father in a non-professional occupation, (4) father who did not finish high school, and (5) mother who did not finish high school. These variables identified students who were presumably less suited for academic and school life; they were the marginal students of the present study. Regular students did not have these handicaps. Subjects were selected according to their positions in the distributions of students on each of the five variables; marginal subjects were low in the distributions and regular subjects were high. Appendix 8.1 gives details of the variables and the methods followed in identifying the marginal and regular students. The final sampling was performed by collecting pools of suitable subjects for each cell in the research design (Figure 8.1), separating sexes within pools, assigning serial numbers to subjects, and sampling without replacement five males and five females per cell. Sex of subjects was controlled because sex differences in rates of participation in behavior settings had been found earlier (see Chapter 6).

Choice of Behavior Settings

Behavior setting surveys that had been made in the other studies yielded data on the exact behavior settings available to the subjects. The settings used in the present study were selected from these surveys.

Five actual settings. The five actual settings were selected so that each one had a counterpart of the same variety in all the schools, had occurred prior to gathering the data, was reasonably important and noticeable to all students, was open to Juniors of both sexes, was voluntary, and was extracurricular. Table 8.1 shows the five actual behavior settings chosen for each school; all of these settings had occurred at least once during an equivalent preceding period of three and a half months.

Settings that had been entered. One set of analyses dealt with the

TABLE 8.1. FIVE ACTUAL BEHAVIOR SETTINGS IN EACH SCHOOL
FOR WHICH STUDENTS REPORTED FORCES TOWARD PARTICIPATION

School	Athletic Contests, Indoors	Dances	Plays, Concerts, Programs	Volunteer Work and Fund-Raising	Fairs, Carnivals, Parades
Malden	Basketball Game, Home	Post-Game Dance	Junior Play	Jrs. Sell Magazines	Pep Club Outdoor Rally
Midwest	Basketball Game, Home	Post-Game Dance	Junior Play	Jrs. Sell Magazines	Jr. Carnival & Chili Supper
Vernon	Basketball Game, Home	Home-coming Dance	Junior Play	Jrs. Sell Hats	Pep Parade
Walker	Basketball Game, Home	Student Council Post-Game Dance	Junior Play	Jr. Car Wash & Odd Jobs	Band Parade & Collection
Capital City	Basketball Game, Home	Varsity Post-Game Dance	"Your Show"	Jrs. Sell Xmas Cards	Home-coming Parade

five settings regardless of participation; a separate analysis was performed on those settings among the five that each subject had entered.

Hypothetical setting. The hypothetical setting, in terms of which each subject projected his anticipated experience of forces toward participation, was All School Banquet, that had not occurred in any one school.

Most meaningful setting. This was the first setting a subject identified in the study reported in Chapter 7 as being "especially good, worth while —'plus.'" It was assumed that this setting maximized attractiveness and meaning for the subject.

Procedures for Gathering and Coding Data

In standardized, individual interviews, the subjects were asked to think of the selected behavior settings one at a time and to report the forces they experienced toward participating in the settings. Following appropriate background remarks (the settings were called "activities"), two separate but parallel sets of data were gathered.

Open-ended data. One set of data was obtained by recording the subjects' responses, for each setting, to the simple open-ended question, "What, if any, were ('would be' for the hypothetical setting) for you real reasons for or pulls toward attending this activity?" Subjects were asked to report their experiences of forces, whether or not they had in fact participated in the setting. Responses were coded into categories of own and foreign forces. These operations yielded the total number of forces, the number of own forces (attractions), and the number of foreign forces (pressures). Two independent coders obtained 84 per cent agreement on placing responses in specific categories.

Examples of students' open-ended responses coded as own forces were "I like to dance," "It sounded like an interesting play"; these were the attractions the settings held for the students. Foreign forces toward participating were reflected by such responses as "I was required to go," "I had to go; they needed girls," and "I was assigned to work there"; these were the pressures that the students experienced. Appendix 8.2 shows further examples of units coded as own and foreign forces.

To study responsibility felt and reported by the students, a separate content analysis was performed on the data by two independent analysts. Responses in the subjects' open-ended protocols were scored as indicating *responsibility* to a behavior setting, to persons, or to groups, if they fell into one of the following descriptive categories:

1. Statement of an obligation or expectation to participate in a setting; e.g., "Pep Club Members were expected to go"; "The town expects us to go."

2. Expression of loyalty because of membership in some group; e.g., "The class needed money; they were in the hole"; "It was a Junior class activity, and I'm a Junior."

3. Assertion of need to maintain the stability of the setting or group; e.g., "It would bring the class closer together"; "To uphold the name of the school."

4. Statement of previously determined job or connection with the setting; e.g., "I was in the skit"; "I was responsible for it."

The number of responses coded into these categories made up the responsibility score of a student.

In the case of the hypothetical setting, in addition to the question about forces, the subject was asked if he would participate in the setting if it were to occur.

Card-sort data. After the open-ended data were secured from a subject, a parallel set of data was obtained by a modified Q-sort method. On each of a set of 16 cards, a statement describing a possible force toward participation in a behavior setting was written, e.g., "I was asked to go," "I like that activity," "I saw that activity needed people." The content of the statements was kept as general as possible, and they were categorized as representing own or foreign forces before the data were gathered. Appendix 8.3 shows the card-sort items for the actual and the hypothetical settings.

A sorting sheet with Yes and No boxes was placed in front of the subject. The subject was asked to think of the settings, one at a time, and was instructed: "Take these cards, and if there are any among them that were (or 'would be' for the hypothetical setting) for you real reasons for or pulls toward attending this activity, sort them into the Yes box. Those that weren't, sort into the No box."

These operations yielded the total number of responses that indicated forces toward participation in the settings, the number of own forces, and the number of foreign forces. These data are called *card-sort data*. In a replication after five days of the card-sort operation in a pilot study, an 89 per cent intra-subject agreement on the sorting of specific cards into the Yes and No boxes was obtained.

Methods of Analysis

Scores. The total number of own and foreign forces toward participation was determined for each individual by both the open-ended and the card-sort methods, and for each of the classes of settings: (*a*) the five actual settings, whether or not the subject had entered them, (*b*) the settings among the five which the subject had entered, (*c*) the hypothetical setting, and (*d*) the most meaningful setting. For the five actual settings, scores were obtained by summing across the five settings; in the case of settings entered, the average frequency per entered setting was calculated. The force scores for the hypothetical setting and the most meaningful setting were the number of forces reported.

Statistical techniques. Two-variable statistical procedures were employed on the data, in keeping with the two-by-two design of the study. When the data met the assumption of homogeneity of variance, analysis-of-variance procedures were used. When this assumption was not met, the data were split at the overall median, frequency counts were made for the various cells, and the Sutcliffe multivariable chi-square procedure was used (Sutcliffe, 1957).

Adequacy of the scores. The relationship between the verbal symptoms of forces toward participation in behavior settings and actually entering and participating in the settings was investigated by means of correlations. Correlations were calculated between the numbers of forces reported in the interview by the subjects and coded as forces (own, foreign, and total forces) and (*a*) the number of behavior settings entered among the five actual settings, (*b*) the number of entrances into behavior settings belonging to the same varieties as the five actual settings, (*c*) the number of performances in the latter settings, and (*d*) the total number of participations (entrances and performances) in the latter settings. The data on participation in these varieties of settings were gleaned from data in the investigation reported in Chapter 6.

RESULTS

The results will be presented in two ways. A representative set of data will first provide an overview of the trends of the findings, and a second section will give the results in more detail. In the presentation the terms attractions and pressures will often be used in place of own and foreign forces, respectively.

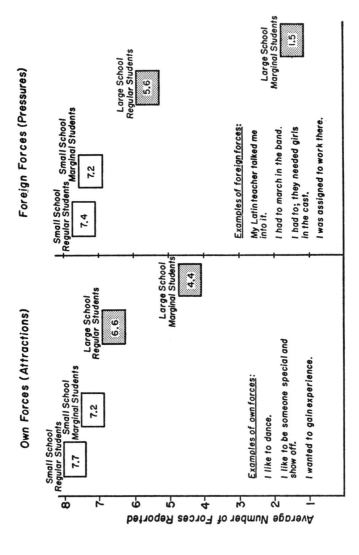

Own Forces (Attractions) Foreign Forces (Pressures)

Small School
Regular Students Small School
Marginal Students

7.7 7.2

Large School
Regular Students

6.6

Large School
Marginal Students

4.4

Examples of own forces:

I like to dance.

I like to be someone special and
show off.

I wanted to gain experience.

Small School
Regular Students Small School
Marginal Students

7.4 7.2

Large School
Regular Students

5.6

Large School
Marginal Students

1.5

Examples of foreign forces:

My Latin teacher talked me
into it.

I had to march in the band.

I had to; they needed girls
in the cast.

I was assigned to work there.

Average Number of Forces Reported

8
7
6
5
4
3
2
1

Fig. 8.2. Mean numbers of forces reported toward participation in five behavior settings by regular and marginal students in large and small schools.

Representative Results

Analyses of the open-ended responses to the five actual settings are provided in Figures 8.2 and 8.3.

Figure 8.2 shows the average numbers of attractions and pressures reported by the various subject groups: small school regular, small school marginal, large school regular, and large school marginal. Students of the small schools, where settings were relatively underpopulated, reported both more attractions ($p < .05$) and more pressures ($p < .001$) toward participation in the school settings than students from the large school; the small school advantage was greater in the case of pressures than in the case of attractions. Regular and marginal students within the small schools did not differ appreciably in either the number of pressures or the number of attractions reported; but within the large school, marginal students reported both fewer attractions and fewer pressures than regular students, and in the case of pressures the deficit was marked (the statistical interaction for pressures had an associated probability of less than .10).

We find here, as was found in the data on participation reported in Chapter 6, that the large school had a sizable group of "outsiders" not found in the small schools. One regular and three marginal students of the large school reported no pressure to participate, while all students of the small schools, regular and marginal alike, reported some pressures. It appears that the small school environments, made up of relatively underpopulated behavior settings, produced less discrimination between the two kinds of students we studied than the large school environment, made up of relatively overpopulated settings. According to the reports of the students, "everyone" in the small schools felt that he had a chance at the rewards provided by the settings and that the settings, and the other persons in them, needed his contribution.

Figure 8.3 reveals the same relationship between the schools in the pattern of responsibility responses as in forces toward participation. Students of the small schools gave more responses indicative of acceptance of responsibility than did students of the large school ($p < .001$). Again, school size acted differentially, the difference between regular and marginal students being greater in the large than in the small schools; the statistical interaction was significant at less than the .05 level. The large

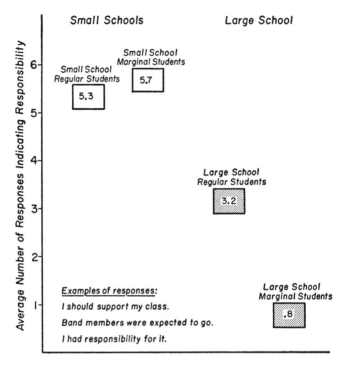

Fig. 8.3. Mean numbers of responsibility responses reported by regular and marginal students in large and small schools.

school produced outsiders. One regular and five marginal students of the large school reported no feelings of responsibility, while all students of the small schools reported at least one instance of responsibility.

The data on forces and responsibilities are relevant to the question of the comparative efficacy of personal variables and ecological variables in influencing behavior. The absence of differences between regular and marginal students in the small schools and the presence of such differences in the large school indicate that school size, as well as the kind of person, is a determinant of forces toward participation. The fact that marginal students of the small schools reported more forces than did the regular students of the large school is relevant too. In the large school the academically marginal student appeared to be truly an outsider, while in the small schools being marginal made no apparent difference on the experience of pressures, attractions, and responsibilities. This issue will be dealt with in more detail later.

The findings reported so far represent a prototype of the major results of the study. School size and its correlates in behavior setting population produce differences in forces to participate experienced by students. Further, it appears that the relatively overpopulated behavior settings of the large school consistently gave rise to a group of outsiders who experienced little attraction, pressure, or responsibility toward participation.

Detailed Results

Big school vs. small schools. Total forces. The total numbers of forces toward participation in the different classes of behavior settings are presented in Table 8.2. Students of the small schools reported more forces than students of the large school for every class of setting and for both kinds of data (card-sort and open-ended). In every case the probability that the obtained difference was not a chance difference was less than .05, and in five of the seven classes of data the probability was less than .01. Results of further analyses of the data are given in Table 8.3.

TABLE 8.2. SUMMARY OF STATISTICAL TESTS OF RELATIONS BETWEEN (P/D) SCHOOL SIZE AND TOTAL NUMBERS OF FORCES REPORTED

Classes of Data	Mean Number of Forces		Statistic	p
	Small Schools	Large School		
Five actual settings				
Card-sort	38.75	19.95	$F = 27.69$	$< .01$
Open-ended	14.75	8.55	$F = 19.32$	$< .01$
Settings entered*				
Card-sort	8.10	4.97	$F = 17.41$	$< .01$
Open-ended	3.01	2.26	$F = 7.11$	$< .05$
Hypothetical setting				
Card-sort	8.35	4.85	$F = 13.84$	$< .01$
Open-ended	3.15	2.20	$F = 4.99$	$< .05$
Most meaningful setting				
Card-sort	9.30	6.10	$F = 12.74$	$< .01$

* The data for this class of behavior setting are the mean number of forces per setting entered; all other data in the table are total numbers of forces for the stated class of settings.

TABLE 8.3. RESULTS OF STATISTICAL TESTS OF RELATIONS BETWEEN SCHOOL SIZE AND NUMBERS OF REPORTED FORCES, RESPONSIBILITY, AND EXPECTATION TO ENTER A HYPOTHETICAL SETTING

	Types of Behavior Settings			
Classes of Data	Five Actual	Settings Entered	Hypo-thetical	Most Mean-ingful
1. Own forces (attractions)				
Card-sort	S > L*	S > L	S > L*	S > L*
Open-ended	S > L	ns	—	—
2. Foreign forces (pressures)				
Card-sort	S > L*	S > L*	S > L*	S > L
Open-ended	S > L*	S > L*	—	—
3. Proportion of foreign to total				
Card-sort	S > L*	S > L*	S > L*	ns
Open-ended	S > L	S > L*	—	—
4. Responsibility, open-ended				
No. of responses....	S > L*	—	—	—
Proportion of total..	S > L*	—	—	—
5. Expected entry into hypothetical setting, open-ended	—	—	S > L*	—

Note: Indicated results were significant at the .05 level or less; an asterisk indicates the .01 level or less. Ns means not significant. A dash indicates that no analysis was available. S and L indicate small and large.

Own forces, attractions. Students of the small schools reported more attractions toward participation than students of the large school in all classes of data except the open-ended data from settings actually entered.

Foreign forces, pressures. Students of the small schools reported more pressures toward participation than students of the large school. This was true in all sets of data.

Attractions and pressures compared. *Proportion of foreign to total* in Table 8.3 is an analysis in terms of the ratio of number of foreign forces reported by each subject divided by total forces the subject reported. All comparisons by means of these ratios, except those for the most meaningful setting, show that the students of the small schools reported higher proportions of foreign forces to total forces than students of the large school. Not only did the small school students report more pressures than the large school students (items 2 and 3, Table 8.3), but foreign forces made up greater proportions of their total reported forces.

Responsibility. Students of the small schools gave more responses indicative of responsibility than the students of the large school, and responsibility responses made up greater proportions of the total responses reported by students of the small schools.

Hypothetical behavior setting. When asked whether or not they would expect to participate in the hypothetical setting if it were to occur, 19 of the 20 students of the small schools and 10 of the 20 students of the large school responded with a clear, unequivocal Yes.

Marginal students vs. regular students. Total forces. The total numbers of forces toward participation in the different classes of behavior settings are reported in Table 8.4. One of the seven differences between marginal and regular students approaches statistical significance.

Combined effect of school size and kind of student. Figure 8.2 shows that the *order* of the mean number of forces toward participation in the five actual behavior settings was, for both attraction and pressures, as follows: small school, regular students; small school, marginal students; large school, regular students; large school, marginal students. Total reported forces (own and foreign) in both the card-sort and open-ended data were used to test the statistical significance of this order among the cells of the research design (Figure 8.1). The statistical test used was the Jonckheere test of ordered alternatives (Jonckheere, 1954), which allows one to test the null hypothesis—that there are no differences among the groups of subjects—and to accept the hypothesis of a predicted order. Table 8.5 summarizes the results of this test. Both the card-sort and open-ended data yielded the above order at a statistical level far above chance. In the lower part of the table, mean (total) numbers of forces reported in the open-ended data illustrate the pattern.

TABLE 8.4. SUMMARY OF STATISTICAL TESTS OF RELATIONS BETWEEN REGULAR
AND MARGINAL STUDENTS AND TOTAL NUMBERS OF FORCES REPORTED

| | Mean Number of Forces | | | |
Classes of Data	Regular	Marginal	Statistic	p
Five actual settings				
Card-sort	29.30	29.40	—	ns
Open-ended	13.15	10.15	$F = 4.58$	$< .05$
Settings entered*				
Card-sort	6.62	6.61	—	ns
Open-ended	2.85	2.46	$F = 1.87$	ns
Hypothetical setting				
Card-sort	6.70	6.50	—	ns
Open-ended	2.90	2.45	$F = 1.12$	ns
Most meaningful setting				
Card-sort	7.45	7.95	—	ns

Note: A dash denotes an F ratio of less than 1.00. NS means not significant.

  * The data for this class of behavior setting are the mean number of forces per
setting entered; all other data in the table are total numbers of forces for the stated class
of settings.

TABLE 8.5. SUMMARY OF STATISTICAL FINDINGS ON THE ORDER
OF CELLS, BASED ON TOTAL REPORTED FORCES

Classes of Data	Z	p	Direction
Five actual settings			
Card-sort	3.80	$< .00007$	Small-Reg > Small-Marg > Large-Reg > Large-Marg
Open-ended ..	3.67	$< .00016$	Small-Reg > Small-Marg > Large-Reg > Large-Marg

Mean numbers of total forces: open-ended data

	Small	Large
Regular	15.1	11.2
Marginal	14.4	5.9

TABLE 8.6. CORRELATIONS BETWEEN THE NUMBER OF SETTINGS
PARTICIPATED IN AND NUMBERS OF FORCES TOWARD ENTRY
INTO THE FIVE ACTUAL SETTINGS

Behavior Setting Data	Open-Ended Data			Card-Sort Data		
	Own	Foreign	Total	Own	Foreign	Total
No. of settings entered among the five actual settings	.61	.85	.87	.48	.58	.54
Participation data, Chap. 6						
Entries only	.49	.38		.12	.05	
Performances only	.30	.69		.48	.60	
Entries plus performances						
Total participation	.53	.66	.67	.35	.38	.39

Note: In the table Spearman rho's, corrected for ties, were computed for the first row; Pearson r's were computed for the other rows. Behavioral data for rows 2, 3, and 4 were obtained from Chapter 6 for the subjects of this study; scores were totals for the varieties of settings from which the five settings of this study were selected.

Relations between forces and behavior. The correlations reported in Table 8.6 (first row) indicate that a positive relationship far above chance exists between reported forces and actual behavior (all p's $< .005$). These data provide a kind of validation of the number of reported "reasons" or "pulls" as a measure of forces toward participation. The open-ended data tend to correlate more strongly with actual behavior than the card-sort data, and foreign forces (pressures) tend to be more highly correlated to participation than own forces (attractions), especially in the case of performances.

Partial Replication

In the study reported above, the large school had 20 times as many students as the small schools. Data were subsequently gathered in a new set of schools, in which the larger school (Haven) had 229 students and a P/D ratio of 2.29 while the small schools (Dorset and Hearn) each had 53 students and an average P/D ratio of 1.00. Thus, the predictions were tested in schools that fell at different points on the size continuum (see Chapter 6).

All subjects in the replication were Juniors. The 15 Juniors in the combined Dorset-Hearn group and the 39 Juniors in Haven were classified by sex and IQ quartile to assure similar distributions of students. As it turned out, only Juniors in the three upper quartiles were used, since the small schools contained no Juniors in the lowest quartile.

The method for eliciting the selected subjects' experiences of forces toward participation was a modified version of the card-sort technique used in the main study. Data were gathered from groups rather than in individual interviews. The original card-sort items (see Appendix 8.3) were printed on questionnaire sheets.

Five such sheets, one for each of the five actual behavior settings, were given to each subject. Subjects filled out the questionnaire sheets under the direction of a research worker. After background remarks, subjects wrote the name of a setting at the top of the first page, and circled Yes if they had attended this setting at least once, and were then instructed: "Read each item in the list carefully, and if it was *for you* a real reason for, or pull toward, attending (*setting*), write in a Yes in the blank after it. If it wasn't, write in a No. Even if you didn't attend this activity, there may have been some pulls toward going, so work through the list, putting either a Yes or a No in each blank." The same procedure was repeated for another setting until all subjects finished all five settings.

This technique provided data on the number of forces toward entry into each setting (the responses marked Yes). These were summed across the five settings, yielding, as in the main study, individual scores of the number of own forces and foreign forces. A ratio of pressures to total forces was then computed for each subject.

Since the distributions of scores for total, own, and foreign forces met the assumption of homogeneity of variance, analysis-of-variance procedures were used. The distribution of ratio scores was dichotomized at the overall median, and chi square was used for the analysis. Pearson product moment correlations were then calculated between the total number of forces and the number of participations in the varieties of settings from which the five settings were selected. Such correlations were calculated separately for the small and larger schools, and then for the combined sample.

Table 8.7 summarizes the results of analyses relating numbers of forces to school size.

As predicted, Juniors from the small schools reported greater numbers of pressures toward participation in the five settings. Not only did they report greater numbers of pressures, but pressures made up greater pro-

TABLE 8.7. SUMMARY OF STATISTICAL TESTS OF RELATIONS BETWEEN
SCHOOL SIZE AND FORCES TOWARD PARTICIPATION IN
FIVE BEHAVIOR SETTINGS

Classes of Data	Mean		Statistic	p	Direction
	Small*	Larger			
Own forces	18.31	15.67	$F = 3.90$	ns	none
Foreign forces	32.30	22.23	$F = 12.93$	$< .01$	S > L
Proportion of foreign to total ..			$X^2 = 3.97$	$< .025$	S > L

Note: S—small; L—larger.
  * Hearn and Dorset are combined into a "small" category.

portions of their total reported experiences. The students from the small schools tended to respond with more own forces, but the differences did not reach statistical significance.

Results of correlations between numbers of forces and numbers of participations were as follows: for the overall combined sample, $r = .24$ (ns); for the small school group alone, $r = .30$ (ns); for the larger school group alone, $r = .33$ ($p < .05$).

In this extension of the main study, school populations differed by a factor of 4 to 1, and P/D ratios by a factor of 2 to 1, rather than by 20 to 1 and 4 to 1, respectively, as in the main study. Results from these studies indicate that the theory predicts differences in experienced forces which are sensitive to both wide and narrow differences in school size and P/D ratio. In both the earlier study and in this extension, pressures varied significantly with size. In the earlier study, attractions tended not to vary as widely with size as did foreign forces, and in this extension own forces did not differ significantly. This finding suggests that foreign forces are more sensitive to size differences, or are a stronger correlate of size.

One purpose for using the modified technique was to test the possibility of using group sessions rather than individual interviews to gather data on forces toward participation. The correlations between forces and participation suggest that the modified technique yielded data that were less valid than the data obtained by the earlier methods, especially less valid than the technique yielding open-ended data. The correlations for the whole group of subjects in this extension of the study did not reach significance. Methodologically, these findings suggest that the three basic techniques used fall in the following descending order of validity of the data they yield: (*a*) unaided recall of forces, i.e., open-ended data, $r = .67$ ($p < .01$); (*b*) stimulated but forced choice recall with sorting of items, i.e., card-sort data, $r = .39$ ($p < .05$); and (*c*) stimulated but forced choice recall with simple Yes-No marking of responses, i.e., questionnaire data, $r = .24$ (ns). The three correlations reported here are based on numbers of forces for the five settings and total frequency of participation in the varieties of settings from which the five were selected.

DISCUSSION

Asch, in his book *Social Psychology* (1952), points out that the social order becomes "objectified" in the form of material objects and institutional relations, and that it is one of the important tasks of the psychologist to study how such stubborn environmental facts act upon and alter the behavior of persons. The studies reported in this volume focus on one such stubborn fact, the ubiquitous, coercive behavior settings that students in high schools inhabit. The present investigation shows that the number of persons present in behavior settings not only alters overt behavior in predictable ways, but also determines, within limits, the nature of the psychological experience of students.

The results support the theory that guided the research. Although the theory is treated in detail in Chapter 2 and elsewhere (Barker, 1960; Willems, 1963), in its simplest form it predicts the effects of behavior setting population as follows.

First, behavior settings contain valent, attractive opportunities for involvement. When manpower diminishes, there will be more such opportunities, or higher valence, per person, and individuals will experience more own forces, or attractions, toward participation.

Second, behavior settings have functions the carrying out of which imposes obligations on the inhabitants. There are, then, manpower requirements necessary to meet the obligations and thus to keep the settings functioning properly. When available manpower falls below the requirements, each remaining person will be the locus of more of the settings' obligations. Individuals will then perceive the necessity of their own, and others', participation to avoid crippling the settings. There will be more invitations, demands, and requirements to take part. Increases in such obligations and demands generate more foreign forces, or pressures, toward participation in relatively underpopulated settings.

Third, there will be differences in behavior coupled with these effects of differences in the ecological environment upon forces toward participation in underpopulated settings. Individuals in underpopulated settings who might otherwise attend only to watch or participate peripherally will be pressed into service in important functions (performances) more often; they will have a larger share of responsibility for the setting and will experience more feelings of responsibility and obligation.

Finally, in underpopulated settings, persons who might otherwise be seen as unsuitable or marginal will also be pressed into service, and experience forces toward participation. In other words, when persons are in short supply and high demand, each will experience many forces toward participation; there will be less discrimination according to kind of person.

Results from this study and the partial replication yielded general support for the theory of the effects of behavior setting size, indicating that the theory is a powerful predictor from ecology to the experience and behavior of individual persons. Students from the small schools, where settings were relatively underpopulated, reported more own forces (attractions) and foreign forces (pressures) toward participation in behavior settings than did students from the large school. Furthermore, a sizable group of students emerged in the large school who experienced few, if any, forces toward participation. The small schools in the present study did not contain any such outsiders; all of the small school students reported experiencing many forces toward participation. Preselected marginal students in the small schools experienced as many forces as did regular students, while in the large school, the preselected marginals experienced very few forces, far fewer than the regular students.

Another important finding is that the responses of the small school students reflected more felt responsibility and obligation. Many persons feel that the development of a sense of responsibility is essential to good citizenship, and that it is one task of schools to encourage this sense of responsibility in students. The frequency of responsibility responses in this study followed the same pattern as the data on forces, with extreme differences between schools and the emergence of outsiders, persons in the large school who reported no felt responsibility.

Pressures (foreign forces) varied more with school size than did attractions (own forces), and pressures correlated more highly with actual participation and involvement than did attractions. These findings suggest that self-generated pressures of behavior settings are more powerful than attractions in mediating the relationship between size and participation reported in other chapters of this volume.

Quite apart from support for a particular theory, several implications stand out from the findings of this study, which impinge radically upon some commonly held ideas about psychological experience, motivation, and development.

First, it seems clear that school size is an important variable in the lives of students. On the basis of the present studies as well as other relevant studies (Chapter 3), effects of size seem to be facts of life which must be reckoned with. Not only is the overt behavior (participation) of students altered by school size, but their experience is altered as well. In Lewinian terms, not only are behavioral locomotions affected by size, but the very structure of the life space is altered. The data on the hypothetical setting are especially interesting in this regard (Table 8.3). Here was a setting that no one had entered, because it had not occurred in any of the schools. Yet when students were asked to project ahead their experience of forces ("What would be real reasons for or pulls . . . ?"), the students of the small schools expected more attractions, more pressures, and a greater proportion of pressures; and more of them definitely expected to enter the setting when it did occur.

Second, motivation is often seen as purely a function of the person. Attraction and sense of responsibility, especially, are often seen as such "inside-the-skin" variables. Yet, when similar persons were compared in different environments in the present study, attraction and felt responsibility were found to vary with the outside environment also. The data (Figures 8.2 and 8.3, and Table 8.5) offer some evidence on the question of the comparative influence of ecology and kind of person in determining the experience of forces. Within the limits of the methods used to identify and select regular and marginal students, one would expect, if the kind of person were more important than the ecology of the school, that similar groups of students would report similar experiences in different ecologies. Table 8.5 shows that this was not the case. Marginal students from the small schools reported more forces than regular students from the large school. Marginal students from the large school were a group apart, a group of outsiders. These findings indicate that the academically marginal students had very different experiences in the two ecologies. In the small school, marginal characteristics made no difference; marginal students experienced almost as many forces toward participation as the nonmarginal students. In the large school, however, the marginal students experienced relatively very few attractions and pressures toward participation.

The correlations between forces and participation provide further evidence that ecology is a powerful factor in determining participation. The consistently high correlations between foreign forces and participation suggest that ecology was a powerful determinant of participation among the subjects of the present study. The studies reviewed in Chapter 3 almost entirely disregarded this variable so strongly associated with size.

Third, there are implications for developmental theory. If it is assumed that "the best way to learn is to *do*," or "the best way to learn responsibility is to have it," then the implications of the present study are clear. Individual students in small schools, with their relatively underpopulated settings, live under greater day-to-day attraction, pressure, and responsibility felt toward taking active part in the voluntary activities of their school environments. They are more motivated to take part.

EXPLORATORY STUDIES

THE BYWAYS encountered in the course of exploratory research are often pleasantly refreshing, even invigorating, with their easy promises when the main line of the research is difficult and discouraging. They sometimes enrich the main discoveries, point to profitable directions for further study, and, with luck, turn up stray, unexpected scientific nuggets. Scientific byways can also be dangerously impeding by pre-empting too much of the available time and energy.

Our efforts to balance the pleasures, rewards, and hazards of research are reported in Part III of *Big School, Small School*, where the results of our digressions are presented. These were all quick reconnoitering efforts. They were not carried out as thoroughly, and they were not pursued as far, as will ultimately be necessary. They are reported as they were done, for their enriching, suggestive, and serendipitous values. Footnotes have been added at points where special cautions are required to evaluate properly some of the findings.

Chapter 9 reports a first attempt to disentangle the strands involved in rural school consolidation. It is a reconnaissance of the out-of-class experiences of students living in very small communities and attending very small local high schools, of students living in comparable small communities but attending a relatively large district high school located in a distant community, and of students living in the community where the district school was located.

The business, governmental, religious, and social life of a community are widely considered to have educational values for its young people. Assertions are sometimes made about the greater educational advantages of students of the more varied and specialized life of cities, but on the other hand the rural culture is sometimes extolled as more accessible to adolescents. However, few facts have been available. Chapters 10 and 11 provide some facts upon the degree of participation of several samples of town and city high school students in both school and out-of-school activities with potential educational values. Chapter 10 provides comparative data on the employment and participation of town and city adolescents in churches and organizations and in music and specialized academic activities. Chapter 11 is a general study of the place of adolescents in the total life of four small towns; it makes methodological as well as substantive contributions.

9

Some Effects of High School Consolidation

W. J. CAMPBELL

CONSOLIDATION is variously defined, but as used in this study, it signifies the transportation of high school students from their local communities to a school in a neighboring community. The essential elements are (a) commuting, and (b) attendance at a larger school than the one that had previously existed, or could exist, in the local community.

Consolidation of high schools, like most educational issues, has given rise to considerable controversy. On the one hand, its supporters claim that *students benefit* through better and more varied curriculums, better classifications, better facilities, especially in such subjects as science and music, contact with better teachers, opportunities to participate in better and more varied extracurricular activities, wider social opportunities and experiences, and more regular attendance as a result of being, in some cases, transported from door to school; *parents benefit* through reduced expenditure on education; the *community benefits* through the creation of closer ties with neighboring communities.

On the other hand, the opponents of consolidation claim that *students lose* through increased breaks in their education, loss of contact with local teachers who know the community and the families well, spending time on commuting which might be spent with greater profit on other activities, and fewer opportunities to participate in extracurricular activities; *parents lose* through being denied opportunities to participate in the control of their school; the *community loses* through being denied the facilities of an active school, which could serve as a cultural and educational center, and through the breakdown of community cohesion and participation, especially in youth activities.

These and other similar arguments have customarily been advanced by those who enter the controversy on consolidation. However, few systematic attempts have been made to examine the assertions empirically. Apart from studies on school size (reviewed in Chapter 3), almost all of the literature on consolidation deals with alleged economies and administrative procedures. The few reports involving student reactions that we found dealt with changes in intelligence quotients and the like. These are important reports, but our interest lies rather in the experiences and processes that underlie changes such as these, and the published work has been of little direct benefit to us.

SCOPE

Our investigations were focused upon the out-of-class experiences of the students and can be divided into three categories: (a) nature of the forces that led to participation in extracurricular behavior settings; (b) the extent and level of participation in these settings; (c) the satisfactions gained from these participations. We sought answers to questions such as the following: In comparison with students attending local schools, are students in consolidated schools under more or less pressure to participate in school activities? Does the nature of the pressures differ? Do students in consolidated schools participate to a greater or lesser extent in school activities? Do they miss out or gain in particular kinds of activity? Do students in consolidated schools report more or less satisfaction with school activities?

The state of Kansas presented an excellent field laboratory for the study of questions such as these. In many districts consolidation at the high school level had already taken place, and schools that were formerly used for secondary students were being used for grade students or were standing idle. On the other hand, there was no dearth of small local high schools that were still functioning actively.

For purposes of the study we selected three groups of students:

Study Group 1, *small local.* Students in attendance at small rural high schools within the boundaries of their own communities. There were two schools involved here and each had a student population of 53. Each, too, was situated within a small town of about 200 persons.

Study Group 2, *consolidated.* Students who came from communities that were similar in size to those of Group 1, but who were transported daily by bus to a county high school with an enrollment of 370 students within a larger district. These students, like the previous ones, came from two different communities, each of which contributed 41 students.

Study Group 3, *larger local.* Students in attendance at the larger county high school referred to above, but who came from the community within which the school was situated. There were 84 students in this group, and the total population of the community was 551 persons.

The schools are identified in Chapters 4 and 8. Dorset and Hearn were the small local schools; they provided the subjects of Group 1. Eakins was the consolidated school to which Group 2 students were transported by bus a distance of eight and nine miles, respectively, from the small towns of Lang and Media. The students living in the town of Eakins and attending Eakins District High School constituted Group 3.

We began by drawing up a combined list of the 82 consolidated students, and then attempted to match each student on the list with one from each of the small local and larger local groups, yielding a matched three. This matching was undertaken on the basis of sex, class in school, and percentile rank on the Differential Aptitude Test (DAT). By maintaining fairly rigorous standards in the percentile rank matching, it was possible to form 61 matched threes, who were distributed as shown in Table 9.1.

The study was designed to isolate the effects of the two variables listed earlier, namely, commuting and size of school, but it was impossible to

TABLE 9.1. DISTRIBUTION OF MATCHED SUBJECTS FROM SMALL LOCAL, CONSOLIDATED, AND LARGER LOCAL SCHOOLS

Percentile Ranks: DAT	Fresh-men	Sopho-mores	Juniors	Seniors	Total
Upper quartile (Q1)					
Girls	2	3	3	2	10
Boys	2	4	1	2	9
Second quartile (Q2)					
Girls	4	2	2	2	10
Boys	3	4	2	3	12
Third quartile (Q3)					
Girls	4	0	0	0	4
Boys	2	2	3	0	7
Lower quartile (Q4)					
Girls	2	2	1	1	6
Boys	2	1	0	0	3
Totals	21	18	12	10	61

Note: A number in the table denotes the frequency of matched threes.

avoid the inclusion of a third variable—size of community. Thus Group 1 students came from very small communities (about 200 in population) and attended very small local schools (enrollment about 50); Group 2 students also came from very small communities but attended a larger consolidated school (enrollment 370); Group 3 students came from a somewhat larger community (population about 550) and attended the same larger consolidated school that was, for them, the local school.

It seems likely that the three variables, and perhaps others, interact in a complex manner, so that to treat them as distinguishable causal elements is to do less than justice to the complexity of relationships. Nevertheless, as a first step, it seems reasonable to make the following assumptions:

1. No differences between any two of the groups would suggest that the effects of consolidation in the areas studied are negligible.

2. A difference between small local students, on the one hand, and consolidated and larger local ones, on the other, would suggest the influence of some school factor.

3. A difference between consolidated students, on the one hand, and small local and larger local ones, on the other, would suggest the influence of commuting.

4. A difference between larger local students, on the one hand, and small local and consolidated ones, on the other, would suggest the influence of community size.

As suggested above, these are merely reasonable assumptions to guide the analyses and interpretations.

FORCES TO ENTER SCHOOL BEHAVIOR SETTINGS

Data on forces were obtained from the questionnaire used in the partial replication study described earlier (pp. 115–35) and in Appendix 8.3.* In this, students are presented with a number of school behavior settings and

---

* The data in this and following sections differ in several important ways from those of Chapters 6, 7, and 8. In the present investigation all data were gathered in one continuous session, whereas students were approached on two different occasions for the data in Chapters 6 and 7. Material for the main study reported in Chapter 8 was derived from interview sessions, whereas group questionnaires were used in the study reported here. There were indications that student replies were less rich in the present situation. Finally, all subjects in the previous studies were Juniors; the present study ranged across four high school classes. The relation between school class standing and participation in school activities has not been investigated.

are asked to indicate for each what were for them real forces or "pulls" toward participation. The settings used in this study were Home Basketball Game, Homecoming Dance, Christmas Music Program, Magazine Sale, and Pep Rally. These were chosen because of their occurrence in each of the schools during the current school year.

In the analysis of the data, no attempt has been made to retain the identity of each setting; rather, responses have been summed across the five settings in order to find the frequency with which each student has reported the existence of each force.

Students in all three groups reported the existence of a considerable number of forces associated with entry into the settings: a mean of 10.48 per setting for small local students, 9.60 for consolidated students, and 9.67 for larger local ones. Overall differences here were not significant. The three groups did not differ either with respect to the relative potency of the forces: #6—"I like to be active and do things," #15—"I knew this activity needed people," and #7—"I like this activity" were consistently at the top of the lists, while #5—"It gave me a chance to be someone special," #12—"I saw that everyone else was going, and it's not fun to be left out," and #14—"This activity is required for students like me" were invariably given few affirmative markings.

In the previous work the forces were classified according to own (arising from within the personality of the respondent: "I thought I might learn something") and foreign (originating from without the respondent: "I was expected to go"). As a first step, we have made a similar breakdown here, and the data are presented in Table 9.2.

TABLE 9.2. NUMBER OF OWN AND FOREIGN FORCES, BY STUDY
GROUPS AND SCHOOL CLASSES

| Subgroups | Study Groups | | | | | |
| | Small Local (1). | | Consolidated (2) | | Larger Local (3) | |
	Own	Foreign	Own	Foreign	Own	Foreign
Freshmen	434	713	474	563	483	539
Sophomores	340	516	392	489	348	434
Juniors	271	439	238	340	271	383
Seniors	210	274	183	255	209	283
Total	1,255	1,942	1,287	1,647	1,311	1,639

This analysis revealed no overall or subgroup differences in the number of own forces, but small local students reported more foreign forces than did those from the other two groups.* F values were: Groups 1 and 2—8.894 ($<$ .01); Groups 1 and 3—11.293 ($<$ .01); Groups 2 and 3—ns.

In an attempt to examine the broad difference in greater detail, further subdivisions into the following clusters of behavior setting forces were made:

1. Items suggesting intellectual attraction: #1—"I thought I might learn something there" and #2—"It was a chance for me to do or see something new and different."

2. Items suggesting external pressures: #9—"Others wanted me to go," #10—"I was expected to go," #13—"I was told or urged to go," and #14—"This activity is required for students like me."

3. Items suggesting anticipated enjoyment: #17†—"I thought it would be lots of fun," #7—"I like this activity," #6—"I like to be active and do things," #7—"In general I like this activity; by going I could help to see to it that it would be there for me to enjoy again," and #8—"In general I like this activity; by doing something there I could see to it that it would be there for me to enjoy again."

4. Items suggesting social attractions: #11—"Everybody else was going, so I wanted to go too," #3—"It gave me a chance to be with the other kids," and #12—"I saw that everyone else was going, and it's not fun to be left out."

5. Items suggesting personal responsibility: #18†—"I had a responsibility with the activity," #15—"I knew this activity needed people," and #16—"I knew this activity needed to have certain things done."

6. Items suggesting opportunity to acquire primary status: #5—"It gave me a chance to be someone special."

The cluster totals for each of the three study groups are shown in Table 9.3.

As Table 9.3 shows, significant intergroup differences were found with respect to *external pressures* and *personal responsibilities*.

From this examination of entry forces we can draw two conclusions: (1) Students attending small local schools are more aware than others of

---

* Unless otherwise stated, an F value based on the formula for the matched-pair design has been used to assess significance levels.

† This item was added to the list shown in Appendix 8.3.

TABLE 9.3. NUMBER OF FORCES, BY STUDY GROUPS AND
CLUSTERS OF FORCES

Clusters	Small Local (1)	Consoli- dated (2)	Larger Local (3)	Significance
1. Intellectual	250	303	313	ns
2. External pressure	669	533	560	Gps. 1 : 2 < .01; Gps. 1 : 3 < .01
3. Anticipated enjoyment	1,096	1,061	1,059	ns
4. Social	508	501	489	ns
5. Personal responsibility	619	483	473	Gps. 1 : 2 < .01; Gps. 1 : 3 < .01
6. Primary status	55	53	56	ns

claims associated with wishes, expectations, demands, and requirements
of other persons, and they also mention more frequently claims associated
with personal responsibilities which they hold or perceive themselves as
holding. (2) The differences noted clearly appear to be associated with
school size.

PARTICIPATION IN EXTRACURRICULAR BEHAVIOR
SETTINGS OF THE SCHOOL

To assess the extent and level of student participation in the extracurricular behavior settings of the schools, a careful survey of all settings that
had occurred from September 1961 to March 1962 was made, and then
students were asked to complete a questionnaire of the kind described in
Chapter 6 and Appendixes 6.1 and 7.1, in which they indicated (a)
whether or not they attended the settings at least once during the period
under review, and (b) exactly what they did in the settings they attended.
The statements given in the second part of this questionnaire were then
used to determine levels of penetration. Thus:

Level 1: "watched," "listened," "danced," "ate"
Level 2: "practiced football," "practiced my part in the play"
Level 3: "sold popcorn at the game," "worked with the other Juniors in the
stand," "was a prompter at the play"
Level 4: "played on the team," "sang a solo," "had a part in the play," "kept
minutes of the meeting"

In general terms, these levels range from just being present at the setting, through more active participation, to taking a responsible part in the proceedings. A score corresponding to the level penetrated was awarded each response.

As a first step in the analysis of the data, we considered each student's *grand total* score of participation, i.e., number of behavior settings in which participation occurred on any level. This revealed the following means: small local, 33.43; consolidated, 36.79; larger local, 39.31. F values were: Groups 1 and 2—6.011 (< .05); Groups 1 and 3—14.606 (< .01); Groups 2 and 3—ns.

Thus, on first glance, students attending the larger school appear to record greater participation than do those from the smaller ones. However, a breakdown of the grand total score into *entries* (Levels 1 and 2) and *performances* (Levels 3 and 4) shows that the apparent superiority of the larger school arises from the many more entry participations that its students experience. Group means for this category were: small local, 21.29; consolidated, 29.41; larger local, 30.75. F values were: Groups 1 and 2—53.746 (< .01); Groups 1 and 3—66.653 (< .01); Groups 2 and 3—ns.

Performance scores, on the other hand, suggested the superiority of the small schools, for group means were: small local, 12.14; consolidated, 7.38; larger local, 8.56. F values were: Groups 1 and 2—5.085 (< .05); Groups 1 and 3—7.862 (< .01); Groups 2 and 3—ns. These differences among the three groups of students are shown in Figure 9.1.

To determine whether these findings were consistent within the different types of setting, we have made further analyses among ten super-varieties: Athletics, Operational settings, Parties and Dances, Student Government settings, Voluntary Work settings, Journalism settings, Outings, Club Meetings, Required Assemblies, and Voluntary Programs (see Chapter 6). The findings can be summarized here as follows:

a) Settings concerned with Student Government and Journalism did not feature prominently among extracurricular activities, and differences from one study group to another were negligible throughout.

b) Operational settings almost invariably demanded entry levels only, and most students participated in these to that extent; no differences were found among the groups.

c) Athletic and Party settings were entered by most students, and it was

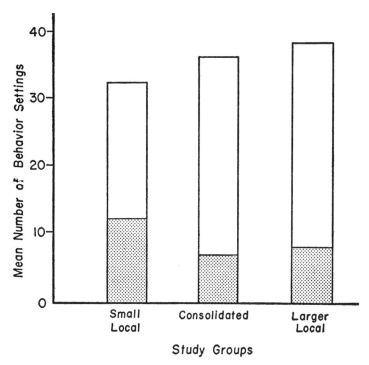

Fig. 9.1. Frequency of participation by study groups in behavior settings at entry and performance levels.

in these two supervarieties that the overall trends were shown most clearly, i.e., students from the larger school recorded many more entries, but students from the small schools recorded many more performances.

d) Required Assemblies were more prominent in the larger school, and this applies to both entries and performances, but Voluntary Work settings, again at both levels of penetration, were more prominent in the smaller schools.

e) Outing entries appeared more frequently on the records of the small local students, and so did Outing performances, but this difference was not statistically significant.

f) Students from the larger school reported more Club Meeting entries, but differences on performances were not significant.

g) No significant differences were found for entry into Voluntary Programs, but students from the small local group scored higher on performances.

In general the supervariety analysis is found to support the two main trends: more entries by consolidated and larger local students; more performances by small local students.

Finally, although students from the larger school had a higher grand total score than did those from the smaller schools, the reverse was true for *scope* score. Students from the smaller schools participated in a greater number of behavior setting supervarieties. The mean numbers of supervarieties were: small local, 7.00; consolidated, 6.49; and larger local, 6.39. F values were: Groups 1 and 2—5.085 (< .05); Groups 1 and 3—7.862 (< .01); Groups 2 and 3—ns.

If only those supervarieties in which performances were recorded are taken into consideration, the small local students are found to widen the distance between themselves and the others. Thus, from a total of ten supervarieties, the mean number of supervarieties in which performances occurred were: small local, 4.49; consolidated, 3.06; larger local, 3.18. F values were: Groups 1 and 2—26.762 (< .01); Groups 1 and 3—27.978 (< .01); Groups 2 and 3—ns.

These findings on extracurricular behavior suggest that: (*a*) students in attendance at larger schools are likely to report more entry participations; (*b*) students in attendance at small schools are likely to report more performance participations; and (*c*) students in attendance at small schools are likely to report participation in a broader range of supervariety settings.

SATISFACTIONS DERIVED FROM THE MOST VALUED SETTINGS

After reporting participations in extracurricular settings, the students were asked (*a*) to record those settings that were for them especially good, satisfying, and worth while, and (*b*) to indicate alongside each selected setting precisely what made it especially good, satisfying, and worth while.

The first finding is that the small local students were inclined to list more settings as especially worth while than were students from either of the other two groups. Mean numbers were: small local, 3.86; consolidated, 2.67; larger local, 2.92. F values were: Groups 1 and 2—21.161 (< .01); Groups 1 and 3—13.560 (< .01); Groups 2 and 3—ns.

A closer examination showed that this difference in favor of small local students arose mainly from the larger number of performance settings they listed.

F values on entry settings were not significant, but those for performance were: Groups 1 and 2—27.535 ($<$ .01); Groups 1 and 3—9.581 ($<$ .01); Groups 2 and 3—ns.

In addition to these differences in total number of settings mentioned as satisfying, there were others concerned with supervarieties. Athletic settings headed each list, Parties and Dances were second in each case, and at the bottom one tended to find the supervarieties of Student Government Journalism, and Voluntary Work settings. Within the top and bottom groups some differences were evident, but the main variation occurred within the middle block of supervarieties. Thus Voluntary Programs, Outings, and Operational settings were mentioned more frequently by the small local students, while Club Meetings and Required Assemblies were mentioned very much less frequently by this group.

In the first-level analysis of the values data, use was made of the code discussed in Chapter 7. The use of this code requires, first, that the responses be broken up into single value units, and, second, that the units be assigned to appropriate categories. It was not anticipated that many of the 40 categories would yield significant intergroup differences, but on the basis of both theory and previous research (Chapter 7), differences were predicted within a small number of supercategories. For this reason a special examination was made of Competence, Learn About, Novelty, Large Entity Affiliation, Big Action and Test, and Vicarious Enjoyment. The findings showed that the study groups did not differ significantly with respect to the first four of these, but that the small local students were more inclined to mention values denoting Big Action and Test and Vicarious Enjoyment (both at the .05 level) than were the other two groups.

Emphasis placed upon Big Action and Test by the small local students confirms one of the findings in Chapter 7 regarding satisfactions of small school Juniors. However, the more frequent mention of Vicarious Enjoyment is not in line with results from the previous study; in that investigation, Vicarious Enjoyment was more typical of large school Juniors.

The analysis by supercategories tends to be mainly descriptive in nature and tells little about the dynamics of behavior. For this reason it was decided in this consolidation study to proceed to a second-level analysis in which use was made of the developmental-task concept. It was assumed that (a) in the process of growing up, adolescents (as well as children and adults) are faced with a series of developmental tasks, and (b) they will tend to seek out and report as most worth while those settings that contribute to the achievement of these developmental tasks. Accordingly, the value categories were further grouped into ten clusters on the basis of inferences made about the nature of the developmental tasks being satisfied. These clusters and the categories they encompass are given below. For the description of the categories and sample responses see pp. 96–101.

Clusters	Categories
Physical: participating in activities that improve physical health, increase fitness and physical skill	1. Physical Competence 6. Learn About—Skill
Social: getting along with others	3. Social Competence 5. Learn About—Social 28. Informal Affiliation 16. New People
Knowledge: acquiring knowledge concerning future educational and vocational choices, developing intellectual interests, experiencing novel events and new and interesting situations	4. Other Competence 7. Learn About—Cognitive Areas 8. Learn About—Vague 9. Learn About—Future 15. New Experience 37. Milieu Knowledge
Responsibility: developing social responsibility and group loyalties, contributing to group success	13. Contribution to Others 24. Support Indication to Others 31. Affiliation—School 39. Others Get Value
Philosophy: acquiring a philosophy of life and an ethical code	35. Uplift
Self-Concept: developing a self-concept	10. Challenge 11. Competition 12. Success 19. Competition—Vicarious
Primary Status: achieving primary status, enjoying the feeling of support by others	27. Be Valued 14. Big Participation 32. Little Participation
Derived Status: achieving derived status, enjoying the feeling of support by others	25. Support from School Adults 26. Support from Others 29. Affiliation—Group 30. Affiliation—Crowd

Clusters	Categories
Self-Expression: having the opportunity and ability to express oneself	2. Emotional Competence
	38. Psychological Release
	17. Escape
	18. Something to Do
	33. Have-a-Say
Zest for Living: developing a zest for living, enjoying an activity, having fun	20. Excitement
	21. Vicarious Valence
	22. Action Valence
	23. Unspecified Valence

After arranging the value categories into these developmental-task clusters, we have considered (a) the number of students from each study group who recorded at least one value that has been assigned to a particular cluster; and (b) the number of mentions recorded by these students. The findings are summarized in Table 9.4. (In the case of (a) above, the chi-square test has been used to assess significance levels, and in the case of (b), the sign test.)

As the summary in Table 9.4 shows, the groups did not differ with respect to their responses associated with Responsibility, a Philosophy of Life, Primary Status, Derived Status, and Self-Expression. However, (a) more students from the small local group than from the others mentioned values concerned with Physical Well-being and the development of a Self-Concept, and the number of times that these were mentioned by small local students was correspondingly higher; (b) while the number of small local students who mentioned values associated with Knowledge and Zest for Living was not very much higher than the number of students in the other two groups, the small local group did tend to mention these values more frequently; and (c) while the number of students mentioning Social values did not differ from one group to another, the small local and consolidated students made use of this cluster more frequently than did those from the larger community.

What do these findings tell us about the schools, commuting, and communities? Presumably any differences found might point to differences in the significance of the task, differences in the provisions for the satisfaction of these, or a mixture of both. Our study was not designed to unravel these factors, but the community difference associated with the Social cluster would appear to reflect either a paucity of social experiences within a small community, and hence a greater need to seek out such experiences else-

TABLE 9.4. NUMBER OF SUBJECTS IN EACH STUDY GROUP MENTIONING
EACH DEVELOPMENTAL TASK, AND NUMBER OF TIMES MENTIONED

Developmental-Task Cluster	Study Groups			Significance
	1	2	3	
1. Physical				
No. of persons	13	5	4	Gps. 1 : 3 < .02; Gps. 1 : 2 < .05
No. of mentions	17	7	5	Gps. 1 : 2 < .05; Gps. 1 : 3 < .01
2. Social				
No. of persons	34	32	24	ns
No. of mentions	68	65	38	Gps. 1 : 3 < .01; Gps. 2 : 3 < .01
3. Knowledge				
No. of persons	25	15	17	ns
No. of mentions	37	19	22	Gps. 1 : 2 < .05; Gps. 1 : 3 < .05
4. Responsibility				
No. of persons	16	14	13	ns
No. of mentions	21	16	19	ns
5. Philosophy				
No. of persons	8	5	9	ns
No. of mentions	13	7	12	ns
6. Self-Concept				
No. of persons	23	11	11	Gps. 1 : 2 < .02; Gps. 1 : 3 < .02
No. of mentions	28	13	19	Gps. 1 : 2 < .05; Gps. 1 : 3 < .05
7. Primary Status				
No. of persons	18	13	18	ns
No. of mentions	27	23	27	ns
8. Derived Status				
No. of persons	6	3	3	ns
No. of mentions	9	4	3	ns
9. Self-Expression				
No. of persons	7	5	4	ns
No. of mentions	9	6	5	ns
10. Zest for Living				
No. of persons	51	40	45	Gps. 1 : 2 < .05
No. of mentions	159	78	101	Gps. 1 : 2 < .01; Gps. 1 : 3 < .01

where, or a stronger demand from smaller communities for the development of social competence. On the other hand, differences in values associated with Physical Well-being, Knowledge, Self-Concepts, and Zest for Living appear to be related to the factor of school size. A small school would appear to provide, within its extracurricular settings, more opportunities for the satisfaction of these particular personality needs.

SUMMARY AND IMPLICATIONS

Summary

This study of consolidation effects suggests that if the small local students were transferred to a county high school they would probably undergo the following changes in experiences: an increase in the number of school settings penetrated to the entry level; and a decrease in (1) external pressures aimed at increasing their participations in extracurricular activities; (2) sense of personal responsibility associated with extracurricular activities; (3) number of school settings penetrated to the performance level; (4) range of supervariety settings penetrated; (5) number of school settings judged to be most worth while; and (6) number of satisfactions associated with physical well-being, acquiring knowledge and developing intellectual interests, developing a self-concept, and zest for living.

Implications

These findings suggest that the current assumption of consolidated school superiority is, in at least some aspects, like the first report of Mark Twain's death—exaggerated. If we discount the Canute-like act of trying to halt the consolidation wave, two main courses are open to us. One is to take the advantages of the consolidated school to the small rural high school, and the other is to take the advantages of the small school to the consolidated one. Our research makes no contribution to the former of these programs, but it does seem to have certain implications for the latter.

In broad terms, the effects of consolidation demand special efforts from both the school and the local community. Through its structural organization, its instructional procedures, and its extracurricular activities, the larger school needs to ensure that *all* its students participate actively and acquire a genuine sense of attachment and contribution to group goals. There is a temptation in a larger school to concentrate upon extracurricular goals and standards which can be achieved by only the most talented students at the expense of the rest. Similarly the "consolidated community" must take special pains to so arrange its recreational programs and community tasks that its young members are appropriately challenged and stimulated. Once consolidation has taken place, there is a temptation for the community to discard some of its obligations to its adolescents, whereas the data presented here suggest the need for a still more determined effort to meet those obligations.

10

Community Size and Activities of Students

ROGER G. BARKER

BEHAVIOR settings that provide an opportunity for young people to participate in the business, government, religious, and organizational life of a community are widely thought to have educational values. This is specifically recognized, for example, by apprenticeship, internship, and school-work programs. But most education of this kind is not formally arranged; it is a consequence of youth's place within the larger community. Little is known about educational opportunities of these sorts and how they vary between localities. We have investigated aspects of this problem in four small towns of Midwest County (Walker, Malden, Midwest, and Vernon) and in neighboring University City and Capital City. The communities are identified in Chapter 4, and studies of their schools are reported in Chapters 6, 7, and 8. The four towns of Midwest County had populations ranging from 450 to 1,150, with a total population of 2,888; University City had 23,296, and Capital City 101,155 inhabitants.

The comparative value of breadth and specialization in the education of adolescents is an issue around which controversy is unending. The studies reported in this chapter add to the little that is known about the school and community conditions that foster these controversial educational objectives.

Four studies are reported. The first two were concerned with the extent to which adolescents were responsible participants in public, non-school behavior settings of four towns and two cities. The third study dealt with music education and participation in the towns and Capital City, and the fourth with academic specialization among intellectually able students in small and large schools.

EMPLOYMENT OPPORTUNITIES FOR ADOLESCENTS IN UNIVERSITY CITY AND IN THE TOWNS OF MIDWEST COUNTY

In 1958–59 there were 267 behavior settings in the four Midwest County towns where business and professional activities occurred. This number did not include settings whose primary function was the welfare of children and adolescents, such as school classes; and it did not include one-person business behavior settings, e.g., James Jones, Painter. The settings were discovered by means of complete community surveys, as described by Barker and Wright (1955), and the settings were classified according to the varieties identified by them. The complete roster of the 267 business and professional settings present in the four small towns was included in the study.

A comparable *sample* of the behavior settings of University City was secured in the following way:

All behavior settings of each variety occurring among the 267 settings in the Midwest towns were identified in University City. To these were added all business and professional settings of varieties not present in the towns of Midwest County. In all, 938 business and professional behavior settings were identified in University City. Data concerning employment of adolescents were secured from a sample of these settings by selecting at random 15 per cent of the settings (to the nearest whole number) in every variety containing 11 or more settings, and by selecting at random one setting from every variety containing fewer than 11 settings. In this way, every variety of behavior setting in the Midwest list was represented in the University City list by at least a 15 per cent sample of all the settings in the variety; in addition, all behavior setting varieties unique to University City were included. The behavior settings finally selected for study were a 21 per cent sample of the business and professional settings of University City. These settings were identified, via the University City telephone directory and the 1960 Cross Reference for University City compiled by the local Credit Bureau. As the field work proceeded, settings not discovered in either directory were added. Very few settings were added in this way; some were deleted because they no longer existed.

Information regarding the employment of adolescents in the behavior settings selected for study was obtained by interviewing the person in charge of each of them. Interviews were done in the month of July 1960. The data reported here were secured from the answers to the following questions:

Is high school help used here at all now or during the past year (September 1959–July 1960)? If the answer was affirmative to this question, the following questions were asked:

How many high school students are employed at one time?

TABLE 10.1. EMPLOYMENT OF ADOLESCENTS IN BUSINESS AND
PROFESSIONAL BEHAVIOR SETTINGS IN FOUR MIDWEST
COUNTY TOWNS AND IN UNIVERSITY CITY

	Midwest County	University City
Number of business and professional behavior settings.....	267	938
Number of behavior settings in sample..................	267	195
Behavior settings employing adolescents		
Number of behavior settings......................	73	55
Per cent of sample of behavior settings..............	27%	28%
Adolescents employed at time of interview		
Number of adolescents	95	105
Mean number per behavior setting		
employing adolescents	1.3	1.9
Total adolescents employed during year		
Number of adolescents	147	155
Mean number per behavior setting		
employing adolescents	2.0	2.8
Total persons employed during year		
(behavior settings employing adolescents)		
Number of persons	516	1006
Mean number per behavior setting		
employing adolescents	7.1	18.3
Per cent of all employees of behavior settings employing		
adolescents who were adolescents...................	28%	15%

How many different high school students were employed during the past year?

How many different people were employed here last year?

The behavior setting varieties involved in the study and number of settings in each are reported in Appendix 10.1. It should be noted that no distinction was made between full- and part-time employment.

The data are reported in Table 10.1. They show that high school employees were found in 27 per cent and 28 per cent of the behavior settings of the towns and the city respectively; i.e., in both cases just over one-quarter of the business and professional settings used adolescent help. Within the behavior settings that employed adolescents the following held: (1) there were about 50 per cent more adolescent employees in the city settings than in the town settings; nevertheless, because of their still greater total number of employees, (2) adolescent employees constituted 15 per cent of the working force of the city settings and 28 per cent of the working force of the town settings. If the 938 business and professional settings in University City employed high school students at the same rate as the settings in the sample, as is to be expected, adolescents constituted $.27 \times .28 = .075$ of Midwest's total working force in these settings, and $.28 \times .15 = .040$ of University City's working force. Relative to all positions in business and professional behavior settings, positions for adolescents in these settings were 187 per cent more frequent in towns than in the city.

The business and professional behavior settings of University City that employed adolescent workers generated one full- or part-time adolescent position for every 6.5 positions within them, and Midwest County settings generated a high school position for every 3.5 positions. University City provided one employment possibility for adolescents within its business and professional settings for every 33 of its inhabitants, and the towns provided one employment possibility for an adolescent for every 20 of their inhabitants. Relative to total community population, positions for ado-

TABLE 10.2. NUMBER OF ADOLESCENT EMPLOYEES IN BEHAVIOR
SETTINGS WITH VARYING TOTAL NUMBERS OF EMPLOYEES

Total No. of Employees of Behavior Setting	Midwest County Towns		University City	
	No. of Settings with Designated No. of Employees	Mean No. of Adolescent Employees per Setting	No. of Settings with Designated No. of Employees	Mean No. of Adolescent Employees per Setting
3	15	1.2	6	1.0
4	10	2.0	6	1.1
5	14	1.6	6	1.3
6	3	1.3	3	1.6
7	7	1.7	5	1.4
8	5	3.0	1	1.0
9	6	3.1	2	2.0
10	5	2.6	4	2.0
11+*	6	5.8	7	4.3

* The Midwest behavior settings in this class had total employees as follows: 11, 11, 16, 24, 35, 54; the University City behavior settings that most closely matched these had total employees as follows: 11, 12, 16, 23, 27, 28, 100.

TABLE 10.3. VARIETIES OF BEHAVIOR SETTINGS USING HIGH SCHOOL
HELP IN MIDWEST COUNTY AND UNIVERSITY CITY

Variety No.	Variety Name	Uses High School Help	
		Midwest County	University City
3	Attorneys and Real Estate Offices	x	x
5	Auctions, Livestock		x
6	Banks	x	
8	*Book Stores		x
9	Builders and Builders' Suppliers	x	x
11	Cemeteries		x
13	Courts	x	x
14	†Dairy Barns	x	
15	Dances and Schools of Dancing		x
18	Doctors' Offices and Clinics	x	
19	Drug and Department Stores	x	x
27	Factories	x	
34	Food and Feed Distributors	x	x
37	Funeral Homes	x	
39	Government, School, and Business Offices	x	x
42	Hardware and Home Furnishers	x	x
45	Hospitals		x
46	Hotels, Rooming Houses, and Nursing Homes	x	
47	Ice Companies	x	
50	Kennels	x	
51	Laundries and Cleaners		x
52	Libraries	x	x
53	Meat Packing Companies	x	
59	Motor Vehicle Sales and Service	x	x
60	Movies	x	x
63	Newspapers and Printers	x	x
71	Police Stations and Jails		x
72	Post Offices	x	
80	Restaurants and Taverns	x	x
87	Shoe Shops, Repair and Sale		x
88	†Slaughter Houses	x	
93	Truck Lines, Heavy	x	x
94	Veterinarians	x	
96	Watch Repair and Jewelry Shops	x	
98	Water Plants		x
155	*Music and Musical Instruments, Sales and Service ...		x
156	*Office Supply Stores		x

* Varieties unique to University City.
† Varieties unique to Midwest County towns.

lescents in business and professional settings were 167 per cent more frequent in Midwest towns than in University City.

Data for settings with comparable numbers of employees in the towns and the city are given in Table 10.2. From these data it appears that the greater rate of adolescent employment within the small towns occurred for settings of all sizes.

The different varieties of behavior settings reporting high school employees in the towns of Midwest County and in University City are given in Table 10.3. It is obvious that adolescents were not restricted to a limited variety of work situations in either the towns or the city: 26 town varieties and 24 city varieties reported using high school help, 37 varieties in all. Thirteen varieties were common to the towns and the city, 13 were unique to the towns, and 11 were unique to the city. The data are given in Table 10.3.

The evidence we have secured indicates that the responsible participation of adolescents was as widely distributed among the business and professional behavior settings of the city as of the towns, but that within the settings, adolescent employees were relatively less numerous in the city settings. The data show, too, that jobs for adolescents were less frequent relative to the total community population in the city than in the towns.

EMPLOYMENT, CHURCH, AND NONSCHOOL SOCIAL ACTIVITIES OF

HIGH SCHOOL JUNIOR STUDENTS IN CAPITAL CITY AND

IN FOUR TOWNS OF MIDWEST COUNTY

The high school students involved in the studies reported in Chapters 6, 7, and 8 of this report were asked questions about their out-of-school activities. See Appendix 6.1 for complete report form. The items that elicited this information were as follows:

Church activities. Students sometimes take part in groups and organizations outside of school. Let's take church as one possibility. Students could attend Sunday School, Church, Mass, Synagogue, or Young People's Group Meeting, etc. They might be performers in some of these: sing in Church Choir, teach Sunday School, lead Young People's Worship Service, etc. If you took part in any church-related activities *this semester,* would you write them in below? If you performed in any, please write in the performance.

Organization activities. Students might also take part in other organizations. Examples would be Scout meeting, Bowling Team contests, 4-H meetings, music group meetings, Rainbow girls party, etc. Students might be performers in some of these: serve as assistant scoutmaster, handle refreshments at club party, etc. Would you write in any of these affairs you have attended and put in any performances?

Work. Have you worked for pay this semester? What kind of work did you do? If you worked for a company or organization, please name it. Did you work for pay *last summer*? What kind of work did you do? If you worked for a company or organization, please name it.

Information was secured by means of these questions from the 18 boys and 24 girls who were high school Junior students *living within the town limits* of the four Midwest County towns and from the 605 Capital City Junior students. Each Midwest student was matched with a Capital City Junior of the same sex, race, and IQ. Selection from among the Capital City subjects who matched Midwest County subjects on the three variables was done via random numbers. The data were collected on December 12–15, 1960.

Employment Reported by Midwest County and Capital City Subjects

Employment that the subjects reported is presented in terms of two categories: (*a*) employment in business and professional behavior settings equivalent to those involved in the survey of Midwest County and University City (reported above), and (*b*) employment in all other settings. The latter category is called "odd jobs" in the tables and discussion; "baby sitting" was the most common odd job reported by the girls, and lawn work and paper delivery by the boys. A *position* is employment reported by one subject in a business or professional behavior setting or an odd job. For example, the subject who reported "street work for the city" and "stocked shelves at Smith's Supermarket" reported two positions; the same is true of the subject who reported "baby sitting" and "worked in jewelry store."

The data regarding employment are presented in Table 10.4. These data show that the Midwest County students, when questioned regarding their work experience in December 1960, confirmed, in general, the data on employment obtained in the Midwest towns via the behavior setting survey in 1959 and reported above. That survey identified 147 positions for adolescents in business and professional behavior settings (see Table 10.1). In the direct questioning of the high school Juniors, employment in 31 business and professional positions was reported. The informants, who

TABLE 10.4. EMPLOYMENT REPORTED BY MIDWEST COUNTY AND CAPITAL
CITY HIGH SCHOOL JUNIOR STUDENTS, SUMMER AND AUTUMN, 1960

Employment	Midwest County	Capital City
ALL SUBJECTS		
1. Number of subjects reporting	42	42
2. Number of positions reported	45	31
3. Positions in business and professional settings	31	22
4. Positions in other settings (odd jobs)	14	9
5. Number of subjects reporting employment	35	29
6. Employment in business and professional settings	23	21
7. Employment in other settings only (odd jobs)	12	8
8. Number of subjects reporting no employment	7	13
BOYS		
9. Number of subjects reporting	18	18
10. Number of positions reported	26	12
11. Positions in business and professional settings	25	9
12. Positions in other settings (odd jobs)	1	3
13. Number of boys reporting employment	18	12
14. Employment in business and professional settings	17	9
15. Employment in other settings only (odd jobs)	1	3
16. Number of boys reporting no employment	0	6
GIRLS		
17. Number of subjects reporting	24	24
18. Number of positions reported	19	19
19. Positions in business and professional settings	6	13
20. Positions in other settings (odd jobs)	13	6
21. Number of girls reporting employment	17	17
22. Employment in business and professional settings	6	12
23. Employment in other settings only (odd jobs)	11	5
24. Number of girls reporting no employment	7	7

constituted about 25 per cent of the high school students of the towns, reported filling 21 per cent as many positions as had been identified by the
survey.

The questionnaire data and the behavior setting survey data were also
in accord in discovering more positions for adolescents in the business and
professional behavior settings of the small towns than in those of the city,
in this case, Capital City. The high school Juniors of Midwest County

TABLE 10.5. VARIETIES OF BUSINESS AND PROFESSIONAL BEHAVIOR SETTINGS
WHERE EMPLOYMENT WAS REPORTED BY MIDWEST COUNTY AND
CAPITAL CITY HIGH SCHOOL JUNIORS

Variety No.	Variety Name	Employment Reported	
		Midwest County	Capital City
6	Banks	x	
9	Builders and Builders' Suppliers.............	x	x
15	Dances and Schools of Dancing..............		x
18	Doctors' Offices and Clinics.................	x	
19	Drug and Department Stores................	x	x
27	Factories		x
34	Food and Feed Distributors.................	x	
39	Government, School, and Business Offices......	x	x
42	Hardware and Home Furnishers.............	x	x
46	Hotels, Rooming Houses, and Nursing Homes..	x	
52	Libraries		x
59	Motor Vehicle Sales and Service.............	x	
80	Restaurants and Taverns...................		x
93	Truck Lines, Heavy.......................	x	
96	Watch Repair and Jewelry Shops............	x	
155	*Music and Musical Instruments, Sales and Service........................		x
162	*Day Nurseries		x
163	*Swimming Pools		x
	†Farms	x	

* Varieties unique to Capital City.
† Varieties unique to Midwest County.

towns reported filling 31 positions during the summer and autumn in business and professional settings; the Juniors of Capital City reported filling 22 positions (Table 10.4, line 3). The same direction and order of difference occurred in the number of "odd jobs" reported (line 4), in the total number of positions reported (line 2), and in the number of subjects reporting employment (line 5).

The city-town difference in the employment of high school Junior students was limited almost entirely to the boys. All Midwest County boys were employed, and they reported 2.2 times the number of positions as the Capital City boys; but equal numbers of Midwest County and Capital City girls reported employment and they reported identical numbers of positions. The Midwest County girls reported half as many positions in business and professional settings as the Capital City girls.

The varieties of business and professional behavior settings within which the subjects reported employment are listed in Table 10.5. There are 19 varieties in the list; four are common to the Midwest County and Capital City subjects, seven are unique to the Midwest County students, and eight are unique to the Capital City students.

Church Activities Reported by Midwest County and Capital City Subjects

An *activity* in a church organization is participation reported by one subject in one behavior setting. "Attended Sunday School and Church" constitutes two activities. Performance and attendance are treated separately: a performance involves filling a position of some responsibility within a behavior setting, such as teacher, chairman, or singer; it is more important to the functioning of the setting than simple attendance.

Data on participation in church-connected activities are presented in Table 10.6. The Midwest County Juniors reported more church activities (line 2), both performances (line 3) and attendances (line 4), than Capital City Juniors; and more of the Midwest subjects reported some church-connected activities (line 5) and some performances (line 6) than did Capital City Juniors. This was true for both the boys and the girls, with one exception: equal numbers of Midwest County and Capital City girls engaged in some church activity (line 21).

Out-of-School Social Organization Activities Reported by Midwest County and Capital City Subjects

The criteria of an activity in a nonschool social organization are the same as for an activity in a church organization.

Data on participation in out-of-school social organizations are given in Table 10.6. They provide a picture of differences in the participation of town and city adolescents that is very similar to that for church activities. More of the Midwest County high school Juniors engaged in more activities within social organizations not connected with the school than did Capital City Juniors.

TABLE 10.6. CHURCH AND OUT-OF-SCHOOL ORGANIZATION ACTIVITIES
REPORTED BY MIDWEST COUNTY AND CAPITAL CITY HIGH SCHOOL
JUNIOR STUDENTS

	Church Activities		Social Organization Activities	
Activities	Mid-west Co.	Capi-tal City	Mid-west Co.	Capi-tal City
ALL SUBJECTS				
1. Number of subjects	42	42	42	42
2. Number of different activities reported	87	56	28	21
3. Number of performances	36	17	16	10
4. Number of attendances, only	51	39	12	11
5. Number of subjects reporting activities	28	24	16	15
6. Number reporting performances	21	11	14	8
7. Number reporting attendance only	7	13	2	7
8. Number of subjects reporting no activities	14	18	26	27
BOYS				
9. Number of subjects	18	18	18	18
10. Number of different activities reported	27	15	15	10
11. Number of performances	9	3	9	7
12. Number of attendances, only	18	12	6	3
13. Number of boys reporting activities	9	5	8	6
14. Number reporting performances	6	2	8	5
15. Number reporting attendance only	3	3	0	1
16. Number of boys reporting no activities	9	13	10	12
GIRLS				
17. Number of subjects	24	24	24	24
18. Number of different activities reported	60	41	13	11
19. Number of performances	27	14	7	3
20. Number of attendances, only	33	27	6	8
21. Number of girls reporting activities	19	19	8	9
22. Number reporting performances	15	9	6	3
23. Number reporting attendance only	4	10	2	6
24. Number of girls reporting no activities	5	5	16	15

Community Activities in Town and City

We have computed a community activity index for each subject by
rating his activities in employment, church, and social settings, as shown
in Table 10.7. Each different job, church activity, and social activity reported by a subject was rated according to these scales. For example, a

TABLE 10.7. COMMUNITY ACTIVITY RATINGS

Employment Rating		Church Rating		Social Org. Rating	
No employment	0	No attendance...	0	No attendance...	0
Odd job, summer........	2	Attendance only .	1	Attendance only .	1
Odd job, autumn........	2	Performance	3	Performance	3
Business and Professional setting, summer	4				
Business and Professional setting, autumn	4				

subject who worked as a mechanic (4) and as a janitor (4) in the summer, and at odd jobs in the autumn (2) received an employment rating of 10, which is the sum of the separate activity ratings given in the parentheses. A subject who attended church (1), was Sunday School secretary (3), and was a member of the youth fellowship (1) received a church activity rating of 5. The community activity index for a subject was the sum of the three separate ratings.

Employment ratings of individual subjects actually varied from 0 to 12, church ratings varied from 0 to 11, and social ratings varied from 0 to 7. The separate credits given for summer and autumn employment and the rating of work in business and professional settings as 4 instead of 3, as performances in church and social organizations were rated, amounted to weighting employment activities considerably higher than either of the other activities. This appeared to be in accord with both the time devoted to employment and the importance attached to employment by the community as a whole and by the adolescents themselves.

The mean community activity indexes are presented in Table 10.8. An analysis of variance showed that the difference between the Midwest

TABLE 10.8. MEAN COMMUNITY ACTIVITY INDEXES

Students	Midwest County	Capital City	Total
Boys	12.00	5.61	8.81
Girls	9.29	7.08	9.36
Total	10.45	6.45	

County and Capital City ratings when the total distributions were considered was significant at the $p < .01$ level. The subgroup differences (Midwest boys vs. Capital City boys, Midwest girls vs. Capital City girls, and boys vs. girls) did not reach acceptable level of significance. It is of some interest to note, however, that although the mean community activity indexes were greater in Midwest County for both boys and girls, the index of the Midwest boys exceeded that of the girls while the reverse was true in Capital City. This constitutes a slight suggestion that extra-school community life may have been richer for boys in the towns and for girls in the city.

The differences in community activity can be made more concrete, perhaps, by presenting the activities reported by subjects whose ratings fell near to the mean ratings of their class:

Midwest County girl:
  Taught Sunday School
  Sang in church choir
  Was member of girl scouts
  Did summer baby sitting

Midwest County boy:
  Sang in church choir
  Member, Explorer Scouts
  Clerked in grocery store, summer
    and autumn

Capital City girl:
  Was church youth group leader
  Day nursery aid, summer

Capital City boy:
  Attended Sunday School and youth
    group
  Clerked in auto supply store,
    summer

These findings and those concerning employment in University City and Midwest County agree in indicating that the adolescents of Midwest County towns participated more widely than those of neighboring cities in out-of-school activities that are widely presumed to have potential educational values.

MUSIC SPECIALIZATION IN SMALL AND LARGE SCHOOLS AND COMMUNITIES

The subjects were all the Junior students of the large school (304 boys and 300 girls) and of the four small schools (45 boys and 46 girls) that were involved in the studies reported in Chapters 6 and 7. The data, given in Table 10.9, were obtained from the class schedules of the students and from the questionnaires on out-of-school activities (see Appendix 6.1).

TABLE 10.9. NUMBER AND PER CENT OF JUNIOR STUDENTS IN
MUSIC ACTIVITIES OF LARGE AND SMALL HIGH SCHOOLS

	Boys		Girls	
Activity	Small Schools (45 boys)	Large School (304 boys)	Small Schools (46 girls)	Large School (300 girls)
Students enrolled in one or more music classes...	10 [22.2%]	29 [9.5%]	35 [76%]	48 [16%]
Also performers in nonclass music settings	10 (100%)	29 (100%)	35 (100%)	48 (100%)
Also performers in church music settings	3 (33.3%)	7 (24.1%)	20 (57.1%)	24 (50%)
Also musical performers in nonschool social settings	0	4 (13.8%)	0	3 (6.2%)
Also employed as professional musicians .	0	6 (21%)	0	0
Mean number of school music performances in a three-month period	2.3	3.6	2.7	1.1
Students enrolled in two music classes	3 [6.7%]	5 [1.6%]	15 [33%]	3 [1.0%]

Note: Figures in brackets are percentages of the number of Junior students in the schools; figures in parentheses are percentages of music students (line 1).

From these data it is clear that many more of the small school than the large school Juniors were receiving some formal classroom instruction in music; for boys and girls combined, the proportions were 49 per cent (small schools) and 13 per cent (large school). The proportions enrolled in two music classes were still more different, namely, 20 per cent and 1.3 per cent for the small and large schools, respectively. All students who were enrolled in music classes participated in nonclass musical performances within school behavior settings, and the average number of performances per student did not differ greatly for the small and large school students. Furthermore the overall proportions of the music students who participated in out-of-school music settings did not differ greatly, though some large

TABLE 10.10. MUSIC "SPECIALISTS" IN THE LARGE SCHOOL AND
IN THE SMALL SCHOOLS

Student	Music Classes	School Music Perform-ances	Nonschool Music Performances	Professional Music Employment
		LARGE SCHOOL		
1 (boy)	Band and orchestra	10	Instructs drum corps	Dance band; gives drum lessons
2 (boy)	Band and orchestra	10	Church brass choir	——
3 (boy)	Band and orchestra	7	——	Dance band
4 (boy)	Band and orchestra	6	Youth symphony	——
5 (boy)	Band and orchestra	9	Church choir	——
6 (boy)	Band	6	——	Combo band
7 (boy)	Band	5	——	Dance band
8 (boy)	Band	5	——	Dance band
9 (girl)	Orchestra and choir	6	Church organ, youth symphony	Dance studio
10 (girl)	Orchestra and glee club	4	Church choir, and songleader, youth symphony	——
		SMALL SCHOOLS		
1 (girl)	Band, mixed chorus, girls chorus	4	Church choir, special choir, piano for Sunday school	——
2 (girl)	Band, mixed chorus, girls chorus	3	——	——

school boys, and no small school boys, engaged in professional musical activities and participated in nonschool social settings. The evidence adds up to the fact that musical education and participation within the schools and communities were much more widely distributed among the small school than among the large school Juniors.

However, when the individual students are considered, we find that ten of the 77 music students in the large school and two of the 45 music students in the small schools were music "specialists." Table 10.10 gives the music participation records of these specialists.

Nine of the large school "music specialists" far exceeded in degree of specialization any small school music specialist. In fact, the large school music specialists dominated the school music activities; 44 per cent of the school music performances of the large school Juniors who were enrolled in music classes were performed by these ten students. The two music specialists of the small schools contributed only 6 per cent of the small school, nonclass music performances. Not only was musical participation less widespread among the Junior students of the large school; there was greater concentration of that which did occur within a small circle of relatively few specialists.

THE SCHOOL CLASSES IN WHICH INTELLECTUALLY ABLE STUDENTS
OF SMALL AND LARGE SCHOOLS WERE ENROLLED

These data refer to 28 pairs of intellectually superior Juniors in the small and large schools, identified in Chapter 6. The subjects comprise all the small school Juniors with IQ above 110, and an equal number of large school Juniors matching them, subject by subject, with respect to IQ and sex. Data on school class enrollments are presented in Table 10.11.

The superior Junior students of the large school were enrolled in a somewhat smaller total number of school classes but a somewhat greater number of academic classes than the equally superior Juniors of the small schools. There were eight "academic specialists" among the large school Juniors, who were enrolled in five academic courses each; there were three

TABLE 10.11. SCHOOL CLASS ENROLLMENTS OF INTELLECTUALLY SUPERIOR JUNIORS IN THE LARGE SCHOOL AND IN THE SMALL SCHOOLS

Enrollments	Small Schools		Large School	
	Number	Average	Number	Average
Number of Juniors..............	28		28	
Total class enrollments	165	5.9	143	5.1
Academic class enrollments........	97	3.5	113	4.0
Total nonacademic class enrollments	68	2.4	30	1.1
Music classes	26		5	
Art classes	0		2	
Commercial classes	25		3	
Home economics classes......	3		5	
Shop classes	1		6	
Physical education classes.....	13		7	
Driver education classes......	0		2	

similar specialists among the small school Juniors. The greatest difference relating to school size was the large number of nonacademic classes taken by the small school Juniors, amounting to 38 additional courses. Nonacademic classes made up 41 per cent of the classes taken by the small school students and 21 per cent of the classes taken by the large school students. In short, the education that the small school Juniors were receiving, as measured by "classes," was relatively heavier in total, and less academically specialized than the education of the large school Juniors. We have no data on the quality of the classes or the depth of student participation in them.

These data are in accord with those concerning extracurricular behavior settings: although more school classes and more varieties of classes were available for them (see Chapter 4 and Appendix 4.1), the large school students participated in fewer classes and in fewer varieties of classes than the small school students.

The scientific byways explored in this chapter have yielded data which generally agree that there is wider participation by adolescents in the business, organizational, religious, and educational settings of towns than of the city, and that there is greater specialization by a few in the city. The towns appear to foster versatility, and the city, specialization. To what degree the versatility is accompanied by shallowness and the specialization by narrowness, the data give no hint. But the results reported here, within the context of those reported in the other chapters, suggest that more than broadness or limitation of the content of experience is involved.

The findings are in line with the theory of behavior settings, which states that among equivalent behavior settings that differ in number of inhabitants, the settings with the smaller number of inhabitants will, on the average, exert a greater claim over potential inhabitants, including marginal inhabitants such as adolescents. And herein resides a potential educational value of participation in small rather than in large behavior settings. According to the theory, employment and performance in small settings involve a reciprocal, axiological relationship between participant and setting that is inevitably reduced as the number of participants increases. The employee or performer who contributes something of value to the maintenance of the setting receives from the setting something of value to the person. If the person's action is not important to the setting, it is unlikely to be important to him. A condition of personal achievement, self-esteem, and psychological success is the completion of difficult and important actions; and filling an essential, responsible position within a serious community setting constitutes an important and often a difficult action. This is more than versatility and specialization. It has some relation to depth of experience.

For these reasons it has seemed to us important to investigate further the place of adolescents within small towns. We have done this in the case of Midwest County adolescents, and we turn to this study next.

11

Adolescents in the Towns of Midwest County

ROGER G. BARKER · WILLIAM F. LE COMPTE

THE INVESTIGATIONS presented in the preceding chapters of this report discovered that the high school students of the small towns held more responsible positions within the nonclass behavior settings of the schools and that they engaged in church, social, and employment activities outside the schools more frequently, on the average, than the high school students of the cities. It appeared desirable, therefore, to investigate more systematically the place of adolescents in the small towns of the main studies. We do not have comparable data for the adolescents of the cities we have studied; the data to be presented here rounds out the picture of small town adolescent life.

In this study we have included all persons of high school age (14 through 17 years) within four towns of Midwest County. The method has been to determine the place of adolescents in all the community behavior settings of the towns. To accomplish this, the K-21 behavior settings of Malden, Midwest, Vernon, and Walker were identified by means of behavior setting surveys, as described by Barker and Wright (1955). Pertinent demographic data regarding the towns are reported in Chapter 4, and Appendix 11.1 lists the number of behavior settings in each variety in each town. In the present connection, it is important to know that the towns were small (population 450 to 1,150), that each had a complete local school system, including a high school, and that the average number of persons per community behavior setting was low, ranging from 1.2 to 1.83. This means, according to the theory of behavior settings, that people were in short supply relative to the number of settings and relative to the number of jobs to be done in the settings.

TERRITORIAL AND PERFORMANCE RANGES OF HIGH SCHOOL ADOLESCENTS

We first investigated the extent and quality of adolescent participation in the behavior settings of the towns. The territorial range of an age group refers to the number of a town's behavior settings entered in any capacity by one or more members of an age group. Chi-square tests showed that the towns of Midwest County did not differ in the territorial ranges of inhabitants of designated ages; hence, the data for the four towns were combined for the total number of 2,005 community behavior settings. (This figure omits 44 behavior settings in which there were no performers, e.g., Vacant Lots.)

The data on territorial range are reported for various ages in Figure 11.1, in which territorial ranges are expressed as per cents of all the behavior settings of the towns, i.e., as territorial indexes. It will be noted that high school adolescents, age 14 through 17, entered just over 50 per cent of the towns' behavior settings at each age, and that this is the end of a gradual increase in territorial index, which began in infancy at 35 per cent. Figure 11.1 shows that adults were present in practically every behavior setting. It should be noted, however, that the points that represent adults (and aged persons too) are not comparable with those that represent children and adolescents. There were many more adults than children at each of the designated ages.

The performance range of an age group refers to the number of a town's behavior settings in which one or more members of the age group were performers, i.e., carried out actions essential to the immediate functioning of the setting (as chairmen, clerks, teachers, officers, proprietors, soloists, etc.). Performers enter behavior settings at participation levels 3 and 4, as described in Chapter 6, p. 82. Chi-square tests revealed that the towns did not differ in the performance ranges of different age groups.

The combined data for the four towns are given in Figure 11.1 in terms of performance indexes, i.e., per cent of all the behavior settings in the four towns. The data show that adolescents were performers in 11 per cent of the towns' behavior settings at 14 years of age and in 22 per cent at 17 years of age. The high school years were a period of rapid expansion into responsible participation: the increase in the performance index during these four years was as great as in the preceding 14 years. The performance index was much smaller than the territorial index at all childhood and adolescent ages, but the performance index increased with age at a more rapid rate than the territorial index. This is shown in Figure 11.2, in which performance indexes are represented as per cents of territorial index at all ages. The rapid acceleration in the degree to which adolescents became performers in the settings they entered in very evident. Adults were perform-

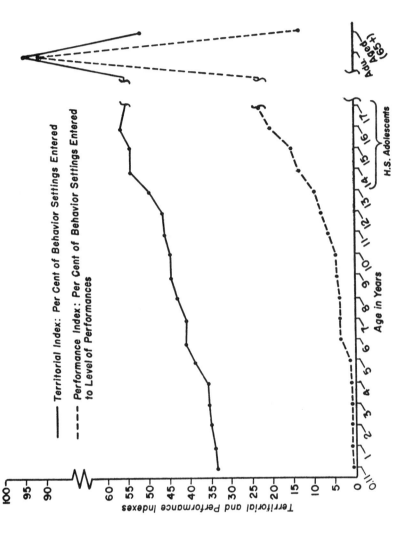

Fig. 11.1. Territorial and performance indexes of selected age groups for four Midwest County towns.

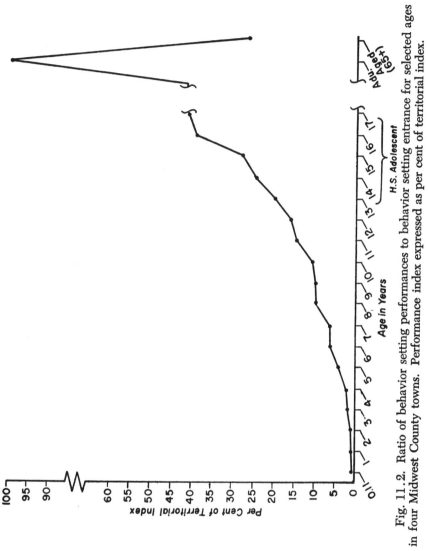

Fig. 11.2. Ratio of behavior setting performances to behavior setting entrance for selected ages in four Midwest County towns. Performance index expressed as per cent of territorial index.

ers in almost all behavior settings. Again, the points representing adults and aged persons are not comparable with those representing children (see p. 173).

In summary, high school adolescents at each consecutive age were inhabitants of about half the behavior settings of the Midwest County towns, and this did not increase during the four years from 14 through 17 years. On the other hand, the settings in which adolescents were responsible participants, i.e., performers, increased at a rate of 2.7 per cent a year during this period to include about one-fifth of the settings at 18 years; during the previous 15 years the rate of increase was 0.8 per cent a year. Adolescents ranged over about half of the town in which they lived, and by the age of 17 they performed in one-fifth of the town's settings. Nevertheless, it is clear that adults dominated the scene in the Midwest County towns; adults were performers in almost all behavior settings.

THE PRIMARY INHABITANTS OF BEHAVIOR SETTINGS

There were many types and classes of behavior settings within the territorial range of adolescents. Two important bases for classifying behavior settings are (*a*) the ages of the primary inhabitants and (*b*) the ages of the performers. The primary inhabitants of a setting are those inhabitants for whom a behavior setting is intended. Some settings are *for* males (Rotary Club Meeting), others are *for* females (Beauty Shop); some behavior settings are *for* children (School Playground) and some are *for* adults (Bridge Club Meeting). The primary inhabitants of a setting are often not the only inhabitants present, and sometimes they do not constitute a majority of the inhabitants. However, the primary population of a behavior setting influences strongly the physical-temporal arrangements of a setting and its standing behavior pattern. The performers, as has been stated, are those who operate a setting.

Six important classes of behavior settings, as defined by these two criteria, are listed in Table 11.1. The settings are listed in order of their primary inhabitants. The list ranges from those that were intended for the capacities and needs of children (class 1), through those that were adapted to the abilities and wants of high school adolescents (classes 2 and 3), through settings whose primary inhabitants were not restricted in age (classes 4 and 5), to behavior settings that were harmonious with the skills

TABLE 11.1. CLASSES OF BEHAVIOR SETTINGS IN ORDER OF MATURITY
OF INHABITANTS AND PERFORMERS

Maturity, BS Class	Primary Inhabitants	Maximal Penetration by		Example
		Adolescents	Adults	
1	Children (under 14 years)	Not present	Performers	1st Grade Music
2	Adolescents (14–17 years)	Members	Performers	High School Science Classes
3	Adolescents (14–17 years)	Performers	Performers	High School District Music Festival
4	All ages	Performers	Performers	Clifford's Drug Store
5	All ages	Members	Performers	Beauty Shop
6	Adults only	Not present	Performers	Presbyterian Session Meeting

and motives of adults (class 6). *Pari passu*, in this list, the performers of the settings change from adults alone (classes 1 and 2), to adults and adolescents (classes 3 and 4), to adults alone (classes 5 and 6).

It will be noted that the classes in this list fall into a rough "maturity order" from behavior settings that are operated by adults for children (class 1), through those that are operated by adults for adolescents (class 2), through settings that are operated by adults and adolescents for adolescents (class 3), through those that are operated by adults and adoles-

TABLE 11.2. NUMBER OF BEHAVIOR SETTINGS IN EACH CLASS

BS Class	Primary Inhabitants	Performers	Number of Settings				
			Malden	Midwest	Vernon	Walker	Total
1	Children	Adults	46	80	92	61	279
2	Adolescents	Adults	33	52	38	38	161
3	Adolescents	Adults and adolescents	44	64	75	45	228
4	All ages	Adults and adolescents	72	143	126	99	440
5	All ages	Adults	87	128	141	69	425
6	Adults	Adults	59	216	139	58	472
All classes			341	683	611	370	2,005

cents for all ages (class 4), through behavior settings that are operated by adults for all ages (class 5), to settings that are operated by adults for adults (class 6).

The number of behavior settings in each town, and in all the towns, are reported in Table 11.2 for each of these classes of behavior settings. When the classes are placed in order within each town according to the number of settings falling in them, the coefficient of concordance (Kendall, 1948) shows that the order does not differ across the four towns. Consequently, the frequencies have been summed across the towns.

BEHAVIOR SETTINGS DEVOTED TO THE WELFARE OF ADOLESCENTS

The data of Table 11.2 show that the settings in which high school adolescents were the primary inhabitants, and which were therefore intended for and tempered to the capacities and needs of high school adolescents (classes 2 and 3), constituted 389 or 19 per cent of all behavior settings. This can be viewed as a measure of the towns' special concern for the well-being of adolescents. The Midwest County towns devoted about one-fifth of their behavior areas to the welfare of adolescents, who constituted one-twelfth of their population. In contrast, adults (including aged persons), who made up over half the population of Midwest County towns, were provided with less than one-quarter of the behavior areas for their use alone, and the children under 14, who constituted one-fourth of the population, were provided with about one-seventh of the towns' settings for their primary use.

When privilege is measured in terms of the behavior setting resources devoted to them, the adolescents of the Midwest County towns were, indeed, a privileged class. However, the high school adolescents were by no means *only* recipients of benefits within the towns' behavior settings; they were responsible performers in more than half of those settings where they were primary inhabitants (classes 2 and 3), and they were performers (classes 3 and 4) in one-third of all the towns' behavior settings.

FUNCTIONAL IMPORTANCE OF ADOLESCENTS IN THE
LARGER COMMUNITY

We were especially interested in the place of adolescents in those behavior settings that were not especially arranged and operated for them as the primary inhabitants, i.e., in the larger, nonadolescent community (all behavior settings except classes 2 and 3). We turn to this next.

When a person carries out a task that is essential to the functioning of a setting, we have called this a performance. If he carries out such tasks in two different settings (e.g., teaches a Sunday school class and sings a solo at a community celebration) he engages in two performances. The total number of a person's performances can be enumerated, and when this is reported as a per cent of all the performances occurring in the community, we term it the Pied Piper index. The Pied Piper index is a measure of the community's loss of essential performances if the person in question were to be piped away; i.e., these are the performances that someone else would have to fill if the community is to maintain its level of functioning. The Pied Piper index is discussed in detail by Barker and Wright (1955).

We have computed average Pied Piper indexes within the larger community for all inhabitants and for high school adolescents. These indexes are presented in Table 11.3. They show, for example, that within Malden's larger, nonadolescent community "the average inhabitant" carried out 0.20 per cent of all the performances occurring within these settings, while "the average adolescent" carried out 0.54 per cent of these performances. In other words, the adolescents of Malden performed 2.2 times as many responsible tasks as did inhabitants in general in the settings of the larger community. The average Pied Piper index of the high school adolescents within the larger community was 2.5 to 5 times as great as that of all inhabitants. Previous work in the town of Midwest (Barker and Wright, 1955) confirms these findings.

These data indicate that, on the average, high school adolescents performed more of the essential tasks within the larger community than the generality of inhabitants. It is obvious that the adolescents of Midwest County towns did not retire to the behavior settings reserved especially for them, and that, in fact, the functional importance of adolescents within the larger community was greater on the average than at other ages.

TABLE 11.3. AVERAGE PIED PIPER INDEX OF ALL INHABITANTS AND OF HIGH SCHOOL ADOLESCENTS IN THE COMMUNITY-AT-LARGE

	Malden	Midwest	Vernon	Walker
All inhabitants	0.20%	0.13%	0.09%	0.22%
Adolescent inhabitants	0.54%	0.46%	0.45%	0.79%

There was the possibility that while individually active as performers, high school adolescents were so much in the minority that their contribution would not be seriously missed. We obtained data regarding this possibility by identifying those behavior settings in which high school adolescents constituted 20 per cent or more of the performers. It was assumed that the absence of adolescent performers would in these cases interfere with the functioning of the settings, i.e., that adolescents were essential performers. This was true for the following per cents of the settings in the larger community of each town (i.e., of all settings except those in classes 2 and 3): Malden, 23.5 per cent; Midwest, 18.5 per cent; Vernon, 20.7 per cent; and Walker, 27.5 per cent. These figures can be viewed as measures of the extent to which the four Midwest County communities were dependent for their functioning upon the performances of high school adolescents, or, conversely, of the degree to which the towns would be crippled for want of performers if the adolescents were removed. The behavior settings created and operated for the particular benefit of high school adolescents were, of course, omitted from these calculations.

BEHAVIOR PATTERN CHARACTERISTICS OF BEHAVIOR SETTINGS

We have approached the question of the nature of the adolescents' environment within the Midwest County towns via the different classes of settings. Now we shall consider the action patterns of behavior settings. We have dealt with the following eight action patterns: Art, Business, Education, Government, Nutrition, Physical Health, Recreation, Religion. An action pattern was rated present in a behavior setting if it was seen by an observer to be a prominent feature of the behavior pattern of the setting. For example, action patterns concerned with Business and Nutrition were rated as prominent features of the behavior patterns of grocery stores, while Recreation, which sometimes occurs in grocery stores, was not rated as prominent. The data on behavior patterns are presented in this research in terms of the per cent of settings in which the action pattern was judged to be prominent. The theory and methods of dealing with action patterns are reported in *Midwest and Its Children* (Barker and Wright, 1955).

Differences and similarities in action patterns were studied across towns and across behavior setting classes. The coefficient of concordance indicated that action pattern rankings, based on per cent of prominent action patterns, agreed across towns at a significant level ($p < .001$). Because of this, the data for the towns were combined. Differences across behavior setting classes were statistically significant ($p < .01$) for all action patterns.

The action patterns are presented in Table 11.4 in order of their occurrence as prominent features of all the settings in the four Midwest County towns. Education and Recreation were the most prominent action patterns; they were prominent in two of every five behavior settings. Nutrition was prominent in one out of three settings; Art, Business, and Religion were prominent in slightly over one-quarter of all settings; Physical Health was prominent in one-sixth of the settings; and Government was prominent in one behavior setting in 14.

The data for the classes of behavior settings are presented graphically in Figure 11.3. Here the great variation between behavior setting classes in the prominence of particular action patterns is dramatically displayed. The data show that the action patterns Education, Recreation, Nutrition, Art, and Physical Health reached their peaks of prominence in settings that were designed for the welfare of adolescents (classes 2 or 3). Business, Religion, and Government, on the other hand, were of very low prominence in these behavior settings. Within those settings of the larger community that high school adolescents inhabited (classes 4 and 5), Business and Religion reached their peaks of prominence. In other words, the behavior settings within the larger community where adolescents participated extensively compensated to an important degree for action pattern deficiencies in those settings where adolescents were the primary inhabitants.

TABLE 11.4. ACTION PATTERNS IN BEHAVIOR SETTINGS
(Per cent of all behavior settings (2,005) in which each action pattern was prominent, and per cent of settings in various classes exhibiting each action pattern prominently)

Class of Setting	Edu-cation	Recre-ation	Nutri-tion	Art	Busi-ness	Reli-gion	Physical Health	Govern-ment
All settings	42	40	33	29	26	26	17	7
BS classes								
1	66	58	23	39	2	27	25	2
2	69	42	20	23	9	20	24	5
3	43	73	47	44	20	14	32	2
4	34	35	37	40	32	36	12	4
5	19	26	28	20	50	18	16	5
6	45	32	37	15	23	29	8	16

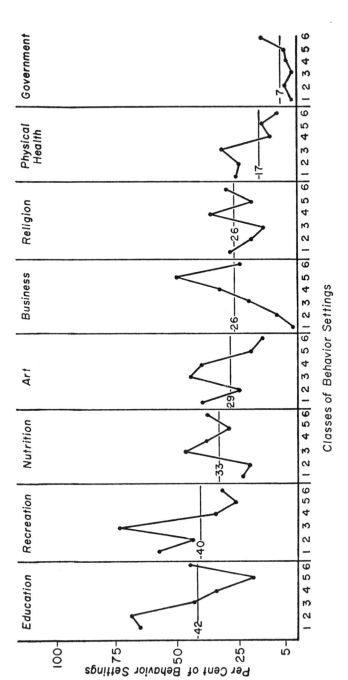

Fig. 11.3. Per cent of all behavior settings (horizontal line) and per cent of settings in each behavior setting class (points) in which action patterns were prominent. Data of four Midwest County towns combined.

Behavior settings of class 6, i.e., the settings to which the high school adolescents were to graduate as sole inhabitants in adulthood, gave highest prominence to only one action pattern, Government. No action pattern reached its greatest prominence in settings of class 1, which comprised the settings from which children emerged into adolescence. However, Education, Recreation, and Physical Health were widely prominent in class 1 behavior settings, and Business, Nutrition, and Government were low.

It appears from this analysis that the behavior settings arranged particularly for high school adolescents, plus those of the larger community which adolescents inhabited, provided adolescents with an environment where all the action patterns we have studied, except Government, were prominent. Action patterns missing from class 2 and 3 settings were provided by class 4 and 5 settings.

POWER, INFLUENCE, AND RICHNESS OF DIFFERENT CLASSES OF BEHAVIOR SETTINGS

The power of a behavior setting refers to the number of other settings over which it has authority. The setting High School Principal's Office in Midwest had the power to control the functioning of the setting School Lunch Room (who used it, how the room was arranged, how much was charged, etc.); it therefore had power over the School Lunch Room. Data are presented in terms of the per cent of behavior settings that had power over two or more other settings.

The power of different classes of behavior settings is reported in Figure 11.4. It is evident that high school adolescents were not inhabitants of the powerful behavior settings of the towns; only one class of the settings they entered (class 3) had power over other behavior settings to a greater degree than the generality of settings. The most powerful behavior settings were those in which adults were both the primary inhabitants and the only performers.

The influence of a behavior setting refers to the importance of the setting to individual people; it is measured by the number of persons whose behavior would be directly changed if the setting were to cease functioning. Almost every literate resident of Midwest read the *Midwest Weekly* and would, therefore, have been directly affected if the setting ceased operation. Data are presented in terms of the per cent of behavior settings with influence upon 92 or more people.

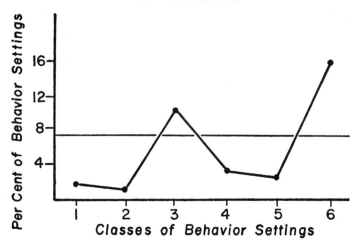

Fig. 11.4. Power of different classes of behavior settings. Per cent of all settings (horizontal line) and per cent of settings at different classes (points) with power over two or more behavior settings.

Data concerning the influence of different classes of behavior settings are presented in Figure 11.5. The picture here differs radically from that for power. Three of the classes of settings that adolescents inhabited had greater influence than behavior settings in general. High school adolescents were inhabitants of influential settings in Midwest County towns,

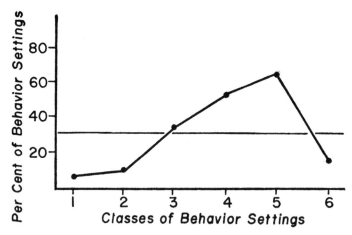

Fig. 11.5. Influence of different classes of behavior settings. Per cent of all settings (horizontal line) and per cent of settings of different classes (points) with influence over 92 or more persons.

and they were performers in most of the influential settings. It is interesting to note that among behavior setting classes 4, 5, and 6 the behavior settings that were influential were not powerful, and vice versa.

Richness ratings describe the variety of people and the variety of behavior occurring in a setting. There are three richness ratings: (*a*) Number of different vocational groups present among the regular inhabitants of the setting. Seven vocational groups were recognized, ranging from professional to unskilled labor. (*b*) Number of different ages among the people who regularly inhabited the setting. This ranged from one age in the case of School Board Meeting, which only adults attended, to 19 in the case of Basketball Game, which aged persons, adults, and 17 different child and adolescent single-year age groups attended. (*c*) Number of different action patterns rated prominent in the setting. Data respecting richness ratings are given in terms of per cent of behavior settings in the class under consideration that exceeded the median rating of all behavior settings.

Data for the three richness ratings are presented in Figures 11.6, 11.7, and 11.8. According to these data, the special adolescent behavior settings (classes 2 and 3) were somewhat below the general richness standard for vocational groups, ages, and action patterns in the case of class 2, where adolescents were members, and they were somewhat above the general richness standard for class 3, where adolescents were performers. The picture was clearer with respect to settings in the community-at-large, which high school adolescents inhabited (classes 4 and 5). These settings were among the richest settings in the towns with respect to the vocational

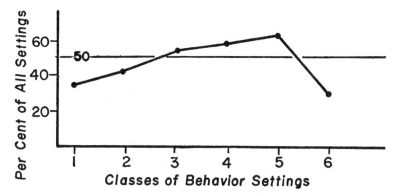

Fig. 11.6. Vocational groups present. Per cent of behavior settings within each class (points) which exceeded the median number of vocational groups present in all behavior settings (horizontal line).

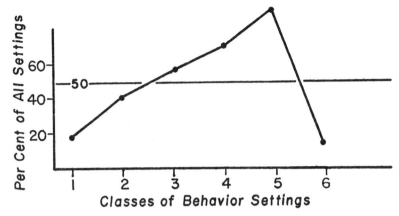

Fig. 11.7. Ages present. Per cent of settings within each class (points) which exceeded the median number of ages present in all settings (horizontal line).

groups and ages of their inhabitants, though action pattern richness was variable. The general indications of these data are that the classes of settings inhabited by the high school adolescents of Midwest County towns were at or above the general community standard with respect to richness. The high school adolescents of Midwest County towns lived in behavior settings that were relatively rich in people and behavior; they were not isolated from the Midwest world.

In summary, we have found that the high school adolescents of small towns in Midwest County participated in behavior settings that were (*a*)

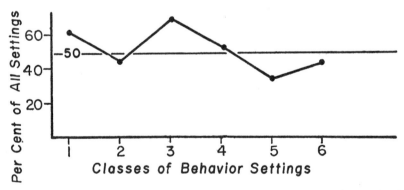

Fig. 11.8. Action patterns present. Per cent of settings within each class (points) which exceeded the median number of action patterns present in all settings (horizontal line).

low in power, (b) high in influence, and (c) high in the variety of people and behavior occurring within them.

In an effort to make the findings more concrete, we have listed in Table 11.5 the different kinds of performances in which the 47 high school adolescents of the town of Midwest engaged during the survey year. We have used the definitions of occupations given in the *Dictionary of Occupational Titles* (1949) as the basis for identifying the "kinds of performances." Eighty-six per cent of all the performance positions filled by the adolescents of Midwest are described in the *Dictionary of Occupational Titles* as standard occupations in American culture. Performances not defined as occupations in the *Dictionary* are appended at the end of Table 11.5.

In the table each "occupation" (kind of performance) is identified by its *Dictionary* title and by its *Dictionary* code number. The number of behavior settings in which each "occupation" occurred is then given separately for those settings where high school adolescents were the primary inhabitants (class 3) and for those settings within the larger community (class 4). Finally, examples of actual settings within both classes are provided. An example that involved paid employment is indicated by an asterisk beside the setting in which it occurred.

This study has shown that the high school adolescents of the small towns of Midwest County, Kansas, participated in almost two-thirds of the public behavior settings of the towns, and that they were the primary inhabitants of one-fifth of the towns' settings. The latter settings were devoted to the welfare of high school adolescents, and it was in them that the "adolescent culture" occurred. It is obvious, however, that the "adolescent culture" comprised only a part of the high school students' lives, for the behavior settings that accommodated this culture amounted to only 30 per cent of the settings in which they participated. Within the larger community, beyond the bounds of the settings devoted to them, the high school adolescents were functionally important people in influential, but not powerful, behavior settings that were rich in people and rich in behavior. The life of the high school adolescents outside their own culture area supplemented the environment within it by providing exposure to different action patterns.

In these small towns, adolescence was a time of important progress toward full attainment of adult status by means of responsible participation in behavior settings within the larger community.

TABLE 11.5. PERFORMANCES ENGAGED IN BY THE HIGH SCHOOL
STUDENTS OF MIDWEST CLASSIFIED ACCORDING TO THE
DICTIONARY OF OCCUPATIONAL TITLES

DOT Classification	Code No.	Setting Class	No. of Settings	Examples of Settings
Actor and Actress	0-02.11(15)	3	2	H.S. Senior Class Play
		4	6	Amateur Program, Old Settlers
Athlete	0-57.01	3	11	H.S. Football Games
		4	2	Town Team Baseball Games
Announcer	0-69.22	3	1	H.S. Football Games
		4	0	
Automobile Service Station Attendant	7-60.50	3	0	
		4	3	Bethel Service Station*
Bus Boy	2-29.51	3	1	Presbyterian Covered Dish Supper
		4	2	Father-Son Banquet
Butcher Helper	9-59.01	3	0	
		4	1	Kane's Grocery*
Buyer I (Collector: Used Clothing)	1-61.60	3	0	
		4	1	H.S. Home Economics Bundle Day Program
Cashier II	1-01.53	3	0	
		4	3	Old Settlers Reunion— Midway*
Character Men (Pantomime)	0-02.11	3	0	
		4	1	Mother-Daughter Banquet
Character Man	0-02.11(15)	3	0	
		4	2	School Christmas Vespers
Child Monitor	2-07.01	3	0	
		4	2	Presbyterian Nursery during Church
Chorus Girl (Cheerleader)	0-45.21	3	8	H.S. Basketball Games
		4	0	
Cleaner III	9-85.02	3	0	
		4	3	Junior Class Car Wash
Clergyman (Worship Leader)	0-08.10	3	8	Westminster Fellowship Retreat
		4	1	Methodist Easter Sunrise Service
Clerk, General Office	1-05.01	3	0	
		4	1	Chest Unit X-Ray

* Employment for pay.

TABLE 11.5 (*continued*)

DOT Classification	Code No.	Setting Class	No. of Settings	Examples of Settings
Clerk-Typist	1-37.34	3	0	
		4	1	Bank of Midwest*
Compositor I (Typesetter)	4-44.010	3	0	
		4	1	Midwest Weekly*
Concert Singer (Soloist)	0-24.02	3	5	Senior Class Commencement
		4	19	World Day of Prayer Service
Concession Attendant	2-40.21	3	0	
		4	3	Boy Scouts Pop Stand at Old Settlers
Cook Apprentice	2-47.01	3	0	
		4	1	County Principals' Dinner with Wives
Contribution Solicitors	1-55.40	3	0	
		4	2	Red Cross Fund Drive
Counterman, Cafeteria (Food Servers)	2-27.21	3	2	Valentine Formal
		4	2	Grade School Lunch Program*
County Agricultural Agent (Demonstration Leader)	0-12.20	3	3	Jolly Juniors 4-H Meeting
		4	0	
Custodian, Athletic Equipment	5-56.92	3	6	H.S. Football Games
		4	0	
Cylinder-Press Man	4-48.010	3	0	
		4	1	Midwest Weekly*
Dramatic Reader	0-02.25	3	1	Methodist Watch Night Service
		4	4	Methodist Church School Christmas Program
Floor Layer	5-32.752	3	0	
		4	1	Chase Floor Layer*
Frame Assembler I	8-39.81	3	0	
		4	1	Wherry Sash and Door Factory*
Funeral Attendant	2-43.91	3	0	
		4	3	Sherwin's Funeral Home*
Gardener	3-40.01	3	0	
		4	1	Senior Class Jobs for Fund Raising

* Employment for pay.

TABLE 11.5 (*continued*)

DOT Classification	Code No.	Setting Class	No. of Settings	Examples of Settings
Group Worker (Song Leader)	0-27.40	3	6	Jolly Juniors 4-H Meeting
		4	6	Baptist Worship Service
Hostess, Restaurant and Coffee Shop	2-27.14	3	7	Methodist Y.F. Weiner Roast
		4	3	Presbyterian Watch Night Party
Home Demonstration Agent	0-12.30	3	2	4-H Club Sewing Meeting
		4	0	
Instrument Players	0-24.12	3	7	Band to K.U. Band Day
		4	3	Halloween Parade
Janitor	2-84.10	3	0	
		4	5	U.S. Post Office*
Kennelman	3-17.60	3	0	
		4	1	Crawford Kennels*
Mechanic Helper	7-81.10	3	0	
		4	1	Beyet Implement*
Laborer, Construction	9-32.01	3	0	
		4	1	Nading, Contractor*
Lecturer (Speaker or Panel Member)	0-39.91	3	2	Junior-Senior Banquet
		4	3	County Teachers Institute
Make-up Man (Performer's Helper)	2-32.41	3	1	All School Assemblies
		4	0	
Make-up Assistant	2-32.42	3	0	
		4	2	H.S. Junior Class Play
Manager, Stage	0-02.37	3	0	
		4	2	H.S. Senior Class Play
Manager, Athletic Team	0-57.51	3	4	Coach's Room
		4	0	
Manager, Recreation Establishment	0-98.54	3	7	Teen Town Dances
		4	0	
Manufacturing Assembly Helper (Favor Makers)	8-94.41	3	0	
		4	1	Father-Son Banquet
Master of Ceremonies	0-62.51	3	2	Junior-Senior Banquet
		4	5	Home Economics Fashion Show
Mechanic and Repairman, Radio	5-83.445	3	0	
		4	1	Midwest TV and Radio Repair*

* Employment for pay.

TABLE 11.5 (*continued*)

DOT Classification	Code No.	Setting Class	No. of Settings	Examples of Settings
Model	2-43.41	3	1	County 4-H Style Revue
		4	1	Home Economics Fashion Show
Musical Entertainer	0-24.07	3	3	School Assemblies
		4	8	School Christmas Vespers
Musician, Instrumental	0-24.12	3	3	Presbyterian W.F. Regular Summer Meeting
		4	11	Baptist Worship Service
Musical Occupation, Miscellaneous (Drum Major)	0-24.9	3	2	H.S. Football Games
		4	0	
Newspaper Carrier	1-58.10	3	0	
		4	2	Capital City Paper Route*
Office Girl	1-23.02	3	0	
		4	1	H.S. Principal's Office
Parade Attendant	2-40.93	3	0	
		4	2	Halloween Parade
Painter	5-27.010	3	0	
		4	1	Presbyterian Work Days
Piano Accompanist	0-24.12	3	3	Junior-Senior Banquet
		4	16	Eastern Star Men's Night
Prompter	1-49.04	3	2	Senior Class Play Practice
		4	1	Senior Class Play
Repairman and Mechanic Helper, Tractor	7-81.040	3	0	
		4	2	Midwest Hardware & Implement Co.*
Routeman Helper	9-35.10	3	0	
		4	1	Pearson Dairy Barn*
Sales Clerk	1-70.10	3	0	
		4	11	Variety Store*
Salesperson	1-75.71	3	0	
		4	2	Cabell Department Store*
Secretary	1-33.01	3	0	
		4	1	County Superintendent of Schools Office*
Scientific Helper (Research Assistant)	0-50.23	3	0	
		4	1	Child Study Project Office*
Soda Dispenser	2-27.61	3	0	
		4	1	Denton Drug Store*

* Employment for pay.

TABLE 11.5 (*continued*)

DOT Classification	Code No.	Setting Class	No. of Settings	Examples of Settings
Solicitor	1-55.40	3	0	
		4	1	School Magazine Sale
Story Teller	0-69.92	3	0	
		4	1	Story Hours, Library
Tap Dancer	0-45.11	3	0	
		4	2	Amateur Show, Old Settlers
Teacher, First Aid (Demonstrator)	0-32.91	3	0	
		4	1	Boosters Club Regular Meeting
Teacher, High School (Bible)	0-31.01	3	3	Methodist H.S. Class
		4	0	
Teacher, Kindergarten	0-30.02	3	0	
		4	1	Methodist Kindergarten Vacation Church School
Taxi Driver	7-36.040	3	1	Methodist Y.F. to Emporia
		4	0	
Ticket Taker	2-40.91	3	0	
		4	1	Teachers' Conference
Umpire, Referee	0-57.61	3	1	Pony and Little League Teams
		4	1	Grade School Basketball Games
Usher	2-48.10	3	0	
		4	3	H.S. Senior Class Play
Waitress	2-27.12	3	0	
		4	6	Hotel*
Waiter, Informal	2-27.11	3	1	Junior-Senior Banquet
		4	2	Gwynn Cafe*
Window Cleaner	2-82.30	3	0	
		4	1	Senior Jobs for Fund Raising

Note: Performances not defined as occupations in the *DOT*:
         Attendant, Methodist Wedding
         Award Recipients, H.S. Awards Assembly
         Bride, Methodist Wedding
         Bride, Charivari
         Club or School Officer, H.S. Student Council Meeting
         Initiation Directors and Planners, H.S. Freshman Initiation
         King, Queen, and Attendants, Valentine Formal
         Offenders, City Court
         Witness, District Court Session
  * Employment for pay.

PART IV

SUMMING UP

OUR REPORT began with some concepts for describing environments and with certain expectations about the relations between school enrollment, number of school parts, and the behavior of students. A series of investigations utilizing the concepts and developing methods for checking upon the expectations were subsequently described and their results presented. The time has come to summarize what has been done and to consider implications of the methods and findings for educational research and policy. This is the task of Part IV of *Big School, Small School*.

12

Overview and Prospects

PAUL V. GUMP • ROGER G. BARKER

THE LARGE school has authority: its grand exterior dimensions, its long halls and myriad rooms, and its tides of students all carry an implication of power and rightness. The small school lacks such certainty: its modest building, its short halls and few rooms, and its students, who move more in trickles than in tides, give an impression of a casual or not quite decisive educational environment.

These are outside views. They are illusions. Inside views reveal forces at work stimulating and compelling students to more active and responsible contributions to the enterprises of small than of large schools. The inside views also show that the small school does not lack as many parts as enrollment alone would imply. Comparison of the largest school, Capital City, with the four small schools of Midwest County reveals that the large school had 20 times as many students but only 5 times as many settings and 1.4 times as many varieties of settings. A small school is not so small in terms of the number and variety of its behaviorally significant parts as it is in terms of students; like a small engine or small organism, it possesses the essential parts of a large entity, but has fewer replications and differentiations of some of the parts.

Our investigations of the behavior and experiences of students were guided by the hypothesis that the essential equivalence of small and large high schools with respect to kinds of parts, together with their difference in number of students per part, provides a crucially different environment for students. A prototype of this difference is the Junior Class play of a small school, where each member of the class is essential to the play's successful presentation, versus the Junior Class play of a large school, where at most only 15 per cent of the members of the class have more than a spectator's involvement in the play. According to the theory that guided the research, the behavior settings Junior Class Play, Senior English Class, Football Game, Student Council Meeting are not passive stages upon which behavior may occur, but they are extra-individual entities with power over participants and potential participants. Detailed predictions regarding the expected behavior and experiences of small and large school students were made before the investigations were begun (Chapters 1 and 2).

Voluntary school behavior settings occupied a large place in the investigations because attendance and participation can be easily observed, and they are crucial indicators of motivation and involvement. In the case of school classes, on the other hand, where attendance and participation are required, methods of assessing motivation and involvement are very difficult. It is for this technical reason that many of the investigations were limited to nonclass (extracurricular) settings.

Investigations were made in high schools varying in enrollment from 35 to 2,287 students; the most crucial studies compared high school Juniors in four schools of 83 to 151 students with those in a high school of 2,287 students. The schools were located in eastern Kansas with a homogeneous economic, cultural, and political region; all schools met the standards of the same state authority (Chapter 4).

EXTENT OF PARTICIPATION IN SCHOOL ACTIVITIES

The proportion of students who participated in district music festivals and dramatic, journalistic, and student government competitions reached a peak in high schools with enrollments between 61 and 150. The proportion of participants was 3 to 20 times as great in the small schools as in the largest school. The average number of extracurricular activities and kinds of activities in which students engaged during their four-year high school careers was twice as great in the small as in the large schools (Chapter 5).

The large high school provided its Junior students with a larger number and more varieties of nonclass behavior settings than the small schools (Chapters 4 and 6). In spite of this, the small school students participated in the same number and in more varieties of the available settings, on the average, than the students of the large school. Furthermore, a much larger proportion of the small school students held positions of importance and responsibility in the behavior settings they entered, and they occupied these positions in more varieties of settings than the students of the large school. The number of settings in which students participated varied more among students of the large than of the small schools (Chapters 6 and 9).

EXPERIENCES REPORTED BY STUDENTS

Rewards achieved by Juniors in their nonclass settings were topics of investigation for Chapters 7 and 9. Our hypothesis predicted that small and large school Juniors would report different kinds of satisfactions from their experiences in the behavior settings they inhabited. This prediction was confirmed. Specifically, Juniors from the small schools reported more satisfactions relating to the development of competence, to being challenged, to engaging in important actions, to being involved in group activities, and to achieving moral and cultural values; while large school Juniors reported more satisfactions dealing with vicarious enjoyment, with large entity affiliation, with learning about their school's persons and affairs, and with gaining "points" via participation. It was further predicted that these school differences would be causally related to differences in occupancy of important and responsible positions in school settings. This prediction was verified: the satisfactions reported were significantly influenced by the positions the student respondents occupied within settings, and most of the differences between large and small schools in this regard were eliminated when differences in setting position were held constant. The burden of the evidence supports the conclusions that large and small school Juniors experienced different satisfactions and that most of these differences were due to differences in the number of students who occupied important, responsible positions (Chapter 7).

Students of small schools reported experiencing more attractions and more pressures toward participation in school nonclass behavior settings than students of large schools, and their responses reflected more involvement and more feelings of responsibility. Furthermore, the small schools did not produce such great individual differences in experienced attractions and pressures as did the large school; the small schools contained fewer "outsiders." The findings indicate that the small school students lived under greater day-by-day attraction, obligation, and external pressure to take active part in the various behavior settings of their schools (Chapters 8 and 9).

COMMUNITY ACTIVITIES

Part-time and summer employment in business and professional behavior settings and responsible participation in church and out-of-school social organizations are widely believed to have educational values. These community activities were more frequent for the small school–small town adolescents than for the large school–city adolescents. In these respects, the differences were clearer for the boys than for the girls. In general, the schools and communities were harmonious: the small communities, like the small schools, provided positions of functional importance for adolescents more frequently; and the cities, like the large schools, provided such positions less frequently. The data provide no evidence that the urban environments of the large schools compensated by means of their greater resources and facilities for the relatively meager functional importance of students within their large schools (Chapter 10). In the two instances studied where students were removed from small communities and transported to a central, district school, there was some evidence that participation in voluntary school settings was lower than in the case of students attending small schools in small communities (Chapter 9). The high school adolescents of the small communities made functionally important contributions to their towns in behavior settings beyond the borders of the schools; and these settings, in turn, supplemented the school settings (Chapter 11).

CLASSROOM ACTIVITIES

For the technical reasons that have been mentioned, most of the findings of the research refer to nonclass (extracurricular) activities. The question arises if the findings hold, as well, for classroom activities. This is a very important question, and we shall summarize the limited data of this study that bear upon it. But the fact that classroom activities are important does not detract from the educational significance of the findings with respect to nonclass activities. In high schools of all sizes, classroom behavior settings comprise about 20 per cent of all school settings; this is true, also, of two English schools we have studied. Evidently the educational enterprise as it is organized in many schools today involves substantial arrangements for nonacademic activities. Whether or not these activities are presumed to have positive educational value, schools provide behavior settings for them, and the settings demand the time and attention of students; they therefore contribute in one way or another to the schools' influence upon students, and it is important to know what behavior and experiences they are eliciting.

The study of school structure showed (a) that formal educational behavior settings constituted about the same proportion of the settings of schools of all sizes; (b) that there were fewer varieties of formal educational behavior settings in the small schools; and (c) that within the variety concerned with academic subjects the number of different subject-matter classes (cytosettings) was smaller in the small schools (Chapter 4). In spite of the greater numbers and varieties of educational behavior settings in the large schools, the available evidence indicates that, as was true with the nonclass settings, the large school students participated in fewer classes and varieties of classes than the small school students (Chapter 10). The problem of specialization was investigated in the case of the single subject matter, music, with the findings that musical education and experience were more widely distributed among the small school than among the large school students, but that there were more music specialists among the large school students (Chapter 10).

Within a broader context, the studies reported here have relevance for two issues: the methodological problem of how to study institutions, such as schools, as environments; and the substantive problem of the relation between institutional size and individual behavior.

THE ISSUE OF METHOD

The high schools of the United States provide a significant segment of the environment of the nation's adolescents. It is practically important, therefore, to study high schools as environments. How does one do this? These studies provide one answer.

The basic unit of the school environment is the behavior setting. To put it plainly: A school *is* its behavior settings. With this unit and associated measures it is possible to study the school in terms of its first-order reality for its inhabitants. The distinction between this approach and others is worth making explicit. For example, it is possible to study schools in terms of such variables as the social class of students, the training of teachers, and the extent of curricular offerings; but students do not respond directly to these variables. Students respond to the sectors of the school environment in which they live. The effects of social class and of other variables may impinge upon events within behavior settings, but students react to them as they are transformed within behavior settings. Differences in social class, for example, may have quite dissimilar consequences in small and large settings.

Behavior settings can enter research in three ways. First, they can be used as sampling units. If one wishes to know what happens in one kind of school as opposed to another, it is necessary that these schools be sampled in a representative and equitable fashion. A behavior setting survey maps the school environment; once the map is developed, decisions about areas from which to take measurements can be made with confidence. This "situational sampling" involves a different principle from person sampling and is an essential aspect of environmental research.

Second, the number, kind, and organization of settings can be viewed as sets of dependent variables. If one is interested in the effects of consolidation, one can observe what this move does to the behavior settings of the schools involved: what happens, for example, to after-school settings when all students must ride the bus? Or, one can study effects of variation in educational philosophy upon the behavior settings of schools: how do secular versus religious, public versus private, American versus European schools differ in the number, kind, and interrelation of settings?

In the third place, behavior settings can be used as the independent variables. The target of such investigation is the response of the inhabitants of behavior settings to the settings. One aspect of school behavior settings was selected in the present effort, namely, population. There are, however, certainly other behavior-coercive properties of settings: e.g., the number of "performance niches" they contain, the amount of interdependence they require, the specific types of effort they demand, the kinds of human beings they include. Variations in setting qualities have implications for educational strategy. School learning occurs at the mutual boundary between the school and the individual student; this boundary is located in the school's behavior settings. Educators wish to create good schools, and this, then, means to create settings consonant with their educational goals. The attainment of this consonance requires methods of identifying and characterizing settings and methods of describing the behavior that is responsive to setting contexts.

THE ISSUE OF SIZE

A basic problem for the immediate future is to investigate the degree to which the relations we have discovered between school size, school settings, and student participation are inevitable. Not only the present research, but all other research known to us, indicates that the negative relationship between institutional size and individual participation is deeply based and difficult, if not impossible, to avoid (Chapter 3). It may be easier to bring specialized and varied behavior settings to small schools than to raise the level of individual participation in large schools. Furthermore, the current method of broadening educational offerings by moving hundreds of bodies to a central spot may be both unnecessary and old-fashioned. Already a technical revolution with respect to teaching devices and educational facilities is upon us. Self-teaching machines, taped school courses, TV classes, wired TV linking separate schools, new ideas about teaching personnel (e.g., school aides), new conceptions of inter-school cooperation (e.g., transporting teachers and equipment rather than students), new conceptions of the contributions of the community to educational objectives, and new materials and standards for school construction are freeing schools from past molds.

These new developments, taken with the findings reported here, provoke the question: How large should a school be?

The present research, in itself, cannot answer this question. Some of the crucial variables such as academic learning were not investigated. Furthermore, "should" in this query implies purpose, and educational purposes differ. For example, the findings of Chapters 5 and 10 indicate that if versatility of experience is preferred over opportunity for specialization, a smaller school is better than a larger one; if specialization is sought, the larger school is the better.

Although a definite answer to the size question cannot be given, the theory developed here can be helpful in deciding particular issues. It often happens, in these days, that population increase in a given area requires sharply increased high school facilities. One solution to this problem lies in the expansion of the facilities and enrollment of the existing school. Our findings show that among the results of this policy is a decrease in responsible student action and experience. A second solution is the establishment of a number of new small schools, thereby keeping enrollments relatively low. A third approach is the campus school, an arrangement by which students are grouped in semiautonomous units for most studies but are usually provided a school-wide extracurricular program. The campus school provides for repeated contacts between the same teachers and students; this continuity of associates probably leads to closer social bonds. A common-sense theory is that the campus school welds together the facility advantages of the large school and the social values of the small school. But the social values of small schools reported in the present research do not rest upon associate continuity; they rest upon low population per setting, a condition difficult or impossible to achieve in the school-wide extracurricular programs of large campus schools. A fourth solution, then, would be another arrangement of the campus school, for example, making the separate units autonomous with respect to voluntary activities as well as for most classes.

Common-sense theories about schools are not adequate bases for policy decisions. Another example of this is the common-sense assumption that there is a direct coupling between the facilities or properties of schools and the behavior and experiences of students. This simple view of reality, so common in education, has been long passed in physical and biological sciences. No one would seriously argue that because one bridge is stronger than another the individual beams of which it is constructed must also be stronger. Good facilities provide good experiences only if they are used. The educational process is a subtle and delicate one about which we know little, but it surely thrives on participation, enthusiasm, and responsibility. Our findings and our theory posit a negative relationship between school size and individual student participation. What seems to happen is that as schools get larger and settings inevitably become more heavily populated, more of the students are less needed; they become superfluous, redundant.

What size should a school be?

The data of this research and our own educational values tell us that a school should be sufficiently small that all of its students are needed for its enterprises. A school should be small enough that students are not redundant.

APPENDIXES

APPENDIX 4.1

High School Behavior Setting Surveys, Midwest and Capital City High Schools, School Year 1959–60

FOLLOWING are behavior setting surveys of two high schools. The Community Behavior Setting Varieties listed in Appendix 11.1 show 99 varieties for four Midwest County communities. Not all the varieties found in communities appear in the high schools, e.g., Banks; therefore, the numbers in the high school lists are not necessarily consecutive, since the numbering is that of the community surveys. The behavior settings within each variety are simply numbered consecutively as listed; a number in one survey is not parallel to the same number in another survey.

MIDWEST HIGH SCHOOL

1. Athletic Contests, Indoors
   1.1 Regional Basketball Tournament
   1.2 District Basketball Tournament
   1.3 County Basketball Tournament
   1.4 Basketball Games, Boys A and B Teams and Girls
   1.5 Basketball Games, Boys A and B Teams and Girls at other school
   1.6 Basketball Practice, Boys
   1.7 Basketball Practice, Girls
   1.8 Gymnasium for Noon Freetime
2. Athletic Contests, Outdoors
   2.1 County Track Meet at other school
   2.2 Track Practice
   2.3 Football Game
   2.4 Football Game at other school
   2.5 Football Practice
   2.6 Baseball Game at other school
   2.7 Baseball Practice
8. Book Exchange and Rentals
   8.1 Parent-Teacher Book Exchange
15. Dances
   15.1 Dance Following Football Game
   15.2 Dance Honoring Basketball Boys
   15.3 Homecoming Dance
   15.4 Valentine Formal
17. Dinners and Banquets
   17.1 Last Day of School Dinner
   17.2 Junior-Senior Banquet and Dance

20.   Educational Groups, Academic
    20.1 English I, II, III, IV Classes, Teacher 1
    20.2 Social Science and Latin Classes, Teacher 2
    20.3 Algebra, Algebra II, and Geometry Classes, Teacher 3
    20.4 Bookkeeping, Shorthand, and Typing Classes, Teacher 4
    20.5 Science Classes, Teacher 5
    20.6 General Mathematics Class, Teacher 6
    20.7 Health Class, Teacher 3
    20.8 Make-up Day, Teacher 1
21.   Educational Groups, Driver Education
    21.1 Driver Education Class, Teacher 5
22.   Educational Groups, Home Economics
    22.1 Home Economics Classes, Teacher 7
23.   Educational Groups, Music
    23.1 Band Marching Practice, Teacher 8
    23.2 Band Practice, Teacher 8
    23.3 Junior Band Practice, Teacher 8
    23.4 Voice Groups, Teacher 8
24.   Educational Groups, Physical Education
    24.1 Freshman Physical Education Class, Teacher 3
    24.2 Cheerleader Practice
25.   Educational Groups, Shop and Agriculture
    25.1 Boys Shop Classes, Teacher 9
    25.2 Boys Mechanical Drawing Class, Teacher 9
29.   Fire and Tornado Drills
    29.1 Fire Drill
35.   Food Sales
    35.1 Senior Class Food Sale
    35.2 Sophomore Class Food Sale
36.   Fund and Membership Drives
    36.1 Students Magazine Subscription Sale
    36.2 Home Economics Bundle Day Program
    36.3 Junior and Senior Fire Extinguisher Sale
    36.4 Senior Class Candy Sale
39.   Government and School Offices
    39.1 Principal's Office
    39.2 Ditto Room
41.   Hallways and Coatrooms
    41.1 Halls
48.   Initiations
    48.1 Senior Class Freshman Initiation
52.   Libraries
    52.1 Library and Study Hall
54.   Meetings, Executive
    54.1 Student Council Meeting
55.   Meetings, Organization Business
    55.1 Senior Class Meeting
    55.2 Junior Class Meeting

81. Restrooms
    81.1 Boys' Basement Restroom
    81.2 Boys' Basement Locker and Shower Room
    81.3 Girls' Basement Restroom
    81.4 Girls' Basement Locker and Shower Room
    81.5 Home Economics Club Room
83. School, Coaches' Rooms
    83.1 Coach's Room
84. School, Custodians' Rooms
    84.1 Utility Room
85. School, Special Days
    85.1 Enrollment Day
95. Volunteer Work and Fund Raising Projects
    95.1 Senior Jobs for Fund Raising
    95.2 Senior Car Wash
    95.3 Junior Car Wash
    95.4 Juniors Decorate for Junior-Senior Prom
    95.5 Sophomore Car Wash

CAPITAL CITY HIGH SCHOOL

1. Athletic Contests, Indoors
    1.1 Basketball Tournament
    1.2 Basketball Game, A Team
    1.3 Basketball Game, A Team at other school
    1.4 Basketball Practice, A Team
    1.5 Basketball Game, B Team
    1.6 Basketball Game, B Team at other school
    1.7 Basketball Practice, B Team
    1.8 Basketball Game, Sophomore
    1.9 Basketball Game, Sophomore at other school
    1.10 Basketball Practice, Sophomore
    1.11 Wrestling Match, A Team
    1.12 Wrestling Match, A Team at other school
    1.13 Wrestling Match, B Team
    1.14 Wrestling Match, B Team at other school
    1.15 Wrestling Practice
    1.16 Basketball, Boys Intramural
    1.17 Handball, Boys Intramural
    1.18 Bowling, Boys Intramural
    1.19 Playday at other school, Girls
    1.20 Basketball, Girls Intramural
    1.21 Volleyball, Girls Intramural
    1.22 Deck Tennis, Girls Intramural
    1.23 Badminton, Girls Intramural
    1.24 Trampoline Activities, Girls
2. Athletic Contests, Outdoors
    2.1 Football Game, A Team
    2.2 Football Game, A Team at other school

2.3 Football Game, B Team
2.4 Football Game, B Team at other school
2.5 Football Practice, A and B Teams
2.6 Football Game, Sophomore
2.7 Football Game, Sophomore at other school
2.8 Football Practice, Sophomore
2.9 Track Meet
2.10 Track Meet at other school
2.11 Track Practice
2.12 Cross Country Race
2.13 Cross Country Race at other school
2.14 Cross Country Practice
2.15 Tennis Game
2.16 Tennis Game at other school
2.17 Tennis Practice
2.18 Golf Game and Practice, Boys
2.19 Baseball Game
2.20 Baseball Game at other school
2.21 Baseball Practice
2.22 Touch Football, Boys Intramural
2.23 Golf Game and Practice, Girls
8. Book Exchange and Rentals
8.1 Book Rental and Exchange Room
8.2 Library Club Sale of Paperbacks
12. Classrooms, Freetime and Home Rooms
12.1 through 12.74. 74 Home Rooms
15. Dances
15.1 Varsity Dance after Game in Cafeteria
15.2 Annual Election Dance
15.3 Queen of Courts Varsity Dance
15.4 Junior-Senior Prom
15.5 Senior Dance Following Commencement
15.6 Sophomore Party
15.7 Pep Club Roundup
15.8 All School Dance
17. Dinners and Banquets
17.1 Employer-Employee Banquet
17.2 Future Homemakers of America St. Patrick's Tea with Mothers
17.3 Thespian Supper Party and Initiation
17.4 Open House Dinner
17.5 Quill and Scroll Potluck Supper
17.6 Future Nurses Pinning Banquet, New Holiday Inn
17.7 Sunflower Debate League Dinner at Shereton High
17.8 All Sports Banquet, City Hotel
17.9 Football Banquet
17.10 C Club Dinner for Coaches and Wives
17.11 Basketball Game Cadets Breakfast
17.12 Future Teachers Club Installation Banquet

18. Doctors' Offices and Clinics
    18.1 School Nurse's Office
    18.2 Tuberculin Testing Program
    18.3 Vision and Hearing Screen Test
20. Educational Groups, Academic
    20.1 English Classes, Teacher 1
    20.2 English Classes, Teacher 2
    20.3 English Classes, Teacher 3
    20.4 English Classes, Teacher 4
    20.5 English and Journalism Classes, Teacher 5
    20.6 English and Reading Classes, Teacher 6
    20.7 English and Stage Craft Classes, Teacher 7
    20.8 English Classes, Teacher 8
    20.9 English Classes, Teacher 9
    20.10 English Classes, Teacher 10
    20.11 English Classes, Teacher 11
    20.12 English Classes, Teacher 12
    20.13 English and Speech Classes, Teacher 13
    20.14 English Classes, Teacher 14
    20.15 English Classes, Teacher 15
    20.16 English Classes, Teacher 16
    20.17 Math Classes, Teacher 17
    20.18 Math Classes, Teacher 18
    20.19 Math Classes, Teacher 19
    20.20 Math Classes, Teacher 20
    20.21 Math Classes, Teacher 21
    20.22 Math Classes, Teacher 22
    20.23 Math Classes, Teacher 23
    20.24 Physics Classes, Teacher 24
    20.25 Chemistry Classes, Teacher 25
    20.26 Biology Classes, Teacher 26
    20.27 Chemistry Classes, Teacher 26
    20.28 Botany and Biology Classes, Teacher 27
    20.29 Biology Classes, Teacher 28
    20.30 Physics Classes, Teacher 28
    20.31 Biology Classes, Teacher 29
    20.32 Physiology Classes, Teacher 30
    20.33 Biology Classes, Teacher 31
    20.34 General Science Classes, Teacher 31
    20.35 Social Studies Classes, Teacher 32
    20.36 Social Studies Classes, Teacher 33
    20.37 Social Studies Classes, Teacher 34
    20.38 Social Studies Classes, Teacher 35
    20.39 Social Studies Classes, Teacher 36
    20.40 Social Studies Classes, Teacher 37
    20.41 Social Studies and Public Speaking Classes, Teacher 38
    20.42 Social Studies Classes and Debate Classes, Teacher 39
    20.43 Social Studies Classes, Teacher 40
    20.44 Social Studies Classes, Teacher 41

20.45 Social Studies Classes, Teacher 42
20.46 Social Studies Classes, Teacher 43
20.47 Spanish and Latin Classes and Latin Club, Teacher 44
20.48 French Classes, Teacher 45
20.49 Spanish Classes, Teacher 46
20.50 French and Latin Classes and Latin Club, Teacher 47
20.51 Commercial Classes, Teacher 48
20.52 Commercial Classes, Teacher 48
20.53 Typing Classes and Business Arithmetic, Teacher 49
20.54 Typing Classes, Teacher 50
20.55 Bookkeeping Classes, Teacher 50
20.56 Stenography Classes, Teacher 51
20.57 Transcription Classes, Teacher 51
20.58 Typing Classes, Teacher 52
20.59 Stenography and Bookkeeping Classes, Teacher 53
20.60 Commercial Classes, Teacher 54
20.61 Bookkeeping and Typing Classes, Teacher 55
20.62 Typing Classes, Teacher 55
20.63 Office Machine Classes, Teacher 56
20.64 Retail Selling Classes, Teacher 57
20.65 Study Hall, Teacher 58
20.66 Study Hall, Teacher 59
20.67 Study Hall, Teacher 60
20.68 Senior Testing Period
20.69 Junior Testing Period
20.70 Sophomore Testing Period
20A. Educational Groups, Art Education
    20A.1 General Art and Advanced Ceramics Classes, Teacher 61
    20A.2 General Art and Advanced Painting Classes, Teacher 62
    20A.3 General Art and Ceramics Classes, Teacher 63
21. Educational Groups, Driver Education
    21.1 Driver Education Classes, Teacher 64
    21.2 Driver Education Classes, Teacher 65
22. Educational Groups, Home Economics
    22.1 Clothing, Home Decoration, Social Living Classes, Teacher 66
    22.2 Foods Classes, Teacher 67
    22.3 Home Nursing, Home Management and Clothing Classes, Teacher 68
    22.4 Clothing Classes, Teacher 69
    22.5 Clothing, Home Decoration, Social Living Classes, Teacher 70
    22.6 Future Homemakers of America Meeting
23. Educational Groups, Music
    23.1 Girls Chorus Classes, Teacher 71
    23.2 Vocal Music Classes, Teacher 72
    23.3 Instrumental Music Classes
        (Band, Orchestra and Instrumental Ensemble), Teacher 73
    23.4 Instrumental Music Classes
        (Band, Orchestra and Instrumental Ensemble), Teacher 74
    23.5 Band Marching Practice

24. Educational Groups, Physical Education
    24.1 Physical Education Classes, Boys, Teacher 75
    24.2 Physical Education Classes, Boys, Teacher 76
    24.3 Physical Education Classes, Boys, Teacher 77
    24.4 Physical Education Classes, Girls, Teacher 78
    24.5 Physical Education Classes, Girls, Teacher 79
    24.6 Physical Education Classes, Girls, Teacher 80
    24.7 Cheerleaders Practice
    24.8 Troy Janes Meeting
24A. Educational Groups, Physical Education, Swimming
    24A.1 Swimming
    24A.2 Swimming at other school
    24A.3 Swimming Practice
    24A.4 Swimming, Boys Intramural
    24A.5 Swimming Club, Boys
    24A.6 Tadpole Club, Girls
    24A.7 Squid Club, Girls
25. Educational Groups, Shop and Agriculture
    25.1 Woodworking and Advanced Woodworking Classes, Teacher 81
    25.2 Mechanical Drawing Classes, Teacher 82
    25.3 Printing I and II and Vocational Printing Classes, Teacher 83
    25.4 Electronics and Radio Classes, Teacher 84
    25.5 Mechanical Drawing and Stage Classes, Teacher 85
    25.6 Machine Shop Classes, Teacher 85
    25.7 Auto Mechanics Classes, Teacher 86
    25.8 Machine Shop Classes, Teacher 86
    25.9 Photography Classes, Teacher 87
    25.10 Electronics Classes, Teacher 88
    25.11 Welding Classes, Teacher 89
    25.12 Radio Classes, Teacher 90
    25.13 Machine Shop Classes, Teacher 91
    25.14 Auto Mechanics Classes, Teacher 92
26. Elections
    26.1 All School Elections
26A. Elevators
    26A.1 Elevator
28. Fairs, Circuses, and Carnivals
    28.1 Homecoming Parade
    28.2 Senior Spring Carnival
29. Fire and Tornado Drills
    29.1 Fire Drill
    29.2 Tornado Drill
35. Food Sales
    35.1 Future Teachers Cookie Sale
36. Fund and Membership Drives
    36.1 Tag Day—American Field Service Assembly
    36.2 Quill and Scroll Sale of Book Protectors
    36.3 Junior Red Cross Annual Rummage Sale

36.4 Junior Red Cross Chrysanthemum Corsage Sale
36.5 Hi-Y High School Pennant Sale
36.6 C Club Fund Raising Project
36.7 Future Nurses Coke Bar
36.8 Home Room Activity Card Sale
36.9 Honor Pep Club Sale of Movie Discount Tickets
36.10 Girls Pep Club Sale of Game Ribbons
39. Government and School Offices
39.1 General Office
39.2 Principal's Office
39.3 Vice Principal's Office
39.4 Guidance Office
39.5 Visual Aids Office
39.6 Point System Room
39.7 Dean of Girls Office
39.8 Dean of Boys and Adult Education Office
39.9 Consultation Room
39.10 Art Exhibit Room
39.11 Lost and Found Room
39.12 Check Room
39.13 Cafeteria Director's Office
39.14 Girls Gym Office
39.15 Boys Gym Office
39.16 Mathematics Office
39.17 English Office
39.18 Science Office
39.19 Home Economics Office
39.20 Social Studies Office
41. Hallways and Coatrooms
41.1 Hallways and Lockers
48. Initiations
48.1 Future Nurses Club Candlelight Initiation
48.2 Mathematics Club Initiation
48.3 C Club Initiation and Chili Supper
48.4 Quill and Scroll Initiation and Dinner at Kansas University
48.5 French Club Initiation
48.6 Science Club Officers Initiation at Spring Picnic
48.7 Future Homemakers Initiation
52. Libraries
52.1 Library
52.2 Cataloguing Room
52.3 Conference Room
54. Meetings, Executive
54.1 Student Council Meeting
54.2 Student Council Officers Meeting
54.3 Home Room Representative Council Meeting
54.4 Newspaper Staff Meeting
54.5 Annual Staff Meeting
54.6 Senior Class Officers Meeting

65. Outings
    65.1 Band Trip to Perform
    65.2 Band and Orchestra See "The Music Man"
    65.3 String Ensemble Appearance for Women's Club
    65.4 String Ensemble See "My Fair Lady"
    65.5 Music Students Attend "The King and I" at Kansas University
    65.6 Science Students to Science-Math Day at Kansas University
    65.7 Junior and Senior "B" Average Students to New York and Washington
    65.8 Seniors Attend a Movie
    65.9 Home Management Classes Visit Gas Service Company
    65.10 Art, Crafts, Painting, and Ceramics Students to Art Conference at Kansas University
    65.11 Annual and Newspaper Staffs to Journalism Conference
    65.12 Advanced Physical Education Class to Modern Dance Clinic
    65.13 Science Fair at Fair Grounds, Exhibits by Science Students
    65.14 Science Club Field Trip
    65.15 Library Club to Public Library
    65.16 Business Education Club to Convention
    65.17 Latin Convention at Kansas State Attended by Latin Students
    65.18 Future Homemakers of America District Convention at Booth
    65.19 Future Teachers and Future Homemakers Clubs Visit Exhibition Train
    65.20 Future Nurses Club Visits Veterans Hospital
    65.21 Thespians to "My Fair Lady"
    65.22 Open House at Governor's Mansion for Capital City Students
    65.23 Teacher 76 Home Room Members and Friends See A's Baseball Game
    65.24 American Field Service Club Picnic at Lake
    65.25 Junior Red Cross Party at Forbes
    65.26 Junior Red Cross Goes Caroling
    65.27 Junior Red Cross Picnic
    65.28 Future Nurses Club Goes Caroling
    65.29 Quill and Scroll Picnic
    65.30 Hi-Y Overnight
    65.31 Hi-Y Hayrack Ride
    65.32 Band and Orchestra Picnic at Lake
    65.33 Business Club Picnic Party at Lake
    65.34 Key Club Hayrack Ride
    65.35 C Club Hayrack Ride
    65.36 Math Club Picnic
68. Parties
    68.1 Youth for Christ Funspiration
    68.2 Swimming Club Party
    68.3 Boys Senior Council Party
    68.4 Girls Council Coke Party
    68.5 Annual Staff Party Given by Music Department Faculty
    68.6 Honor Pep Ridiculous Party

68.7 Senior Girls Council Reception for Senior Home Room Teachers
68.8 Reception after Senior Vespers
68.9 Reception after Commencement
68.10 Sophomore Party
68.11 Pre-Election Party
68.12 Band and Orchestra Party and Dance
68.13 Math Club Christmas Party
68.14 Future Teachers Tea for Visiting College Representatives
68.15 Government Class Election Party
69. Photographers
69.1 Individual Pictures Taken
69.2 Photographic Rooms
70. Plays, Concerts, and Programs
70.1 Election Rally
70.2 Election Assembly
70.3 Election Assembly Practice
70.4 Regular Assembly
70.5 Pep Assembly
70.6 Christmas Assembly
70.7 Sophomore Induction Assembly
70.8 Junior and Sophomore Spelling Assembly
70.9 State Music Festival
70.10 District Music Festival
70.11 Spring Band Concert
70.12 Orchestra Pop Concert
70.13 Madrigal Singers Program
70.14 Music Department Program for Masonic Family Night
70.15 Band Plays for United Funds Drive Kick-off Dinner
70.16 Annual Orchestra Concert
70.17 Vocal Concert at Kansas State Teachers Association Building
70.18 Ten School Orchestra Clinic at Capital City High School
70.19 Kansas State Choirs Program at Capital City High School
70.20 Debate Tournament, Experienced
70.21 Debate Tournament, Experienced at other school
70.22 Debate Tournament, Novice
70.23 Debate Tournament, Novice at other school
70.24 Dance Drama Company Program
70.25 Homecoming Assembly
70.26 Homecoming Rehearsal
70.27 Induction of Class and All School Officers
70.28 Induction Practice
70.29 Play Practice, "Tish"
70.30 Junior Sponsored Play, "Tish"
70.31 Play Practice, "Mousetrap"
70.32 Senior and Masque and Wig Sponsored WPA Play, "Mousetrap"
70.33 Play Practice, "Pygmalion"
70.34 Play, "Pygmalion"
70.35 Junior-Senior Program before the Prom

70.36 All School Christmas Program
70.37 Play Practice, Christmas Program
70.38 Operetta, "Carousel"
70.39 Operetta Practice
70.40 Fashion Show
70.41 Squid Show
70.42 Daisy Chain Rehearsal
70.43 Class Day Rehearsal
76. Recognition Programs
76.1 Commencement
76.2 Scholarship Assembly
76.3 Athletic Awards Assembly
76.4 Honor C Assembly
76.5 Class Day Ceremonies
77. Religious Services and Classes
77.1 Future Homemakers of America Church Day
77.2 Senior Vespers
77.3 Easter Services
80. Restaurants
80.1 School Cafeteria
80.2 Faculty Lunch Room
80.3 Kitchen
81. Restrooms
81.1 Ladies' Faculty Lounge
81.2 Men's Faculty Lounge
81.3 Girls' Restroom
81.4 Boys' Restroom
81.5 Girls' Shower Room
81.6 Boys' Shower Room
83. School, Coaches' Rooms
83.1 Coaches' Room
84. Custodians' Room
84.1 Custodians' Boiler Room and Lounge
85. School, Special Days
85.1 Student Registration for Elections
85.2 Education-Business Day
85.3 College Representative Day
85.4 Occupational Information Day
85.5 Examination Day
86. School, U. S. Savings Stamps Sales
86.1 Stamp Sales by Retail Selling Class
95. Volunteer Work and Fund Raising Projects
95.1 Junior Red Cross Pack Overseas Boxes
95.2 Junior Red Cross Wrap Gifts for State Hospital
95.3 Future Teachers Club Ushers for Teachers Convention
95.4 Future Homemakers of America Clothing Drive for Needy Children
95.5 Future Nurses Club Assist at Polio Clinic
95.6 Future Nurses Club Assist in Tuberculin Testing Program

Behavior Setting Report

Introduction

HELLO. I'm ———— from the University of Kansas; this is ————, also from the University. We are asking your help today in a second part of a study of various Kansas high schools. As you know, people are showing more and more interest in improving education in schools. One of the biggest problems is that ideas about schools are often just ideas; we need facts—research findings—to help decide which good things need strengthening, which things need changing.

We do hear people say, "Well, schools were a lot different when I went to school." Now, they might be right, but we really don't know this. The best way to know what a school is like is to study it as it exists now. We want to get information from people who are in school now—from students.

A large part of the questionnaire you will be working on today was carefully created by our staff, who made a survey of all the activities and places you might enter in this school, *this semester*. (*Sentence for Capital City only:* Maybe you'll be surprised how many things go on in this school.) What we have, then, is a kind of picture of activities across this school—and over the time extending from the first day of school, this September, until now. What we don't have is a picture of how students fit into this picture. We want you to help us put the students *in* the picture.

Your help to us has two parts. The first part is to tell us which of these activities you were a part of—at least once—*this* semester.

Let's look at the front page of the questionnaire. Notice where it says "Made-up Examples, Part I." Suppose a boy, Joe, were taking the questionnaire: Joe looks at the activity or place—goes across and circles *No* or *Yes* to indicate whether he was at a German Club meeting *this* semester. Joe ignores the number 56 in the parentheses; he also ignores, for the time being, the blank spaces under performances.

Some of these items are obvious and easy to answer. You may have some question about offices. For example, Joe said he had not attended the Scholarship Records Office. To attend or participate in an office means to go there on business of some kind. Of course, it's obvious that if you work in an office you would say Yes, but if you were a person seeking information or help, you also enter the office activity.

So all you have to do for most of this first part is simply ask yourself, Was I a part of this activity or of this setting? and circle Yes or No. (*Sentence for Capital City only:* Since we took everything that exists in the school, there will be a lot of No answers; this is to be expected.) Any questions?

If you do have any questions that come up as you work along, just raise your hand and one of us will come to help you. That's what we're here for—to help you make the information accurate. If it is accurate, then people who are trying to improve education will have real information to go by.

All right, work through the list, answering each item and the material after the list. What did you do *this semester*—from school opening in September until today? Start by filling in the top of the front page. We will tell you about the second part of the job later.

After most people have finished the list—not necessarily the material after the list—say:

We tried very hard to list all the activities that actually happened, but we may have overlooked some. If you added any to our list, will you tell us now, so that we can put them on the board for other students to add to their lists?

Would you mark where you are on the questionnaire and then turn back to the front page? You can finish shortly.

The second part of the job is to fill in the blanks in those cases where you circled Yes. We want you to tell us what you did in the activities and places you attended. We need a special kind of information written in. Let me tell you what we are going to do with it. We are going to try to decide whether you were a performer in the activity.

A performer is one who has a special job in a place or activity to keep it going. Sometimes we are performers; sometimes we are customers, members, watchers.

Let's look at Made-Up Examples, Part II. Here we have some of Joe's Yes answers. For the Baseball Game, Joe writes—"just watched." Joe was a fan. He was not a performer—performers at games between schools would be players, cheerleaders, officials, pep club members, refreshment sellers, etc. Look at Easter Assembly—Joe wrote "sang in choir." At the assembly the people on stage, the stagehands, the musicians would be performers—the audience would not be performers. Look at Checker Club. Joe wrote "recorded winners." Apparently the club had a contest and Joe helped run the contest—he was a performer then. Members of the club who just took part but had no special job would not be performers. And now the Hi-Y Poppy Sale—Joe wrote "bought poppy." He was a customer. Cashiers and salesmen at the sale would be performers.

We want you, then, as the last part of the questionnaire, to fill in the blanks by Yes answers with what you did there; tell us the kind of "what-I-did information" that will let us decide if you were performers. If, at a game, you played in the band, ate a hot dog, and watched the game, we want the playing-in-the-band part, because band members playing for an occasion are performers.

Be sure to ask us if any of this seems confusing—you don't have to decide if you were a performer or not—just give us the information so we can decide. All right, go on and finish.

MIDWEST HIGH SCHOOL

Name_____ Boy　Girl　(circle which)
　　　(last)　　(first)　　(middle)

Address_____

MADE-UP EXAMPLES, PART I

Performance Information

German Club regular meeting	(56)	(No) Yes	
Home Baseball Game	(3)	No (Yes)	
Booster Club candy sale	(25)	(No) Yes	
Scholarship Records Office	(39)	(No) Yes	
Easter Assembly	(70)	No (Yes)	
Tennis matches, another school	(1)	(No) Yes	
etc.			

MADE-UP EXAMPLES, PART II

Home Baseball Game	(3)	No (Yes)	*just watched*
Easter Assembly	(70)	No (Yes)	*sang in choir*
Checker Club	(68)	No (Yes)	*recorded winners*
Hi-Y Poppy Sale	(25)	No (Yes)	*bought poppy*
etc.			

Basketball

Home Basketball Game, Boys A and B Teams and Girls	(1)	No	Yes
Basketball Game, Boys A and B Teams and Girls at another school	(1)	No	Yes
Basketball Practice, Boys	(1)	No	Yes
Basketball Practice, Girls	(1)	No	Yes

Football

Home Football Game	(2)	No	Yes
Football Game at another school	(2)	No	Yes
Football Practice	(2)	No	Yes
Home Football Game, B Team	(2)	No	Yes

Cheerleader

Cheerleader Practice	(24)	No	Yes

Clubs

Harlequin Club meeting	(56)	No	Yes
Harlequin Club try-outs	(70)	No	Yes
Harlequin Club family night show and movie	(70)	No	Yes
Harlequin Club trip to "King and I"	(65)	No	Yes
Harlequin Club trip to "Music Man"	(65)	No	Yes
Thespian and Harlequin Club, Installation Program	(70)	No	Yes
Thespian Club meeting	(55)	No	Yes

Clubs (*Continued*)   Performance Information

Le Bon Ton Club meeting	(55) No	Yes	————
Teen-age Book Club secretaries meeting	(55) No	Yes	————
Girls Pep Club meeting	(55) No	Yes	————

Student Government

Student Council meeting	(54) No	Yes	————
Junior Class meeting	(55) No	Yes	————

School Offices

Principal's Office	(39) No	Yes	————
Ditto Room	(39) No	Yes	————
Custodian's Room	(84) No	Yes	————
Coach's Room	(83) No	Yes	————
Le Bon Ton Club Room	(81) No	Yes	————

Library

Library and Study Hall	(20) No	Yes	————

Plays

Junior Class Play	(70) No	Yes	————
Junior Class Play Practice	(70) No	Yes	————

Journalism

Cub Reporter and Yearbook Staff to K.U.	(65) No	Yes	————
Cub Reporter Poll on national election	(26) No	Yes	————
Cub Reporter Poll on school attitudes	(26) No	Yes	————

Dances and Parties

Homecoming Dance	(15) No	Yes	————
Dance following football game	(15) No	Yes	————

All School Events to Make Money

Students Magazine Subscription Sale	(36) No	Yes	————
Seniors sell sweatshirts	(36) No	Yes	————
Pep Club Food Sale	(35) No	Yes	————
Parent-Teacher Book Exchange	(8) No	Yes	————
P.T.A.-sponsored Carnival and Chili Supper	(28) No	Yes	————
Senior Car Wash	(95) No	Yes	————
Senior Class Candy Sale at School	(35) No	Yes	————

Assemblies			Performance Information
High School Opening			
Assembly	(70) No	Yes	————————
High School Assembly	(70) No	Yes	————————
All School Lyceum			
(Pay Assemblies)	(70) No	Yes	————————
Special Assembly Programs			————————
(Veterans Day,			
Thanksgiving)	(70) No	Yes	
Pep Club Rally	(70) No	Yes	————————
Eating Places			
School Lunch Room and			
Kitchen	(80) No	Yes	————————
Miscellaneous			
Student Panel at P.T.A.	(70) No	Yes	————————
Career Day at Winchester	(65) No	Yes	————————
Le Bon Ton Clothing Drive	(36) No	Yes	————————

We might have overlooked some school activities. If you took part in some school occasions not on this list, would you write them in?

Activity	Performance Information
————————————	————————————

(use back of page if necessary)

(*The following settings were added. They were each put on the blackboard and announced to the group, with the request that any student who had attended add the name to his list.*)

Band Marches in Halloween Parade	(28)	————————
Harlequin Club Officers meeting	(54)	————————
Home Ec. Class Serves Principals Dinner	(17)	————————
Le Bon Ton Dinner	(17)	————————
Science and Math Day at K.U.	(65)	————————

Students sometimes take part in groups and organizations outside of school. Let's take church as one possibility. Students could attend Sunday school, church, mass, synagogue, young people's group meetings, etc. They might be performers in some of these: sing in church choir, teach Sunday school, lead young people's worship service, etc. If you took part in any church-related activities *this semester*, would you write them in below? If you performed in any, please write in the performance.

Church Activity	Performance Information
————————————	————————————
————————————	————————————
————————————	————————————
————————————	————————————

(Use back of this sheet for additional church activities)

Students might also take part in other organizations. Examples would be Scout meeting, bowling team contests, 4-H meetings, music group meetings, Rainbow Girls party, etc. Students might be performers in some of these: serve as assistant scoutmaster, handle refreshments at club party, etc. Would you write in any of these affairs you have attended and put in any performances?

Organization Activities	Performance Information
_____	_____
_____	_____
_____	_____
_____	

(Use back of this page for any additions)

WORK

Have you worked for pay *this semester?* (circle which)   No   Yes
What kind of work did you do? _____
If you worked for a company or organization, please name it:
_____

Did you work for pay *last summer?*   No   Yes
What kind of work did you do? _____
If you worked for a company or organization, please name it:
_____

Would you fill in your present schedule?

Subject	Teacher
1st Period _____	_____
2nd Period _____	_____
3rd Period _____	_____
4th Period _____	_____
5th Period _____	_____
6th Period _____	_____
7th Period _____	_____
8th Period _____	_____
(if any)	

The format, instructions, and questions regarding out-of-school activity and school schedule were identical in all schools. In order to save space, we present the behavior setting list for the Capital City High School Settings Report spaced more closely than it was given the students. The B was not marked in the questionnaire. It indicates bloopers, fictitious but likely-sounding settings, which served to give an indication of the accuracy of the responses as a whole.

CAPITAL CITY HIGH SCHOOL
SETTINGS LISTED ON SCHOOL SETTING REPORT

		Performance Information
Basketball		
Home Basketball Game, A and B Teams	(1) No Yes	_____
Basketball Game, A and B Teams at another school	(1) No Yes	_____
Basketball Practice, A and B Teams	(1) No Yes	_____
Basketball Practice, Sophomore	(1) No Yes	_____
B Sophomore-Junior Basketball Game	(1) No Yes	_____
Wrestling		
Home Wrestling Match, A Team	(1) No Yes	_____
Wrestling Match, A Team at another school	(1) No Yes	_____
Wrestling Team Practice	(1) No Yes	_____
Swimming		
Home Swimming Meet	(24A) No Yes	_____
Swimming Meet at another school	(24A) No Yes	_____
Swimming Team Practice	(24A) No Yes	_____
Swimming Club—Boys	(24A) No Yes	_____
Swimming Team Party	(68) No Yes	_____
Tadpole Club (Girls)	(24A) No Yes	_____
Squid Club (Girls)	(24A) No Yes	_____
Football		
Home Football Game, A (Varsity) Team	(2) No Yes	_____
Football Game, A Team at another school	(2) No Yes	_____
Home Football Game, B Team	(2) No Yes	_____
Football Game, B Team at another school	(2) No Yes	_____
Football Practice, A and B Teams	(2) No Yes	_____
Home Football Game, Sophomore	(2) No Yes	_____
Football Game, Sophomore at another school	(2) No Yes	_____
Football Practice, Sophomore	(2) No Yes	_____
B Sophomore-Junior Touch Football Game	(2) No Yes	_____
Football Banquet	(17) No Yes	_____
Cross Country Racing		
Cross Country Race	(2) No Yes	_____
Cross Country Race at another school	(2) No Yes	_____
Cross Country Practice	(2) No Yes	_____
Girls Intramural Sports		
Basketball, Girls Intramural	(1) No Yes	_____
Volleyball, Girls Intramural	(1) No Yes	_____
Deck Tennis, Girls Intramural	(1) No Yes	_____
Badminton, Girls Intramural	(1) No Yes	_____
Trampoline Activities, Girls	(1) No Yes	_____

			Performance
Cheerleaders			Information
Cheerleader Tryouts	(70)	No Yes	———————
Cheerleader Meetings	(24)	No Yes	———————
Clubs			
American Field Service Regular Meeting	(56)	No Yes	———————
Business Education Club Regular Meeting	(56)	No Yes	———————
Business Education Convention in Emporia	(65)	No Yes	———————
Chess Club Regular Meeting	(57)	No Yes	———————
Coin Club Regular Meeting	(56)	No Yes	———————
B Electronics Club Regular Meeting	(57)	No Yes	———————
Future Business Leaders Regular Meeting	(56)	No Yes	———————
Forensic League Regular Meeting	(56)	No Yes	———————
French Club Regular Meeting	(56)	No Yes	———————
Future Homemakers Regular Meeting	(22)	No Yes	———————
Future Homemakers Cabinet Meeting	(54)	No Yes	———————
Future Nurses Club Regular Meeting	(56)	No Yes	———————
Future Nurses Officers and Committee Chairmen Meeting	(54)	No Yes	———————
Future Nurses Club Visits Veterans Hospital	(65)	No Yes	———————
Future Nurses Club Helps with Health Booth at Fair	(65)	No Yes	———————
Future Nurses Club Visits K.N.I.	(65)	No Yes	———————
Future Teachers Club Meeting	(56)	No Yes	———————
Future Teachers Club Tea for Visiting College Representatives (K.U., K. St., Washburn)	(68)	No Yes	———————
Future Teachers Usher at K.S.T.A. Meeting	(95)	No Yes	———————
Future Teachers Officers Meeting	(54)	No Yes	———————
Hi-Y Regular Meeting	(56)	No Yes	———————
Hi-Y Overnight Trip	(65)	No Yes	———————
Key Club Regular Meeting	(56)	No Yes	———————
Key Club Hayrack Ride	(65)	No Yes	———————
Latin Club Regular Meeting	(56)	No Yes	———————
Library Club Regular Meeting	(56)	No Yes	———————
Library Club to City Library	(65)	No Yes	———————
Masque and Wig Regular Meeting	(56)	No Yes	———————
Mathematics Club Regular Meeting	(56)	No Yes	———————
Mathematics Club Hayrack Ride	(65)	No Yes	———————
Mathematics Club Officers Meeting	(54)	No Yes	———————
Modern Dance Club Regular Meeting	(56)	No Yes	———————
Pep Club Regular Meeting, Boys	(55)	No Yes	———————
Pep Club Regular Meeting, Girls	(55)	No Yes	———————
Honor Pep Club Regular Meeting	(55)	No Yes	———————
B Photography Club Regular Meeting	(56)	No Yes	———————
Radio, Ham Regular Meeting	(25)	No Yes	———————
Junior Red Cross Regular Meeting	(56)	No Yes	———————
Junior Red Cross Council Meeting	(54)	No Yes	———————

Performance
Information

Junior Red Cross Goes Caroling	(65) No Yes	_____
Junior Red Cross Packs Overseas Boxes	(95) No Yes	_____
Junior Red Cross Wraps Gifts for State Hospital	(95) No Yes	_____
Junior Red Cross Helps at Regional Red Cross Meeting	(95) No Yes	_____
Safety Club Regular Meeting	(56) No Yes	_____
Science Club Regular Meeting	(56) No Yes	_____
Science Students to Science-Math Day at K.U.	(65) No Yes	_____
Science Club Field Trip	(65) No Yes	_____
Spanish Club Regular Meeting	(56) No Yes	_____
C Club Regular Meeting	(57) No Yes	_____
C Club Concessions at Junior High Play Day	(36) No Yes	_____
C Club Hayrack Ride	(65) No Yes	_____
Thespian Club Regular Meeting	(56) No Yes	_____
Youth for Christ Regular Meeting	(56) No Yes	_____
Youth for Christ Funspiration Party	(68) No Yes	_____

Student Government Group Meetings

Student Council Meeting	(54) No Yes	_____
Home Room Representative Council	(54) No Yes	_____
Student Congress Meeting	(54) No Yes	_____
Student Council Officers Meeting	(54) No Yes	_____
Junior Home Room Representative Council Meeting	(54) No Yes	_____
Junior Class Officers Meeting	(54) No Yes	_____
Officers Training Meeting	(55) No Yes	_____

Debates

Debate Clinic (September 23)	(20) No Yes	_____
Debate Tournament, experienced	(70) No Yes	_____
Debate Tournament, experienced, at another school	(70) No Yes	_____
Debate Tournament, novice	(70) No Yes	_____
Debate Tournament, novice, at another school	(70) No Yes	_____
B Photography Club Regular Meeting	(56) No Yes	_____

School Offices

General Office	(39) No Yes	_____
Principal's Office	(39) No Yes	_____
Vice-Principal's Office	(39) No Yes	_____
Dean of Girls Office	(39) No Yes	_____
Dean of Boys and Adult Education Office	(39) No Yes	_____
Guidance Office	(39) No Yes	_____
Visual Aids Office	(39) No Yes	_____

Performance
Information

Point System Room	(39)	No Yes _____
Book Rental and Exchange Room	(8)	No Yes _____
School Nurses Office	(18)	No Yes _____
Vision Testing Program	(18)	No Yes _____
Library	(52)	No Yes _____
Cataloguing Room	(52)	No Yes _____
Art Exhibit Room	(39)	No Yes _____
Lost and Found Room	(39)	No Yes _____
Check Room	(39)	No Yes _____
Cafeteria Director's Office	(39)	No Yes _____
Girls Gym Office	(39)	No Yes _____
Boys Gym Office	(39)	No Yes _____
Mathematics Office	(39)	No Yes _____
English Office	(39)	No Yes _____
Science Office	(39)	No Yes _____
Home Economics Office	(39)	No Yes _____
Social Studies Office	(39)	No Yes _____
Biology Office	(39)	No Yes _____
Coaches' Room	(83)	No Yes _____

School Election Activities

Registration for Election	(26)	No Yes _____
Qualification Committee Meeting	(54)	No Yes _____
Election Commission Meeting	(54)	No Yes _____
Election Rally	(70)	No Yes _____
All School Election	(26)	No Yes _____
Annual Election Party	(68)	No Yes _____
Induction Assembly Practice	(70)	No Yes _____
Induction Assembly	(70)	No Yes _____

School Dances and Parties

Varsity Dances after Games	(15)	No Yes _____
Girls Coke Party Given by Honor Pep Club	(68)	No Yes _____
B Girls Fashion Show and Tea	(68)	No Yes _____
WPA Halloween Party and Dance	(15)	No Yes _____
Veranda After-School Dance	(15)	No Yes _____

School Events to Raise Money

Quill and Scroll Sale of Book Protectors	(36)	No Yes _____
Library Club Book Sale	(52)	No Yes _____
Junior Red Cross Chrysanthemum Sale	(36)	No Yes _____
Girls Pep Club Sells Game Ribbons, Sweatshirts, Basketball Pins	(36)	No Yes _____
Junior Class Sells Christmas Cards	(36)	No Yes _____
Future Nurses Cookie Sale	(36)	No Yes _____
Student Council Collects Money, Clothing, and Food for Thanksgiving Boxes	(36)	No Yes _____

		Performance Information
Assemblies		
Pep Rallies	(70) No Yes	_____
Regular Assembly	(70) No Yes	_____
Homecoming Assembly Tryouts	(70) No Yes	_____
Homecoming Assembly Rehearsal	(70) No Yes	_____
Homecoming Assembly	(70) No Yes	_____
Thanksgiving Assembly	(70) No Yes	_____
Christmas Assembly Tryouts	(70) No Yes	_____
Christmas Assembly Rehearsal	(70) No Yes	_____
Plays		
"Your Show" Tryouts	(70) No Yes	_____
"Your Show" Rehearsal	(70) No Yes	_____
"Your Show" Performance	(70) No Yes	_____
"Blithe Spirit" Tryouts	(70) No Yes	_____
"Blithe Spirit" Rehearsal	(70) No Yes	_____
"Blithe Spirit" Performance	(70) No Yes	_____
"South Pacific" Tryouts	(70) No Yes	_____
Music Programs and Activities		
Orchestra Pop Concert	(70) No Yes	_____
All City Orchestra Clinic	(23) No Yes	_____
Orchestra Plays at Capper Junior High	(65) No Yes	_____
Orchestra Plays at Safety Conference	(65) No Yes	_____
Band Business Meeting	(55) No Yes	_____
B Band and Choir Evening Concert	(70) No Yes	_____
Madrigal Singers Perform for Outside Groups	(65) No Yes	_____
Choir Sings at Benefit (Cerf spoke)	(65) No Yes	_____
Journalism and Photography		
Newspaper (World) Staff Meeting	(54) No Yes	_____
Yearbook (Sunflower) Staff Meeting	(54) No Yes	_____
World Staff Conducts Presidential Poll	(26) No Yes	_____
Students to Journalism Conference at Manhattan	(65) No Yes	_____
Individual Pictures Taken	(69) No Yes	_____
Photographic Rooms for School Publications	(69) No Yes	_____
Eating Places		
School Cafeteria	(80) No Yes	_____
Faculty Lunch Room	(80) No Yes	_____
Cafeteria Kitchen	(80) No Yes	_____
Miscellaneous		
B Boys Science and Hobby Show	(70) No Yes	_____
Open House and Dinner for Parents	(17) No Yes	_____
B Victory Carnival	(28) No Yes	_____

Group to See Bellamy Award Representatives
Off to Maine	(65) No Yes _____
Home Room Activity Card Sale	(36) No Yes _____
Smoking Room	(57) No Yes _____
Homecoming Parade	(28) No Yes _____

We might have overlooked some school activities. If you took part in some school occasions not on this list, would you write them in? (*The following settings were added. They were each put on the blackboard and announced to the group, with the request that any student who had attended add the name to his list.*)

Advisory Committee for West High	(54) No Yes _____
All School Party Tryouts	(70) No Yes _____
All School Party Rehearsal	(70) No Yes _____
French Club Christmas Party	(68) No Yes _____
Future Teachers Cookie and Apple Sale	(36) No Yes _____
Y-Teens Meeting	(56) No Yes _____
Library Club Christmas Party	(68) No Yes _____
Boys Glee Club away	(70) No Yes _____
Clarinet Choir away	(70) No Yes _____
Modern Dance away	(70) No Yes _____
Girls Glee Club away	(70) No Yes _____

Appendix 7.1

Instructions for Remembering Last Semester

YOU probably remember that last December you helped us out by filling out a questionnaire about school activities. These questionnaires have all been studied by our group, and we are back today to ask your help in the next important step. Those questionnaires, in a way, were records of students' lives over about a three-month period. It reminds one of the "This Is Your Life" idea on TV. The questionnaires tell what activities you were in and a little of what you did then. The question now is: What did participation in these things mean to you?

We are asking your help in gaining some understanding about what school activities and classes do to or do for students. This is the way we'll handle it: I am going to return your questionnaire. You look it over; try to recall how it was last fall in these activities. Which were the best in terms of what you got out of them? Which were not-so-good?

A second questionnaire will be given out, which you can use to tell what the activities meant to you. You will notice that the second questionnaire has four sheets: one page for "plus," or good activities or settings; one for "minus," or not-so-good activities; one for "plus" classes; and one for "minus" classes.

Let me pass these out now and give you a chance to look them over and get accustomed to thinking about them. Don't start to write yet—just get used to it; I'd like to say something else before you actually start.

(*Pass out sheets; leave about three minutes for perusal of material.*)

The care and thought you invest in answering the part called "explanation" will make a big difference. We are doing the same thing in other schools in a real effort to find out what activities mean to students. We already know from the first questionnaire where you were. The next question is: What did you get out of it? What specifically was good about the plus settings? What specifically was bad about the minus ones? I hope you will be able to say more than "I liked it" or "I didn't like it"—this is some help, but not much!

(*Give following slowly and with clarity.*)

When trying to explain what's good about an activity, there are two ways of thinking that can help. You know that we all have desires, needs, wants. We can think of which of our desires or needs gets satisfied in the activity and explain it that way. The other way to look at an activity or setting is to think about the setting itself; it has a number of parts or aspects. Try to recall which part in particular was good, satisfying, worth while, and write about that. Using these two helps, you should be able to explain in a way so we can understand what the activity or setting meant to you.

In somewhat the same way you can explain about the minus settings or classes. Think of which things you didn't like, which ones were bothersome, and what parts of the setting were not enjoyable or worth while.

You should all feel free to write exactly what you think. We will keep these answers confidential, and when our study on schools is written up, there will be no names used. This material is for our use, and only general information is given to schools.

You notice that we have room for three activities or classes per page. Three is just our guess at how many might be chosen. In other schools, students have chosen as many as six, as few as one. You don't have to do three. Take as many as were real good, and as many as were not so good; this might be two, or three, or six, or whatever. Don't feel you have to stop at three, just because there are three numbered spaces. It is possible to have more for one section than for another.

There have been students for whom a setting was particularly good in some ways and particularly poor in others.   •

This problem can be handled by putting the setting on the plus page and giving the good points, and then putting it on the minus page and giving the bad points. You can do this *if* there is a setting that was definitely *both* plus and minus.

Do you have any questions? (*Answer questions.*)

Okay. Look over your first questionnaire. Pick the best settings for last semester and write about them.

If a question comes up, just raise your hand and I'll talk to you personally—that way we'll not disturb the others.

We appreciate your help very much.

REMEMBERING LAST SEMESTER

NAME————————————————————————

NAMES OF SETTINGS	EXPLANATION
Settings which were especially good, satisfying, worth while—"plus."	What I did, or what went on, that made settings good—"plus." What I enjoyed or got out of the setting.
1. ———————————	1.
2. ———————————	2.
3. ———————————	3.
(Other good settings could be listed on the back)	(Other explanations could be put on back)

Note: The three following pages were identical except that page 2 asked for minus settings and pages 3 and 4 asked for plus and minus classes, respectively.

Appendix 8.1

Variables Used in the Identification of Regular and Marginal Students with Comparative Weights Shown

FORTY subjects (10 per cell) were chosen for the investigation. Procedures and conventions followed in the selection of subjects are discussed below.

From a review of the literature on the identification and prediction of high school dropouts, and drawing especially on a study by Thomas (1954), a cluster of five variables was chosen which appear to be predictive of a tendency to drop out of high school. These variables were used as an operational definition of regular and marginal inhabitants for this study. The variables and the points at which each was divided are discussed below. The ends of the distributions that divided regular and marginal inhabitants were weighted 1 and 2, respectively, in each case.

1. IQ. (The six-point IQ difference between the subject groups was introduced to avoid too great similarity on this variable.)

    105 and higher 1
    99 and lower 2

2. Academic performance during semester of measurement. (Here again the distribution of students was trichotomized and the two extreme groups chosen.)

    No grade lower than C 1
    Two grades of D and lower 2

3. Occupation of father (using a scheme based on the Minnesota Occupational Rating Scale).

    Professional and managerial 1
    Nonprofessional and nonmanagerial 2

4. Father's education.

    Father finished grade 10 1
    Father did not finish grade 10 2

5. Mother's education.

    Mother finished grade 12 1
    Mother did not finish grade 12 2

In the review of the literature on dropouts, it was found that a slight differential in parental education correlated with dropping out and staying in school, i.e., a slightly lower finishing level for fathers than for mothers. This differential was included in items 4 and 5 of the identifying variables.

The minimal weighted score summed across the five variables was 5, and the maximal was 10. To identify pools of regular and marginal subjects, the following conventions were followed: (1) subjects with summed values of 6 and below, and without a value of 2 on either IQ or academic performance, were defined as *regular inhabitants*; and (2) subjects with summed values of 8 and above, and without a value of 1 on IQ, were defined as *marginal inhabitants*, i.e., those inhabitants who manifested traits and histories that made them relatively unsuited for the school milieu.

Identifying data on the five variables were gathered for all 91 Juniors in the small schools, and for a sample of 144 Juniors from the large school, stratified on IQ (see Chapter 6). Values of 1 or 2 were assigned to the data on each variable for each subject, and five-variable summed scores were obtained. In this way pools of regular and marginal inhabitants in schools of low and high P/D ratio were identified. The pools of subjects for each cell were collected, sexes were separated, serial numbers were assigned to the subjects, and sampling without replacement of five males and five females per cell was carried out.

Examples of Units from the Open-Ended Data
Coded as Own and Foreign Forces

Own Forces	Foreign Forces
I like to dance.	Pep Club members were required to go.
It was a chance for me to do something new.	Everyone was supposed to be there.
I wanted to win a prize.	My Latin teacher talked me into it.
I wanted to meet new people.	I had to; they needed girls in the cast.
It's interesting and exciting to go on these rallies.	Band members were required to go.
It sounded like an interesting play.	I was in the Pep Club, so I had to.
I like to *do* things.	I had to march in the band.
I like to act; I like to get in front of people and show them what I can do.	Everyone else was going.
	It was really part of English class activity, so I had to take part.
Dramatics is good for students; you learn confidence and security.	My family urged me to take part.
It was something new for me.	I was asked to sell magazines.
I like to be someone special and show off.	There are only five boys in the class; they had to have me in the play.
I like to play basketball.	I had to bring my sister.
I wanted to gain experience.	I was assigned to work there.
I like to dance with girls.	The home-room teacher asked us to go.

APPENDIX 8.3

Card-Sort Items for the Five Actual Settings

1. I thought I might learn something there.
2. It was a chance for me to do or see something new and different.
3. It gave me a chance to be with the other kids.
4. I liked that specific activity.
5. It gave me a chance to be someone special.
6. I like to be active and do things.
7. In general I like this activity; *by going* I could help to see to it that it would be there for me to enjoy again.
8. In general I like this activity; *by doing something there* I could see to it that it would be there for me to enjoy again.
9. Others wanted me to go.
10. I was expected to go.
11. Everybody else was going, so I wanted to go too.
12. I saw that everyone else was going, and it's not fun to be left out.
13. I was told to go.
14. This activity is required for students like me.
15. I knew this activity needed people.
16. I knew this activity needed to have certain things done.

The card-sort items for the hypothetical setting were identical to the above except that they were put in the future tense where appropriate, e.g.: It will be a chance for me to do or see something new and different.

Setting Variety Number and Name in Midwest County and University City

Variety No.	Variety Name	No. in Midwest County	No. in University City	No. in University City Sample
3	Attorneys and Real Estate Offices	9	91	14
5	Auctions, Livestock	1	1	1
6	Banks	4	20	2
7	Barbers and Beauticians	10	25	5
9	Builders, Repairers, and Suppliers	31	77	16
10	Bus Stops (Station)	1	2	1
11	Cemeteries	5	2	2
13	Courts	4	6	2
15	Dances and Schools of Dancing	1	2	1
18	Doctors' Offices and Clinics	8	78	12
19	Drug and Department Stores	15	50	10
27	Factories	2	10	1
31	Fire Stations	2	2	1
34	Food and Feed Distributors	25	67	14
37	Funeral Homes	3	5	2
39	Government, School, and Business Offices	25	76	13
40	Greenhouses	1	5	1
42	Hardware and Home Furnishers	8	56	8
43	Hatcheries	1	2	1
45	Hospitals	1	3	2
46	Hotels, Rooming Houses, and Nursing Homes	9	18	5
51	Laundries and Cleaners	3	20	4
52	Libraries	2	1	1
59	Motor Vehicle Sales and Service	39	108	20
60	Movies	1	4	1
63	Newspapers and Printers	3	5	2
69	Photographers	1	7	1
71	Police Stations and Jails	1	3	1
72	Post Offices	4	2	2
74	Railroad Freight Stations	1	2	1
80	Restaurants and Taverns	15	65	11

Appendix 10.1 *(Continued)*

Variety No.	Variety Name	No. in Midwest County	No. in University City	No. in University City Sample
87	Shoe Shops, Repair and Sale	3	9	2
89	Storage Buildings	2	2	1
90	Telephone and Electric Offices	5	2	2
93	Truck Lines, Heavy	11	21	5
94	Veterinarians	1	7	1
96	Watch Repair and Jewelry Shops	3	11	2
98	Water Plants	1	1	1
	UNIQUE TO UNIVERSITY CITY			
8	Book Exchanges (Bookstores)		3	1
75	Railway Maintenance Departments ...		2	1
77	Refuse Clean-up, City Routes		1	1
101	Coal Yards		1	1
109	Sewage Disposal Plants		1	1
110	Taxis		2	1
113	Trailer Parks		6	1
136	Florist and Gift Shops		11	2
150	Advertising Agencies		1	1
151	Architects and Engineers		9	2
152	Bicycles, Sales and Service		1	1
153	Bowling Alleys		2	1
154	Dairy Products Distributors		6	1
155	Music and Musical Instruments, Sales and Service		9	2
156	Office Supplies and Repair		7	1
157	Railroad Passenger Stations		2	1
158	Railway Express Offices		1	1
159	Telegraph Offices		1	1
160	Trailer Rentals		2	1
161	Tree Surgeons		2	1
	UNIQUE TO MIDWEST COUNTY			
14	Dairy Barns	1		
47	Ice Companies	1		
50	Kennels	1		
53	Meat Packing Companies	1		
88	Slaughterhouses	1		
	Total	267	938	195

Behavior Setting Varieties Showing Number of Settings in Each of Four Midwest County Communities, 1958–59

Variety No.	Variety Name	Malden	Midwest	Vernon	Walker	Total
1	Athletic Contests, Indoors....	12	14	14	16	56
2	Athletic Contests, Outdoors ..	17	16	18	19	70
3	Attorneys and Real Estate Offices	0	6	2	1	9
4	Auction and Jumble Sales	1	2	2	6	11
5	Auctions, Livestock	0	0	1	0	1
6	Banks	1	1	2	0	4
7	Barbers and Beauticians	2	2	4	2	10
8	Book Exchange and Rentals ..	1	1	1	0	3
9	Builders, Repairers, and Suppliers	6	13	8	4	31
10	Bus Stops (Station)	0	1	0	0	1
11	Cemeteries	1	1	2	1	5
12	Classrooms, Freetime and Home Rooms	8	9	16	8	41
13	Courts	0	6	0	0	6
14	Dairy Barns	0	1	0	0	1
15	Dances	5	8	7	2	22
16	Dead Stock Removers	0	0	1	0	1
17	Dinners and Banquets	13	37	29	17	96
18	Doctors' Offices and Clinics ..	2	3	4	5	14
19	Drug and Department Stores	2	7	9	1	19
20	Educational Groups, Academic	16	48	36	17	117
21	Educational Groups, Driver Education	`1	1	1	0	3
22	Educational Groups, Home Economics	1	6	4	3	14
23	Educational Groups, Music Classes	17	15	9	12	53
24	Educational Groups, Physical Education	1	10	2	2	15
25	Educational Groups, Shop and Agriculture	1	2	4	4	11

Appendix 11.1 *(Continued)*

Variety No.	Variety Name	Malden	Midwest	Vernon	Walker	Total
26	Elections	1	3	3	2	9
27	Factories	0	1	1	0	2
28	Fairs, Circuses, and Carnivals	4	5	9	3	21
29	Fire and Tornado Drills	2	2	4	2	10
30	Fires	0	1	3	0	4
31	Fire Stations	1	1	0*	0*	2
32	Fireworks Sales	0	1	0	0	1
33	Fish Distributing Program, Dept. of Agric.	0	1	0	0	1
34	Food and Feed Distributors ..	5	12	7	3	27
35	Food Sales (for money raising)	3	8	6	5	22
36	Fund and Membership Drives	6	14	7	7	34
37	Funeral Homes	1	1	1	0	3
38	Funeral Services	3	3	6	3	15
39	Government, School, and Business Offices	3	21	2	2	28
40	Greenhouses	0	0	1	0	1
41	Hallways and Coatrooms	2	4	3	2	11
42	Hardware, Home Furnishers .	1	3	3	1	8
43	Hatcheries	0	0	1	0	1
44	Home Handicrafts	0	0	0	1	1
45	Hospitals	0	0	0	7	7
46	Hotels, Rooming Houses, and Nursing Homes	1	4	3	2	10
47	Ice Companies	1	0	0	0	1
48	Initiations	1	2	2	1	6
49	Insurance Agents	3	4	1	1	9
50	Kennels	0	1	0	0	1
51	Laundries and Cleaners	3	9	3	1	16
52	Libraries	1	3	2	1	7
53	Meat Packing Companies	0	0	1	0	1
54	Meetings, Executive	18	51	27	16	112
55	Meetings, Organization Business	11	33	24	19	87
56	Meetings, Social Cultural	21	30	34	11	96
57	Meetings, Social Recreational	3	9	7	4	23
58	Meter Readers	2	3	2	1	8
59	Motor Vehicle Sales and Service	8	11	16	4	39
60	Movies	1	1	5	5	12
61	Music Classes, Individual	1	6	5	1	13

* Occurred as part of another setting.

Appendix 11.1 *(Continued)*

Variety No.	Variety Name	Malden	Midwest	Vernon	Walker	Total
62	National Guard	0	0	1	0	1
63	Newspapers and Printers	0	1	1	1	3
64	Open Spaces	3	8	4	4	19
65	Outings	7	30	14	10	61
66	Paper Routes	4	3	3	4	14
67	Parent-Teacher Conferences. .	0	2	0	0	2
68	Parties	22	22	26	19	89
69	Photographers	0	0	0	1	1
70	Plays, Concerts, and Programs	12	29	24	22	87
71	Police Stations and Jails	0	1	0	0	1
72	Post Offices	1	1	1	1	4
74	Railroad Freight Stations	0	0	1	0	1
76	Recognition Programs	8	10	7	4	29
77	Refuse Clean-up, City	2	2	1	1	6
78	Religious Services and Classes	47	66	123	56	292
79	Reporters	1	0*	0*	0*	1
80	Restaurants and Taverns	3	12	10	2	27
81	Restrooms	6	18	24	11	59
82	Retreats	0	1	0	0	1
83	School, Coaches' Rooms	1	1	1	1	4
84	School, Janitors' Rooms	1	1	2	2	6
85	School, Special Days	2	3	2	2	9
86	School, U.S. Savings Stamps Sale	0	2	0	0	2
87	Shoe Shops, Repair and Sale .	1	1	1	0	3
88	Slaughterhouses	0	0	1	0	1
89	Storage Buildings	0	1	1	0	2
90	Telephone and Electric Offices	1	2	1	1	5
91	Telephone Booths	0*	1	0*	0*	1
92	Trafficways	1	1	1	1	4
93	Truck Lines, Heavy	3	2	4	2	11
94	Veterinarians	0	1	1	0	2
95	Volunteer Work and Fund Raising Projects	2	13	4	6	25
96	Watch Repair and Jewelry Shops	1	1	1	0	3
98	Water Plants	0	1	0	0	1
99	Weddings	1	3	5	0	9
	Total number of settings. .	345	698	630	376	2,049
	Total number of varieties.	67	83	78	62	96

* Occurred as part of another setting.

References

Acton Society Trust. 1953. *Size and morale*. London.

Allport, F. H. 1955. *Theories of perception and the concept of structure*. New York: Wiley.

Anderson, K. E., G. E. Ladd, and H. A. Smith. 1954. A study of 2500 Kansas high school graduates. *Kansas Studies in Education*, Univ. of Kansas, **4**.

Asch, S. E. 1952. *Social psychology*. New York: Prentice-Hall.

Bales, R. F. 1952. Some uniformities of behavior in small social systems. In G. Swanson, T. Newcomb, and E. Hartley, eds., *Readings in social psychology*. New York: Holt, pp. 146–59.

———. 1953. The equilibrium problem in small groups. In T. Parsons, R. Bales, and E. Shils, eds., *Working papers in the theory of action*. Glencoe, Ill.: Free Press, pp. 111–61.

Bales, R. F., and E. F. Borgatta. 1955. Size of group as a factor in the interaction profile. In A. Hare, E. Borgatta, and R. Bales, eds., *Small groups: studies in social interaction*. New York: Knopf, pp. 396–413.

Barker, R. G. 1960. Ecology and motivation. In M. Jones, ed., *Nebraska symposium on motivation*. Lincoln: Univ. of Nebraska Press, pp. 1–49.

———. 1963. *The stream of behavior*. New York: Appleton-Century-Crofts.

Barker, R. G., and Louise S. Barker. 1961a. Behavior units for the comparative study of culture. In B. Kaplan, ed., *Studying personality cross-culturally*. Evanston, Ill.: Row, Peterson, pp. 457–76.

———. 1961b. The psychological ecology of old people in Midwest, Kansas, and Yoredale, Yorkshire. *J. Geront.*, **16**, 144–49.

Barker, R. G., and H. F. Wright. 1955. *Midwest and its children*. Evanston, Ill.: Row, Peterson.

Barker, R. G., H. F. Wright, Louise S. Barker, and Maxine F. Schoggen. 1961. *Specimen records of American and English children*. Lawrence: Univ. of Kansas Press.

Bass, B. M., and Fay-Tyler M. Norton. 1951. Group size and leaderless discussion. *J. appl. Psychol.*, **35**, 397–400.

Baumgartel, H., and R. Sobol. 1959. Background and organizational factors in absenteeism. *Personnel Psychol.*, **12**, 431–43.

Campbell, H. 1952. Group incentive pay schemes. *Occup. Psychol.*, **26**, 15–21. Cited by Hewitt and Parfit (1953).

Cleland, S. 1955. *Influence of plant size on industrial relations*. Princeton: Princeton Univ. Press.

Coleman, J. S. 1961. *The adolescent society*. Glencoe, Ill.: Free Press.

Dawe, Helen C. 1934. The influence of size of kindergarten group upon performance. *Child Devel.,* **5,** 295–303.

Dictionary of occupational titles. 1949. I, *Definitions of titles.* 2d ed. Washington: U.S. Government Printing Office.

Feldt, L. S. 1960. Relationship between pupil achievement and high school size. Research report from College of Education, State Univ. of Iowa, Iowa City.

Fisher, P. H. 1953. An analysis of the primary group. *Sociometry,* **16,** 272–76.

Gaston, G. I., and K. E. Anderson. 1954. The effect of size of high school on achievement of the number-one students. Univ. of Kansas, *Bull. of Education,* **9,** 16–19.

Haire, M. 1955. Size, shape and function in industrial organizations. *Human Organizations,* **14,** 17–22.

Hare, A. P. 1952. A study of interaction and consensus in different sized groups. *Amer. Social. Rev.,* **17,** 261–67.

Harmon, L. R. 1961. High school backgrounds of science doctorates. *Science,* **133,** 679–88.

Heider, F. 1958. *The psychology of interpersonal relations.* New York: Wiley.

Hewitt, D., and J. Parfit. 1953. A note on working morale and size of group. *Occup. Psychol.,* **27,** 38-42.

Hoyt, D. P. 1959. Size of high school and college grades. *Personnel and Guidance Journal,* April, pp. 569–73.

Indik, B. P. 1961. Organization size and member participation. Paper read at Amer. Psychol. Assoc., New York, September.

Isaacs, D. A. 1953. A study of predicting Topeka high school drop-outs one year in advance by means of three predictors. Unpublished doctoral dissertation, Univ. of Kansas.

Jonckheere, A. R. 1954. A distribution-free k-sample test against ordered alternatives. *Biometrika,* **41,** 133–45.

Katz, D. 1949. Morale and motivation in industry. In W. Dennis, ed., *Current trends in industrial psychology.* Pittsburgh: Univ. of Pittsburgh Press, pp. 145–71.

Kelley, H. H., and J. W. Thibaut. 1954. Experimental studies of group problem solving and process. In G. Lindzey, ed., *Handbook of social psychology.* Cambridge, Mass.: Addison-Wesley, pp. 735–85.

Kendall, M. G. 1948. *Rank correlation methods.* London: Griffin.

Kounin, J. S. 1961. Dimensions of adult-child relationships in the classroom. Paper read at Topology Meeting, New York, August.

Larson, Carol M. 1949. School-size as a factor in the adjustment of high school seniors. *Bull. No. 511, Youth Series No. 6,* State College of Washington.

LeCompte, W. F., and R. G. Barker. 1960. The ecological framework of cooperative behavior. Paper read at Amer. Psychol. Assoc., Chicago, September.

Lewin, K. 1938. The conceptual representation and measurement of psychological forces. *Contributions to Psychological Theory,* **1,** No. 4.

———. 1951. *Field theory in social science.* New York: Harper.

Marriot, R. 1949. Size of working group and output. *Occup. Psychol.,* **23,** 47–57. Cited by Indik (1961).

Revans, R. W. 1958. Human relations, management, and size. In E. Hugh-Jones, ed., *Human relations and modern management.* Amsterdam: North Holland Pub. Co., pp. 177–220.

Ross, D. H., and B. McKenna. 1955. Class size: the multi-million dollar question. Institute of Administrative Research, Teachers College, Columbia University, Study 11.

Schoggen, P. 1951. A study in psychological ecology: a description of the behavior objects which entered the psychological habitat of an eight-year-old girl during the course of one day. Unpublished master's thesis, Univ. of Kansas.

Slater, P. E. 1958. Contrasting correlates of group size. *Sociometry,* **21,** 129–39.

Sutcliffe, J. P. 1957. A general method of analysis of frequency data for multiple classification designs. *Psychol. Bull.,* **54,** 134–37.

Tallachi, S. 1960. Organization size, individual attitudes and behavior: an empirical study. *Administrative Sci. Quart.,* **5,** 398–420.

Taylor, D. W., and W. L. Faust. 1952. Twenty questions: efficiency in problem-solving as a function of group size. *J. exp. Psychol.,* **44,** 360–68.

Terrien, F. W., and D. L. Mills. 1955. The effect of changing size upon the internal structure of organizations. *Amer. Sociol. Rev.,* **20,** 11–14.

Thibaut, J. W., and H. H. Kelley. 1959. *The social psychology of groups.* New York: Wiley.

Thomas, E. J. 1959. Role conceptions and organizational size. *Amer. Sociol. Rev.,* **24,** 30–37.

Thomas, E. J., and C. F. Fink. 1963. The effects of group size. *Psychol. Bull.,* **60,** 371–84.

Thomas, R. J. 1954. An empirical study of high school drop-outs in regard to ten possibly related factors. *J. Educ. Sociol.,* **28,** 11–18.

Willems, E. P. 1963. Forces toward participation in behavior settings of large and small institutions: a field experiment. Unpublished master's thesis, Univ. of Kansas.

Worthy, J. C. 1950. Organizational structure and employee morale. *Amer. Sociol. Rev.,* **15,** 169–79.

Wright, H. F. 1961. The city-town project: a study of children in communities differing in size. Interim research report published at Univ. of Kansas.

Index